THE COMPLETE
ONE FOOT
in the GRAVE

First published in hardback in Great Britain in 2006 by
Orion Books
an imprint of the Orion Publishing Group Ltd
Orion House, 5 Upper St Martin's Lane,
London WC2H 9EA

1 3 5 7 9 10 8 6 4 2

A CIP catalogue record for this book is available from the
British Library.

ISBN-13: 978 0 75287 357 2
ISBN-10: 0 75287 357 1

Printed and bound in Spain by Cayfosa-Quebecor

The Orion Publishing Group's
policy is to use papers that are
natural, renewable and recyclable
and made from wood grown in
sustainable forests. The logging
and manufacturing processes are
expected to conform to the
environmental regulations of
the country of origin.

www.orionbooks.co.uk

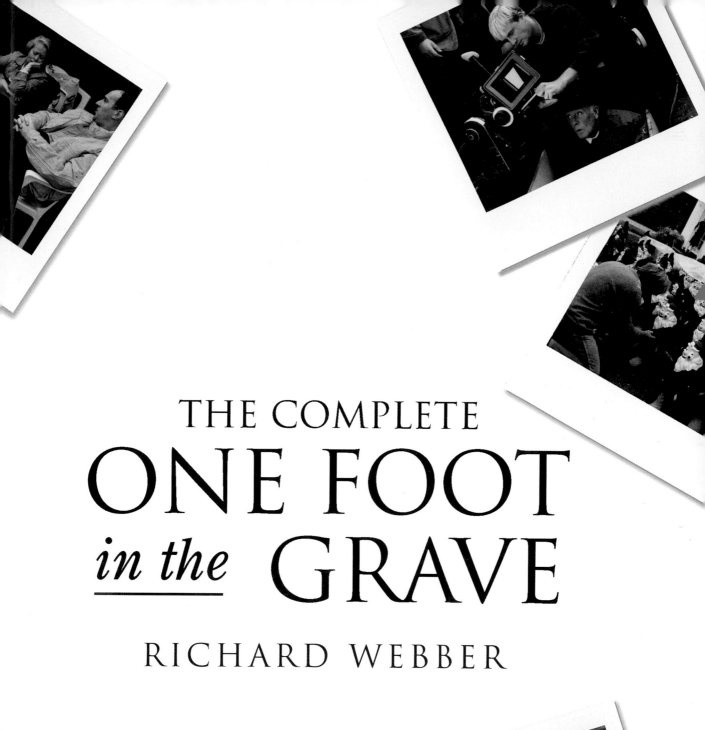

THE COMPLETE
ONE FOOT
in the GRAVE

RICHARD WEBBER

ACKNOWLEDGEMENTS

This book wouldn't have been possible without the generous help and support of David Renwick, who not only gave up much of his time to answer questions and discuss his creation, but allowed me to reproduce entries from his private journals and use photos he took while on location. Thank you, David.

Someone else who allocated a lot of their time to chat about the show, as well as answering many queries during numerous phone calls, was Susan Belbin. Thanks, Susie; I enjoyed our little chats.

But so many people have been extremely helpful during the research and writing of this book. I'd like to thank all the cast and crew who shared their memories of working on *One Foot*, particularly Richard Wilson and Annette Crosbie, who have also written a joint foreword. Here, I'd like to make special mention to the work Annette conducts on behalf of greyhound welfare. Having met her lovely greyhounds and been made aware of the plight of many ex-racing greyhounds, I have made a donation to Wimbledon Greyhound Welfare to help their cause.

I'm also grateful to Owen Brenman, Doreen Mantle, Angus Deayton, Janine Duvitksi, Hannah Gordon, Rula Lenska, Brian Murphy, Richard Winter, Gavin Clark, Christine Gernon, Jean Steward, Nick Wood, Vanessa White, Chris Lawson, Adam Tandy, Duncan Unsworth, Ed Welch, John Record, John Rhodes, Jacky Levy, Laurie Taylor, Martin Kempton, Chris Kempton, Murray Peterson, Nick Somerville, Linda Conoboy, John Asbridge, Chris Wadsworth, Duncan Cooper, Mark Lawrence and Roger Goss. Other people who helped include Sydney Lotterby, Jim Moir, Lin Cook, Carol Rowbrey, Mike Lewis, Kelly Southgate, David Liddiment, Brian Codd, Andrew Marshall, David Hatch, Peter Salmon, Gareth Gwenlan, Neill Gorton, David Landsberg, Simon Brett, Peter Spence, Humphrey Barclay, John Lloyd, Edward Taylor and Tom Werner. Many thanks, also, to Steven Arnold (check out his website, www.kennethwilliams.org.uk), Don Smith, Victoria Kingston, my agent Jeffrey Simmons, everyone at Orion, particularly Ian Marshall, Lorraine Baxter and Sue Michniewicz, all those who allowed me to use their photos and, once again, Hilary Johnson. Thanks for all your expert advice, Hilary.

RICHARD WEBBER
Minehead, March 2006

CONTENTS

FOREWORD

ANNETTE CROSBIE

'The number of times people say to me, "You must have had such laughs doing *One Foot in the Grave*!". Well, you don't want to spoil their illusions, but I had no idea the whole thing was such a sliding scale of angsts, with David at the top, until I read this book. I found it fascinating and what comes across so clearly is just how ridiculously short a time we had in which to do the shows. We didn't have a full five days to rehearse. We had five mornings, because Susie had to spend the afternoons wearing her producer's hat. Then the day in the studio, starting at ten and staggering through the rehearsal for the cameras, when the rhythm and the certainty disappears as you cope with the real props and real doors and how they affect the timing – all the technical stuff that has nothing to do with performance but which you will have to remember when the audience comes in. You do your best on very little food and pure adrenalin. It says a lot for everyone involved, technicians and actors, that the series was as successful as it was, but Susie, being producer and director, and having to deal with everything, including accountants, deserves a medal.'

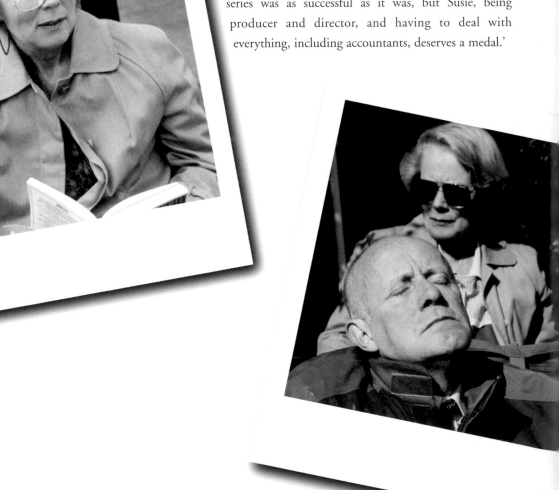

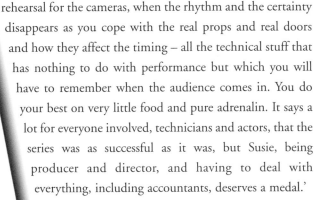

RICHARD WILSON

'Richard Webber has done a masterful and detailed piece of work in documenting the making and the background of the comedy series *One Foot in the Grave*.

I, of course, was absolutely fascinated when reading the book because it told me so much about the genesis of the series: the casting of it, the relationship between the director and writer, etc. Much of this was new to me, and I could look at the show in quite a new way.

I'm sure, however, that not only fans of *One Foot* will find it equally interesting but also anyone interested in situation comedy as a genre. Here, one can find out how a series takes shape and how it is perceived by the public and the press alike.

When I met Richard I realised he has a firm grasp of his subject; he has an encyclopedic knowledge of each and every episode and has already talked to a number of the participants. But as I read the book, I became aware of a great dedication to his subject; no stone was left unturned, no aspect neglected. He was much helped by David Renwick, the writer of the series, who had kept a journal of the whole experience. I hadn't, but now I have the book to remind me of the most important and fulfilling job I have ever done, and to remind me of the many wonderful friends I made on both sides of the camera.

I hope you will enjoy reading the book as much as I did.'

INTRODUCTION

Cast your mind back: what were you doing on the evening of Monday, 20 November 2000? It was a period when the viewing public was torn between two major events. Those who chose ITV were willing on a certain Judith Keppell as she edged nervously towards being first to claim top prize in *Who Wants to be a Millionaire?*, while the 12.8 million tuning in to BBC1 would witness the death of television's most popular grump, Victor Meldrew, in David Renwick's deliciously black comedy, *One Foot in the Grave*.

By the time Judith was delighting in her new-found wealth, Victor was knocking on the Pearly Gates after being killed by a hit-and-run driver; he arrived at his final resting place just five days after another screen favourite, Inspector Morse, had bitten the dust. That November's schedules had

left many heavy hearted viewers slumped in their armchairs and ineffably sad, mourning the loss of sterling programming that would be sorely missed in the coming years.

The curtain coming down on *One Foot in the Grave* marked the end of an era for all concerned: actors, writer, crew and, of course, the legions of fans who'd witnessed the everyday events in the lives of Victor and Margaret Meldrew. For forty-two shows, spanning ten years, the doors of the Meldrews' world were opened to us all. How many fans peering in wish their favourite anti-hero was still around? Life, however, moves on and writer David Renwick was keen to tread pastures new, and to dedicate more time to his other success story of the period: *Jonathan Creek*. Besides, after already providing us with nearly twenty-five hours of first-rate entertainment, Renwick could be forgiven for feeling enervated; furthermore, it was inevitable that his seemingly endless stream of storylines and intricately woven sub-plots, a crucial element in all of the scripts, would eventually begin to run dry. In an interview on the eve of the final series' transmission, he said: 'For the new six half-hour shows I was apprehensive as to whether I'd be able to find the ideas and get to the end. It became an increasing struggle to write him [Victor]. I just got slower and it was making me unhappy.'[i]

The old adage, 'Quit while you're ahead,' should always be adhered to in the world of television, and while he could probably have milked his comedy for one or more additional seasons, with the public undoubtedly lapping it up, Renwick had the foresight to close that chapter of his working life while the show not only ranked among the current elite of British situation comedy, but was guaranteed a place in the pantheon of all-time greats.

As with all successful comedy creations, people have asked over the years why Victor Meldrew became such a hit, and why, even now, six years after his demise, his name remains etched in the national psyche. Only last year it was reported in the *Sun* that astronomers had discovered a constellation resembling Victor's profile; of course, this could all be tongue-in-cheek, but there is no doubting the name has found its way into common parlance to describe

On location: Angus Deayton, David Renwick and Richard Wilson.

maybe, not since. There was so much standard sitcom that took place against a rather middle-class background in a street full of grand suburban houses – *Terry and June*, *Butterflies* and *The Good Life*, for example. Then there was the standard working-class "kitchen-sink" setting, epitomised by *Till Death Us Do Part*, *Rising Damp* and *Only Fools and Horses* to some extent, and of course the very grandiose, upper-crust comedies like *To the Manor Born*. In truth, of course, fewer people than ever now fitted into those categories. In post-Thatcher Britain, the masses were enjoying more affluence, more comfortable lifestyles; they were actually not like Alf Garnett or Rigsby or their rather twee middle-class counterparts, but were somewhere in between. And I just thought it would be more realistic to put those characters on the screen.'

attitudes and behaviour: John Inverdale, writing in the *Daily Telegraph* after a bad week for rugby enthusiasts, stated: 'At the risk of turning into Victor Meldrew, it's not been a good week for rugby-related topics.'[ii]

The overall success of the show can be ascribed to many factors, including perhaps that it was a totally fresh approach in a genre that had largely been rooted in the cosy, middle-class world of suburbia; in *One Foot* David Renwick anchored his scripts in realism and didn't shy away from confronting the stark aspects of life, played out through the lives of the leading characters. Infidelity, death, rejection, violence and vandalism were just some of the unsavoury subjects examined in the show.

I spent a great deal of time talking to David Renwick during the research for this book, discussing every conceivable aspect of his series, and it's clear that he did set out to create a sitcom somewhat different from those that had graced our screens before. While acknowledging the general principles of situation comedies to date, he was also striving to push the form forward. He says: 'What I was trying to achieve more than anything was a neutrality of context, which I felt was an area that hadn't been successfully addressed in comedy shows at that time – and,

Renwick stripped away the standard conventions employed in the vast majority of domestic offerings, replacing them with a situation drenched in reality, its highs and lows tackled in equal measure. He didn't filter out life's uglier elements, allowing his characters to confront them head on, and sometimes they hurt. This was black comedy at its best and, for me, it's these darker moments scattered through the series that provide an extra dimension to *One Foot*, setting it apart from its contemporaries in the genre, heralding a more honest examination of human foibles without losing the all-important subtleties that make for good situation comedy.

Being able to blend laughter with tears is a rare skill enjoyed by a lucky few, and one of those scriptwriters is David Renwick. Let's not forget, *One Foot in the Grave* is primarily a comedy series, and it's much more difficult to deliver the funny lines and humorous situations that make up the lion's share of the scripts than pathos. Nonetheless, the poignant moments are characteristic of Renwick's work: this trait, coupled with an eagerness to shock by pushing the boundaries of expectation helped him reach the zenith of his career. So many scriptwriters spend their working days chasing a chimera, never fulfilling their dream, never achieving the success they so desperately crave, but David Renwick realised his dream with *One Foot*, and if this is his pièce de résistance, it's going to take some beating.

For any situation comedy to be successful, viewers must be able to relate to the characters. Upon first meeting Victor, it was easy to regard him as a crabby old man, a curmudgeon in a world he no longer suited. He always seemed to be ranting and raving about society, driving his wife, Margaret, mad, and his outspokenness did, at times, lead to enmity. Yet closer scrutiny revealed a deeper meaning to the man, a malcontent staunchly supported by a wife forever labelled 'long-suffering', a misnomer that stuck throughout her screen life. Understandably, Victor drove her to the end of her tether at times; she often found his attitudes and beliefs infuriating and was frequently screeching at him, but her devotion never faltered – she loved him to distraction. Even when she strayed, momentarily, into the arms of another man, she soon realised her mistake. A poignant scene in the episode

Margaret's dalliance with Ben (Tristram Jellinek) was short-lived.

'Warm Champagne' revealed that despite a little frisson of excitement, she knew her love for Victor would never wane. Ben, whom Margaret met on holiday, was keen to develop a relationship, trying to convince her that it's never too late to change direction. As the scene unfolded in his flat, Margaret walked over and kissed him passionately.

BEN: What was that for?
MARGARET: Just kissing you goodbye, Ben.
BEN: What do you mean?
MARGARET: It's like Christmas presents, isn't it? They always look so exciting and full of promise, sitting there under the Christmas tree. And once you've opened them all the mystery has gone. It's much better to leave them as they are, with the wrapping paper on. That way you'll never be disappointed, and I think we should leave our wrapping paper on because one of us is going to end up being cruelly rejected, and I couldn't bear that to happen.
BEN: But how can you say that? If you don't reject me, I would never reject you.

MARGARET: I meant one of the three of us. You talk about being sensitive. I'm afraid that's Victor's trouble. He's the most sensitive person I've ever met and that's why I love him and why I constantly want to ram his head through a television screen.

Margaret, who didn't suffer fools gladly, was Victor's moral compass, protecting him from nearing the uncharted world of insanity, despite nearly venturing there herself at times. Victor, meanwhile, was a man riled by the world's ills and the inexorable decline in moral standards. Though frequently cantankerous and obdurate, he wasn't afraid to bemoan the maladies that frustrated him and for that this indomitable man deserved praise. In addition, he spotlighted all those little annoyances in life that frustrate the hell out of us all, like trying to extract videocassettes from the wrappers, setting up answerphones, assembling household appliances and, of course, struggling to make sense of all those notoriously difficult self-assembly products: in 'Threatening Weather', after Victor has spent four hours building his lawnmower's grass box, he jokes, sarcastically, 'Here's your boarding pass for the flight to Rome, Mr Meldrew; you'll find the plane lying in a flatpack at Gate 13, complete with a full set of instructions.'

Yes, Victor had a propensity for moaning and expounding his opinions, and was obviously more susceptible to the stresses and strains of life than most because, as we learnt in 'The Eternal Quadrangle', he suffered a mid-life crisis at thirty, but usually he complained with good cause. He became a mouthpiece for the lion's share of the population, who'd become equally disillusioned with those endless blights on our lives, including litter, disrespect and lack of moral and social standards.

Renwick admits that Victor served as a platform that he could use to comment on matters that infuriated him. He once explained: 'Victor is a victim – I chose the name very deliberately, because Victor is a loser. Essentially he's a character with zero tolerance of the world, of the insanities around him, of all the adversity I spent my time trying to invent to inflict upon him.'[iii] We could all empathise with Victor when two pages of his Sunday supplement stuck together; he struggled to open them but, upon finally prising them apart, discovered to his dismay that it was only a car advertisement inside. 'I threw those kinds of situations in all the time,' says Renwick, who

A rare publicity shot taken by one of the BBC's sloping cameramen.

11

adds that Victor's obsession with litter, which was exploited more frequently in the earlier scripts, is a reflection of his own disgust. 'Litter was driving me to distraction, although there reached a point where I knew I couldn't relentlessly keep going on about it in the scripts,' he says. 'Up the road from where I live, I was so appalled by the volume of crap in the hedgerows that I actually went out and started collecting it up. I filled two or three big black refuse bags, but by the time I got to the car batteries and mangled bits of wrecked vehicles I just gave up in despair.'

Victor was often mistaken for a misanthrope, but he cared about mankind, wanting to protect future generations, although he didn't always show it. He did what we all wanted to do but were usually afraid to: he stood up for what he believed was right, even if he ended up suffering for his cause, as in 'The Wisdom of the Witch', when he told a loud-mouthed diner whose voice was reverberating around a Chinese restaurant to pipe down. Such inconsiderate behaviour deserved condemnation; the trouble, as always, was that Fate was against Victor and

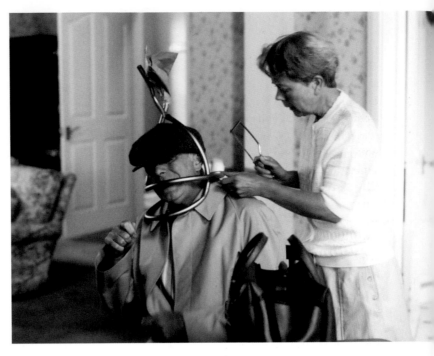

Victor's brush with a litter lout is less than successful.

being dragged down by life.

Other factors that contributed to the show's success included a consummate cast. Richard Wilson invested such energy, feeling and authority into the character that he struck a chord with viewers from day one, and it wasn't long before his unintentional catchphrase, 'I don't belieeeve it!', was being shouted at him in the streets – and still is. Alongside him, the equivalent of the 'straight man' in the Meldrew double-act, was Annette Crosbie, who portrayed Margaret so beautifully. Meticulous casting, even for one-line characters, paid dividends: take the semi-regulars, whom we met during the course of the show – Mrs Warboys, Nick Swaincy, Pippa and Patrick,

> *Litter was driving me to distraction, although there reached a point where I knew I couldn't relentlessly keep going on about it in the scripts.*

DAVID RENWICK

he ended up with a chopstick rammed up his nostril. This was just one example of brave-hearted Victor Meldrew attempting to prevent the slide towards a mannerless world, void of common decencies. Overall, he was essentially a kind individual who found himself

adroitly played by Doreen Mantle, Owen Brenman, Janine Duvitski and Angus Deayton respectively. No one can underestimate the value of their exemplary performances.

And let's not forget those working behind the camera, too, so often overlooked when the accolades are being dished out. The cameramen, make-up designers, costume designers, visual effects designers, assistant floor managers – they all played a crucial role in making *One Foot* the success it became. But teams need a leader, and in Susan Belbin it had one of the best in the industry. An exacting, forthright and innovative woman who helped shape the show's progression, her role was, latterly, taken on seamlessly by one of her protegées, Chris Gernon. Regarded as an 'excellent comedy producer and director' by Gareth Gwenlan, the BBC's head of comedy when *One Foot* got underway, Belbin is a no-nonsense lady, a powerhouse within the corporation, who battled her way up the male-dominated career ladder to become one of the top producer/directors in the business. With Belbin at the helm, the show was in safe hands.

It's very rare that all the essential segments combine to make a programme successful, which explains why the vaults of television stations are littered with long-forgotten failures gathering dust, never to see the light of day again. Thank goodness this isn't the case with *One Foot*, and let's

A finger in every pie? Fate was rarely kind to Mrs Warboys.

hope the BBC's drive to reduce the volume of repeats transmitted on terrestrial television doesn't prevent future generations from meeting the Meldrews.

Here, for the first time, I've told the life story of *One Foot in the Grave*, the jewel in David Renwick's writing crown. Extensive interviews with cast and crew have enabled me to turn the clock back to analyse and revisit events that helped formulate what Peter Salmon, controller of BBC1 in 2000, calls 'the last classic sitcom on the BBC'. Chronicling these years has been made easier by the generosity of David Renwick, who not only gave up so much of his time to talk, but also allowed me access to his meticulous journals, in which he detailed his intimate views and opinions during the show's lifetime. Such thoughts, made public for the first time, also helped me to understand the writer, to appreciate the torment, pain and frustrations he endured while writing *One Foot*. A man of precision and great intellect, Renwick undoubtedly sweated blood whilst crafting his scripts and, hopefully, during the course of this book his sheer commitment will become evident. So sit back and enjoy reading about the life of a true classic.

CHAPTER 1
Before One Foot in the Grave

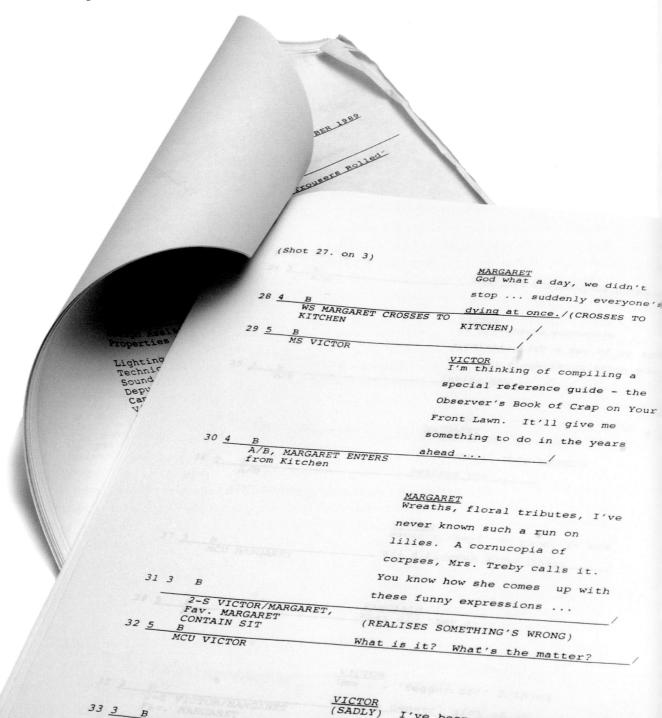

BER 1989

rousers Rolled"

(Shot 27. on 3)

MARGARET
God what a day, we didn't

28 4 B
WS MARGARET CROSSES TO
KITCHEN

stop ... suddenly everyone's
dying at once./(CROSSES TO
KITCHEN) /

29 5 B
MS VICTOR

VICTOR
I'm thinking of compiling a
special reference guide - the
Observer's Book of Crap on Your
Front Lawn. It'll give me
something to do in the years

30 4 B
A/B, MARGARET ENTERS
from Kitchen

ahead ... /

MARGARET
Wreaths, floral tributes, I've
never known such a run on
lilies. A cornucopia of
corpses, Mrs. Treby calls it.
You know how she comes up with

31 3 B
2-S VICTOR/MARGARET,
Fav. MARGARET
CONTAIN SIT

these funny expressions ... /

(REALISES SOMETHING'S WRONG)

32 5 B
MCU VICTOR

What is it? What's the matter?

33 3 B
2-S VICTOR/MARGARET,
Fav. MARGARET

VICTOR
(SADLY) I've been replaced by
a box. /

Every writer has their idiosyncratic way of working: some rely on background music to stimulate the mind, some require open air to get the thought processes going, while others, like David Renwick, need absolute silence to create an atmosphere conductive to literary creativity. Here is an assiduous man for whom writing is an exhausting process, someone who can spend hours, even days agonising over a solitary word; a true perfectionist, he sees that every line of dialogue is carefully crafted and shaped before being committed to paper. The slightest distraction or disturbance can interrupt his train of thought and an inordinate amount of time can pass before he's ready to tackle the task again. This is a writer who, at times, lies face down on the carpet for long periods before even touching his computer keyboard, simply to formulate ideas. He has been known to bury his head in the bed in one of his spare bedrooms in 'agonies of thought'. [i] 'The first part of the process is the thinking, which might be done in an armchair, in the garden or burying my head in the carpet to blot out all distractions,' admits Renwick. 'If I'm having a bad day, just searching for some form of inspiration can be hell, and this stage can go on for weeks.' Only when he's assembled a sufficient number of strong ideas does he begin compiling a running order, moulding it all into some sort of narrative shape.

It would be difficult to find a writer who toils harder in the line of duty than Renwick; his journals reflect the agony he endured while constructing the *One Foot* scripts. The road to success is fraught with pain and the pages of his diaries are peppered with thoughts of despondency, lack of self-confidence and utter frustration as he tried his utmost to produce the goods. On 12 July 1989 after dreaming up 'one or two decent premises' for the third episode of Series One, he spent 'many hours afterwards grinding my brains to a pulp and coming up with nothing further'. Later in the year, on 1 June, after a productive period, he reminded himself that, 'Tomorrow will be the usual business of losing faith in the whole package and then having to rebuild my confidence bit by bit.'

One of the qualities in Renwick's writing is the attention to detail, his ability to go that extra mile to make a scene or line just that little bit funnier. On 6 June 1989 he recorded: 'Head like glue all morning, in a terrible state verging on nausea with all the old tension. I hit upon a nice routine with Victor doing a verbal brain-teaser in the paper, and all the words turn out to be sexually related, but of course it took an

> *Tomorrow will be the usual business of losing faith in the whole package and then having to rebuild my confidence bit by bit.*
>
> DAVID RENWICK

eternity to construct. Several hours wrestling with a million anagrams for a list that will last maybe thirty seconds on screen. You question whether it's worth the effort, but of course the answer is yes.'

Unlike some writers who feel their worries and responsibilities cease upon delivering an acceptable script to the director, Renwick, of his own volition, was involved every step of the way. For him, each piece of the jigsaw was equally important and, therefore, demanded his attention. As his long-term former agent Brian Codd says: 'He's extremely intense about his work, quite rightly so, and he's a very hard taskmaster with himself, setting incredibly high targets; he's professional and expects everyone else to be. He's quite demanding in this way.' This exacting manner ruffled a few feathers from time to time during the show's lifetime, but Renwick only ever had his programme's interests in mind; it's hard to find another sitcom where the writer has exerted so much influence and played such a role in the direction and shape of the programme.

In the company of David Renwick, though, it doesn't take long to realise that he is a courteous, considerate, unassuming, down-to-earth individual who deserves every fragment of success he's achieved; a demure man, he shies away from large social gatherings.

'All my life I've been fairly inhibited by company. I've been away on holiday with groups of friends a few times, but I have to feel really comfortable with those present; if there's even one person I don't feel at ease with, I just tend to clam up. I've always essentially been an introvert.'

Much admired among peers and those connected with the broadcasting industry, his successes have brought not just plaudits but financial security, too. Yet he's never forgotten his working-class roots, keeps his feet firmly on the ground and takes nothing for granted – appreciating the fragility and transient nature of success might go some way to explaining why he's a self-confessed pessimist. One journalist wrote: 'Spend a little time in his doleful company and you'll soon start wondering if there isn't a black storm cloud hovering over his roof alone. His gloomy motto is "prepare for the worst to happen because it probably will".'[ii] Paradoxically, preparing for the worst is what underpins his success because he caters for every scenario, making sure there are no weaknesses or frailties to be exploited.

It was 4 September 1951 when Renwick was born into a working-class family in Luton, the only child of Jim and Winifred Renwick. His father spent his entire working life as a milkman, delivering for the Co-op and Unigate dairies. To help supplement his exiguous income Jim, who originated from nearby Leighton Buzzard, ran his own café for a time and sold newspapers outside Luton railway station during the afternoons. As a result of his various jobs, he became a popular face around town, befriended by people from all walks of life.

'Neither my mum nor dad had a particularly strong education, coming from fairly humble, poor backgrounds. We lived on a council estate and money was tight,' says Renwick, who's convinced his father had a subliminal influence on his writing career. 'He had a very strong sense of humour, which I'm sure I inherited from him – more so than from my mum. It's very difficult, though, defining what that sense of humour is; the most absurd side of my comedy comes from events at school, which weren't necessarily to his taste. But the sense of social humour definitely came from him. He was an uncomplicated man but always great fun.'

Educationally, Renwick progressed well, reaching the highest streams at Stopsley Junior School before passing his Eleven Plus and moving to Luton Grammar School. Although never holding aspirations to pursue a particular career, he was a boy with a creative bent, enjoying, in particular, writing and creating his own comic-book characters. 'Very often I'd help my dad on the milk round, for which he'd always pay me. I'd use the money to buy drawing books and spend hours at home inventing my own superhero characters – blatant rip-offs of the ones I used to read about in D. C. Comics, like *Green Lantern* and *Flash*. That was my earliest bout of creativity, I guess.'

Later in his teens he progressed to penning his own schoolboy stories, influenced by the Billy Bunter and Jennings novels he devoured after emptying the local library of all the titles they had in stock. 'I'd type them up on the typewriter my parents gave me when I was nine – a Remington Home Portable. I prepared my stories in such a way that you could fold them into sections of sixteen pages and then assemble them into a book. Then I'd go to great lengths to design and paint a cover before stitching and sellotaping it all together. The writing, though, was another matter. There wasn't any cohesion to it at all.'

Shows like *The Frost Report* and radio's *I'm Sorry, I'll Read That Again* were at that time considered the cutting edge of comedy and became a seminal influence in Renwick's career. The latter, which enlivened the airwaves between 1964 and 1973, was a salvo of sketches delivered each week by John Cleese, Graeme Garden, Bill Oddie, Tim Brooke-Taylor, Jo Kendall and David Hatch, who'd later play an important role in Renwick's development as a writer. 'The series confirmed my fascination for off-beat humour and I suppose consolidated my ambition to become a comedy writer.' The silly sketches and gags struck a chord with Renwick and his school friends, all of whom were devoted listeners. 'I'd jot down references as I listened to each episode. I wouldn't transcribe the whole joke, just a phrase to remind me of it. And next day at school, we'd compare notes and recall the gags and laugh at them all over again. Most of them were just terrible puns, but they tickled us at the time. The programme had a huge fan club at our school.'

Suitably enthused, it wasn't long before he began writing his own comedy, but instead of kicking off with a few sketches, he jumped in at the deep end and completed several thirty-minute sitcom episodes. Though still a schoolboy, Renwick felt he had nothing to lose by dispatching his scripts to the BBC and regional ITV stations. Reflecting on his endeavours, he admits the material was 'pretty terrible' and wasn't surprised when it led to a flurry of rejection slips dropping through his letterbox. Subsequent offerings met with similar rebuffs until Renwick abandoned conventional comedy and tried his hand at something more anarchic.

Holing himself up in his bedroom at 25 Hallwicks Road, Luton, where he lived with his parents, Renwick produced six 'fairly wacky' five-minute sketches, which he sent to the *Monty Python's Flying Circus* production office at the BBC. The show, which began in October 1969, became a landmark in contemporary television comedy, and its absurd, iconoclastic style greatly appealed to the young Renwick. Although it was another rejection that the postman delivered in February 1970, the letter was accompanied by an inspirational message from John Cleese, who'd particularly liked one of the submitted sketches, titled 'Punch Line'. Explaining that a decision had been made at the programme's inception not to use submitted material because it caused 'a million difficulties, stylistically, administratively and financially', Cleese said he would forward the sketches to Ian Davidson at London Weekend Television, then responsible for *Frost on Sunday*. None of the material was ever used, but Renwick was much encouraged by the handwritten note appended by Cleese in which he gave a brief assessment of his work: 'I think you write good dialogue and good individual lines. What is weaker at the moment is the basic idea of the various sketches. There is no idea here (exc. Punchline) which I would call really good. Getting ideas is very difficult. It's an instinctive and intuitive process. All I can say is these <u>do</u> show promise, unlike 90% of sketches sent to me, so keep writing.'[iii]

Renwick was pertinacious and didn't let the run of rejections dent his confidence; suitably buoyed by Cleese's remarks, he returned to the drawing board and continued generating sketches in the belief that his efforts would be justly rewarded. He took a significant step towards achieving his goal later that year with a script titled *Frederick Dunne's Schooldays*. Reading it today, some thirty years later, he describes it as 'rather more quirky' than previous efforts and 'an attempt at a wacky treatment of the public-school tales I had enjoyed in my early teens – Bunter and Jennings and so on – and stocked with characters based upon my own teachers, who would have meant little to anyone outside Luton Grammar School.' He notes, too, that it's 'full of strange and obscure references and the humour is all a bit primitive'.

He may regard the humour as 'primitive' but it attracted the attention of Edward Taylor, then employed as script editor, Light Entertainment (Radio) at the BBC. Now retired from the corporation, Taylor, a successful playwright in his own right, was based at Aeolian Hall in London's New Bond Street. A famous concert hall during the 1920s and 1930s, this ornate building was taken over by the BBC in the early 1940s to house the headquarters of its variety department after its previous base, St George's Hall, was razed to the ground during the Blitz. Each morning, Taylor's in-tray strained under the weight of unsolicited scripts that arrived in droves from would-be writers. But instead of consigning them to the reject pile after just a cursory glance, Taylor waded through the endless stream conscientiously because occasionally one would sparkle.

Early one fine August morning, Taylor was sipping coffee at his desk as he stretched for the next buff-coloured envelope. This one contained Renwick's submission. 'So much of the material I looked at was total rubbish, and only one in a hundred you could do anything with,' says Taylor. 'David's work fell into the "five in a hundred" category that had something going for it and you wanted to encourage the writer. He sent in this script that was absolutely crazy in the way that young writers were doing *Goon*-like stuff, but then I spotted this very funny scene where someone was arranging for RAF planes to attack the school playground – I can remember it even at this distance. If you come across something that makes you laugh, even if the other 95 per cent is rubbish, you treasure it.'

The script featured schoolboys in its principal roles, and the scene remembered by Taylor reads:

TOLBERT: This place is packed with morons! I'm going out for a stroll in the quad.
(DOOR OPENS AND SLAMS)
CRAWFORD: You needn't hurry back!
(PAUSE) He's a nauser, that bloke. Thinks he's so high and mighty. I hope Fred gets him.
DUNNE: Who's Fred? A bully?
CRAWFORD: No. He's a gorilla. Mr Glossup the Biology Master knocked him up in his prep. room. He's still loose somewhere out there, stalking through the elms, last time I saw him.
DUNNE: He's on the loose outside? Does this kind of thing happen often?
CRAWFORD: All the time. That's the fifth gorilla this term, not to mention three dinosaurs and a pterodactyl.
DUNNE: What happens to them in the end?
CRAWFORD: Some of the science blokes go out in mock-up bi-planes from World War One and shoot them off the clock tower. Then we dissect the bodies in class.

Spotting potential in *Frederick Dunne's Schooldays*, Taylor wrote a letter explaining that he'd found 'one or two quite amusing lines and ideas'[iv], before adding that the script, in its entirety, was some way from being usable. Explaining why the script had no future, Taylor referred to his first-hand knowledge of producing Jimmy Edwards' school comedy, *Whack-O!*, a successful series born in 1956, which spotlighted the shenanigans at Chiselbury, a small public school, with Professor James Edwards as headmaster. Although the show's longevity – it ran to over sixty episodes – proved it was a ratings winner, Taylor knew that working with children wasn't easy. With Renwick's script full of schoolboy characters who'd have to be played by children, Taylor pointed out that: 'Child actors, however talented, simply cannot sustain long scenes between themselves in this sort of world. Apart from four- or five-line sequences essential to the plot, one should always hear them talking to teachers or other adults.'[v] He noted that in Renwick's script, the schoolboys carried the bulk of the action, making it unworkable. Taylor continued his assessment:

The other main objection is that this kind of writing does not sustain half an hour. The gorilla escaping from the Biology Lab and being shot down from the school clock tower by boys in old-fashioned aeroplanes is, to me, a very funny idea: and it would do well in a sketch in *I'm Sorry, I'll Read That Again*, or *Monty Python* on TV. But it's so way-out that it destroys even the slightest degree of credibility that a story-line half-hour must possess to hold the listeners' attention.

There are other snags to your script – the plot, by any standards, is too thin: none of the characters are strong enough to build round: and, for instance, the Head and the teacher who swears are too similar in that they are both self-confessed failures.[vi]

Taylor, however, felt nineteen-year-old David Renwick had a future and invited him to his office. 'We had a nice chat. He was a pleasant and courteous young man who seemed eager to learn. Although our names were never linked on an actual project, I regard David in my little catalogue of privately treasured successes because I did meet him at an early stage and provided encouragement,' says Taylor, who isn't surprised by Renwick's subsequent success.

In correspondence later that year, he told Renwick: 'You have definitely got some comedy-writing talent, and I think you may well eventually succeed. I hope so.'[vii] The letter was written in response to him sending further samples of work for appraisal. After studying two recently rejected television scripts, Taylor highlighted what he believed was Renwick's main problem, which he'd also flagged at their earlier meeting: he referred to the 'uneasy mixture of basic situation comedy (which ought to be credible), and wild *Monty Python*-type craziness'.[viii] Taylor stressed that Renwick had to decide which style to adopt, rather than trying to combine both, suggesting that the 'believable half-hour comedy is a better prospect'[ix]. Of the two scripts supplied, Taylor thought the one based on a policeman's life showed more potential and was surprised it hadn't been picked up, stating: 'I'd have thought with a bit of work from the TV boys it might have been usable.'[x] Of the other, set in the world of horse racing, he found the idea too 'incredible'[xi] and told Renwick bluntly: 'I shouldn't show it around too much if I were you.'[xii]

The writer heeded the advice and, enthused by Taylor's vote of confidence in his long-term future, continued plugging away. Another valuable piece of advice from Taylor saw Renwick directing future sketches to David Hatch, who was producing, among others, *I'm Sorry, I'll Read That Again*. Entertaining listeners since 1964, this anarchic sketch show helped launch the careers of many, including John Cleese, Bill Oddie, Tim Brooke-Taylor and Graeme Garden. After sending material, Renwick received two letters from Hatch, the first dated 4 January 1971, explaining that he wanted to try and use the sketches once he'd found the right vehicle. A week later, another letter arrived, this time inviting Renwick to the BBC.

Renwick began his writing career as a local reporter.

Greeting Renwick when he arrived were David Hatch

and Peter Spence, who would later create and write the sitcom *To the Manor Born*. Back in 1971, the recently graduated writer was scripting *Week Ending*, a twenty-five-minute topical weekend radio show for comedians, with a bunch of other writers. Running throughout the year, it received a well-deserved six-week holiday during the summer and a replacement was still being sought for its late-night slot. 'I think they were proposing a kind of *Comedy Playhouse*, with a different show each week, and one of them was to be a vehicle for David Jason,' recalls Renwick. 'I remember them asking whether I'd heard of David and I said I was a huge fan because at that time he was playing Captain Fantastic in *Do Not Adjust Your Set*, a rather superior children's show on Thames. I'd sent in several sketches, including one about someone being interviewed to take part in a comedy sketch. And Peter Spence had conceived an idea for this programme about a comedy factory, where the staff would walk along a corridor and different sketches would be going on in each room. Absolutely anything could be happening – you could open a door and there would be a scene taking place on a raft in the middle of the ocean. It was all gloriously surreal.'

Hatch and Spence wondered if Renwick wanted to be involved in the project. 'Of course I did; it was incredibly exciting. I'd taken other bits and pieces along which David Hatch read out, and I remember he laughed so much that he went red in the face. It was amazing to just sit there and watch him performing my words.' Over lunch and a few beers, the show's format was discussed further and in due course came to fruition. *The Next Programme Follows Almost Immediately* starred David Jason, Denise Coffey, Jonathan Cecil, Bill Wallis, David Gooderson and, at the piano, Peter Pontzen. Produced by Hatch, the two six-week series ran during the summers of 1971 and 1972 and were mostly written by Spence, who later collaborated with Chris Langham. Although Renwick was invited to submit sketches and jokes, he reluctantly declined an offer to co-write the show. Having recently left sixth-form college (where he'd stayed on for a third year to retake his pure maths A-level, resulting in plenty of free time to devote to the school magazine and his comedy writing) he was now working as a junior reporter on his local weekly, the *Luton News*. 'I'd just finished my six months' probation, and had signed up for

Luton News, May 26, 1971—17

The Professionals fight it out — in a friendly way

How I joined the Army — for one day

DAVID RENWICK REPORTS

19

three years of indentured training. Pete suggested I chucked it all in and wrote the series with him. But being realistic I knew I wasn't remotely qualified at that point in my life and so I said no, though I did continue to feed him jokes and one-liners for the series, and it was great being involved even on a peripheral basis. I attended all the recordings and hung out with everyone on the programme, which was a great thrill.' For his work, Renwick was paid three pounds a minute, and with eight minutes' worth of material used in the first episode, broadcast on Radio 4 on Friday, 9 July 1971 at 11.15 p.m., he pocketed the princely sum of twenty-four pounds. 'As my entire wage on the newspaper was around fifteen pounds a week, it was a very nice supplement.'

Over the next few years, Renwick submitted and sold material to a host of other programmes, while continuing to ply his trade as a journalist. He was, however, never enamoured of the job. 'I became a journalist because I liked writing,' he says, 'but I soon found out that hard news reporting isn't about writing, it's about knocking on doors and ringing people who don't want to speak to you, and generally invading their privacy. I didn't have a knack for it all, and only really survived by bluffing my way through for four years.' One of his earliest assignments was to compile an obituary of a local financier. The problem was, the man was still alive. 'Mercifully, it never appeared in the paper,' smiles Renwick, 'although it got as far as a page proof. The news editor passed me a death notice from the *Daily Telegraph* and asked me to put a story together from the man's cuttings file. And it was only when the deputy editor, who was still struggling to find a decent headline, asked to see the original clipping that he discovered it was, in fact, the wife who had died. I should have checked, of course, but it conjured up a nightmare scenario of this man, who is already grieving over his wife's death, opening the paper to find his own obituary splashed across the page.'

Four years of hard news reporting was enough for the would-be comedy writer.

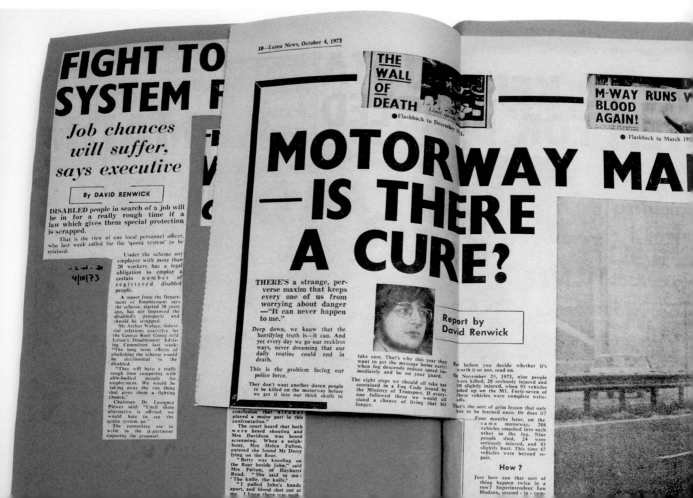

Renwick remained with the newspaper until summer 1974 when, at the age of twenty-two, he took the plunge into the precarious world of full-time comedy writing. People from whom he'd sought advice, including David Hatch, had already been exhorting Renwick to quit journalism, but he remained cautious, lacking the confidence to swap a secure job for the vagaries of freelance writing. Hatch understood his predicament. 'It's difficult to convince yourself that you can actually make it because it's tough out there. David eventually did and we're all glad because he's delighted the nation ever since.'

What eventually convinced him to chance his luck was a commission to write for *Week Ending*, in which he was guaranteed a regular payment, whether his material was used or not. By now, Renwick was contributing sketches and jokes regularly to this show and others, but the offer of relative security provided the impetus he needed. Like all loving parents, Jim and Win Renwick were worried about their son's gamble. 'Yes, they became proud once my career took off,' he says, 'but my mum was always the more sceptical – she always wanted me to get a "proper" job. Anyway, I had my National Journalism Certificate, so knew if it didn't work out, I'd be able to get a job again on a newspaper.' Fortunately, it was never a consideration. 'Once I'd made the break, I was lucky because there was always work coming in – more than I could really cope with, to be honest.'

The popular revue *Week Ending*, which became the longest-running comedy show in the history of British radio, started life on Radio 4 in 1970. Initially Peter Spence wrote the programme, produced by Simon Brett and David Hatch, single-handedly, but when this became unworkable a great number of writers was used, including a big pool of commissioned scribes and hundreds of non-commissioned writers, such as Renwick, supplying material, from the briefest quip to complete sketches. Feisty writing, poking fun at those in power, was the name of the game and Renwick rose to the challenge; it wasn't long before he realised that ditching his job as a reporter had been a wise move.

Week Ending was recorded on Friday mornings in Studio PP1 near Broadcasting House in Portland Place, after which the team would cross the road to the Langham Hotel's salad bar for lunch. 'The regular writers and principals would meet up throughout the week at peak hours to go through the scripts, which I was unable to do when I was on the paper,' says Renwick. 'I'd often write on Sundays and Monday evenings. Tuesday was our press night, so I couldn't post my material off until Wednesday, and usually I wouldn't know if they were planning to use anything until I listened to the broadcast on Friday evening. Whenever I could get Friday morning off, I'd travel up to the studio to make myself known, which was important because so many people contributed to the show. There were all these anonymous writers dotted round the country churning out jokes and sketches, so I thought it was quite useful for the producers to put a face to my name.'

Although co-producer David Hatch doesn't recollect the first time he met Renwick, he soon realised he had what it took to succeed in the field. 'David's material started being used regularly on the show, which was quite an achievement because there was commissioned work from very good writers, and for those who weren't, they had to work hard to get into the scripts.' Hatch spotted a 'remarkable talent, particularly with sketches', so when Kenneth Williams wanted to create his own sketch show, Hatch turned to Renwick for material. 'I got David to write some sketches for him. For Kenneth Williams it was quite a risk to perform sketches written by a new and unknown writer, but he wrote some wonderful stuff – he's a very inventive and imaginative guy. Ken and I were both impressed because whatever you asked David to do, he seemed able to do it.'

Regarding Renwick as a 'shy man who's remained remarkably sane for someone who's had so much success', Hatch is a fan of *One Foot in the Grave*; as he points out, all good sitcoms need one eccentric around whom chaos reigns, and in Victor Meldrew the show had that. 'Things go wrong in ways that you, as an audience, don't always expect. David can see a joke from a long way off and you don't realise he's building towards it until it comes; even if you're an old hand at reading scripts like me, who thinks he can spot plotlines coming, you still miss them because he disguises them so very well.'

Hatch saw David Renwick maturing as a writer and wasn't surprised when he graduated from sketch writing to full-blown situation comedy and crossed media into television, which happened when some of his jokes were accepted for *The Two Ronnies*' newsdesk slot. By this time Renwick had already met Andrew Marshall, with whom he was to forge a successful writing partnership, spawning such series as *Whoops Apocalypse* and *Hot Metal*. Their first meeting had been on *Week Ending*, where they quickly realised they had much in common. Renwick says: 'Most importantly, we had a similar sense of humour, but we weren't part of the public-school set like most of the contributors, and that brought us closer together I think. Also, Andrew was working, as I was: he was at college when he joined *Week Ending* and was still teaching maths when we started writing together.'

Marshall admits feeling 'a little in awe' of his future writing partner when they first met, one lunchtime, in a pub round the corner from the Aeolian Hall. 'I

Renwick (right) with co-writer Andrew Marshall, working on *Whoops Apocalypse*.

worked with a lot of other people on *Week Ending*, and we'd sit in a room and write sketches on the back of old scripts; periodically, somebody would say: "David Renwick has sent in a sketch." I was a student at the time and would often bunk off college and pop over for the afternoon, whereas David was working and couldn't do that. His sketches were always very good. He was, in some ways, advanced on the rest of us with his writing, largely

because he was making a living as a journalist.' Although only a callow reporter, the fact he was

Renwick was an early contributor to the long-running series *The News Huddlines*.

working as a full-time journalist gave Renwick a certain cachet in the eyes of fellow writers in the *Week Ending* team. 'We were quite in awe of him to start with because he was obviously very good while the rest of us felt rather amateurish in comparison.'

The show's original writer, Peter Spence, concurs with Marshall. 'Often the best lines in the shows were David's. They were so good, I wondered why I couldn't write like that.' Hardly a week passed when Renwick didn't produce something Spence wished he'd created. 'It was as if he'd been studying comedy for years – his talent arrived pretty much formed; I don't remember him going through the kind of learning curves I did at that time.'

Spence remembers Renwick's work was always 'beautifully structured and neatly turned out'. 'I recall a conversation I was having with John Lloyd [producer of *The News Huddlines*, to which Renwick supplied material] in a pub. He could tell from looking at a page which writer had submitted the sketch, describing David's as being like a "neat garden trellis dotted very evenly with a beautiful pot of flowers". His work was tight, nicely spaced and his dialogue looked very playable, which it was.'

Renwick and Marshall, who regards his writing partner as being 'like a long-lost brother because we're similar in so many ways', began writing scripts together, including several rejected pilot programmes for David Jason; it was clear from the start that their styles and attitudes were compatible. 'In a way, Andrew pushed for the partnership more than I did, often ringing to encourage me to write something with him. Like any of the best relationships, it just developed, almost without being formalised. It was a very comfortable cohesion of styles and comedy tastes.'

Every writing duo has its own method of working, and Renwick and Marshall never actually sat down together to produce material, preferring instead to discuss ideas exhaustively before going their separate ways to write. 'Writing with another person in the same room is a skill I just don't possess,' admits Renwick, 'so

I would always head back to Luton, and Andrew to Catford, where he was living at the time, and whenever we needed to meet, it would be in London somewhere, perhaps a restaurant, café or pub, and in the summer we'd wander around the parks tossing ideas about.'

The first show they wrote, in conjunction with John Mason, was a spoof on the Open University titled *Half Open University*. Broadcast on Radio 3 in August 1975, it was produced by Simon Brett, who'd worked with Renwick not only on the earlier *Week Ending* but also a failed radio series for comedian Harry Worth. Co-written with David McKellar, the surreal scripts for this show, called *Things Could Be Worse*, were a departure from the more traditional style associated with Worth; when the pilot was well received, a series was swiftly commissioned, but Brett recalls a less than harmonious period for the writers. 'It must have been a nightmare for them because they produced all these scripts, which were very good, but Harry would then contact me with all the things he wasn't happy with. I'd spend hours going through it, replacing this wonderful new stuff with old jokes that had worked awfully well in, say, Oldham in 1932! Having done the pilot, Harry lost his nerve and returned to what worked before, which meant a lot of rewriting – it must have been dispiriting for the two Davids.'

Meanwhile, *Half Open University*, an original idea with a rich mix of wordplay and off-the-wall themes, featured a cast consisting of Chris Emmett, Nigel Rees, Timothy Davies and Christine Ozan; a second episode followed and its impact on an otherwise comedy-starved station led to Marshall and Renwick being invited, in 1976, to submit ideas for a show to step into *Week Ending*'s shoes during its summer recess over on Radio 4. Based on their earlier show, *The Burkiss Way (To Dynamic Living)*, was written primarily by Renwick and Marshall although other writers, including John Mason, contributed. The first of six instalments was

transmitted on 27 August 1976, starring Nigel Rees, Chris Emmett, Fred Harris and Denise Coffey, the latter afterwards being replaced by Jo Kendall. The shows were constructed around the premise of a radio correspondence course run by Professor Emil Burkiss. Six series were commissioned, with Simon Brett producing the first two, John Lloyd seasons three and four and David Hatch the final two, with the closing episode, 'Wave Goodbye to CBEs the Burkiss Way', broadcast on 15 November 1980. Considering the show's success, Brett says: 'The writers were able to

The cast of *The Burkiss Way* – 'written as if Sigmund Freud and A.J.P. Taylor had joined forces with John Cleese,' said Barry Took.

take language and turn it inside out. It was a kind of radio cartoon.' The show's wit, razor-sharp humour and astute observations secured a regular audience. 'At that stage we were getting a lot of films on television with the edges cut off because they didn't quite fit on the screen, so we did *Mutiny on the Bounty* on radio, but as the title didn't fit, it became *Tiny on the Bount*, with all the characters' names truncated – it was a typical Renwick-Marshall idea, and they were full of that kind of invention,' says Brett. At this stage in his career, it was Renwick's prowess at structuring sketches that shone. 'He was so meticulous and must have spent ages working on the shape, so it was a surprise to discover that he could do character as well because normally writers master one or the other.'

While writing the first two series of *The Burkiss Way*, Renwick was still living with his parents in Luton, but the commissioning of another run coincided with the decision to find his own flat. The passage from aspiring writer to full-time scriptwriter had been remarkably smooth for Renwick, who readily admits that he's never experienced financial hardship, even while trying to find his feet in his chosen field, unlike many of his contemporaries who frequently found themselves scratching around for a living. 'I've never been an extravagant person, so the combination of that and the fact I was writing for other shows, including *The News Huddlines* [which began in 1975], meant I've never actually struggled to survive.' By 1978, Renwick was writing for Les Dawson, and was subsequently hired as script editor for some of his shows, while also contributing to other television shows, including Thames Television's *What's on Next?*, as well as vehicles for comics like Bernie Winters and Little and Large.

His developing small-screen career had begun on *The Two Ronnies*, providing jokes for the famous newsdesk sequence. Soon he'd progressed to sketches – the most memorable being the hilarious *Mastermind* sketch – and, eventually, Ronnie Corbett's famous monologues, which became a firm favourite among the show's fans. One of Corbett's earliest memories of Renwick originates from London's Mayfair Hotel, at a drinks party thrown for everyone associated with the show. Corbett recalls: 'We always tried getting together with the writers and newcomers who were contributing

Renwick's television breakthrough: the *Two Ronnies* news desk.

news items, to get them geed up. After starting with news items and sketches, David came to my rescue when Spike Mullins, who'd written my chair spot, could no longer do them; David was waiting in the wings and had said that if ever Spike felt he couldn't continue, he'd love to have a go. He was able to copy Spike's idiom and the join was seamless, so I benefited in a very remarkable way from David's skills.' It didn't take long for Ronnie to spot Renwick's qualities as a writer. 'He's very comic and funny; writing the chair spot wasn't easy, and that's without the added pressure of having to follow Spike Mullins. It had to be full of digression and diversion, with little jokes along the way towards the finish, which was always an old joke. But David was always studious, caring and dedicated, and remains so.'

Writing for *The Two Ronnies* turned out to be an invaluable experience. 'By the time *One Foot in the Grave* came along, my material had already reached audiences of up to twenty million people, because along with *Morecambe and Wise*, it was probably the top entertainment show of the 1980s.' Contributing to the programme provided a good grounding for Renwick, who would always attend recordings every Sunday. 'I'd meet everyone afterwards for a drink, and before long became a member of their close inner circle of friends; I felt very privileged to be there. My sense of humour has always been a hybrid of the conventional comedy of *Hancock, Morecambe and Wise* and *The Two Ronnies*, and the random absurdity of *Python* and early Woody Allen.'

Explosive casting: Richard Griffiths, John Barron, Peter Jones and Barry Morse in *Whoops Apocalypse*.

Among the millions watching *The Two Ronnies* when the famous *Mastermind* sketch was first transmitted was Brian Codd, who worked as an agent for more than forty years. So impressed was he by the quality of the sketch that he phoned the BBC to establish who'd written the piece. Before long, he was not only representing Renwick, but Marshall, too. Barry Cryer, a long-term client of Codd's, recommended the writers contact the agent, who says he'll never forget their first meeting at his office in London's Haymarket. 'They said: "Barry Cryer recommended you and, quite frankly, we don't know anybody else." That's how it all started.' Unbeknown to both writers, Codd christened them 'the prickly pair'. 'They had a reputation for being very tough and rather prickly, so I was surprised to discover they were so friendly – in fact, we got on from the beginning.'

Reflecting on the success they shared before embarking on solo careers, Andrew Marshall feels their writing styles, although different, were complementary. He says: 'David is terribly clever when it comes to structuring, which I'm less good at. He once said I was more ideas and he was more organisation, although over the years it got much more blurred.'

Their first small-screen collaboration was *End of Part One* for London Weekend Television. As Andrew Marshall says, LWT was a 'very classy place to work'. He adds: 'It had great integrity of product and the people there, like Humphrey [Barclay, then head of comedy], were very interested in innovation.'

The first of fourteen episodes of the sketch show, starring Denise Coffey and Tony Aitken as husband and wife Vera and Norman Straightman, was transmitted in April 1979; the Straightmans' lives were continually interrupted by a host of famous people, played by fellow cast members, including Sue Holderness, later of *Only Fools and Horses* fame.

Renwick regards the show as the partnership's big break. 'It was shown on Sunday afternoons and was similar to *Do Not Adjust Your Set*; whereas that was a glorified children's programme, ours appealed primarily to an adult audience.' The programme was launched by Humphrey Barclay. When Renwick and Marshall's speculative script landed on his desk, he appreciated the humour but couldn't foresee an opening for such a programme. As Barclay prepared to return the work, it occurred to him that just like his earlier success, *Do Not Adjust Your Set*, it might stand a better chance of being accepted if it was considered within the schedules allocated for children's programmes. 'As with *Do Not Adjust Your Set*, the only rule was keep it clean,' says Barclay. 'We didn't compromise at all and the joy of writing with a young audience in mind is that you have so much freedom. Not only are you let off the leash because no programme commissioner is looking over your shoulder, but you have a sophisticated audience who aren't jaded and are ready for anything.' Barclay enjoyed producing the show. 'It was a joyous chance to satirise television shows, and marked David and Andrew as brilliant new arrivals on the scene.' He enjoyed working with Marshall and Renwick,

The newspaper satire *Hot Metal* featured Geoffrey Palmer, Richard Kane and Robert Hardy (pictured), and, later, Richard Wilson.

too, remembering them as serious writers. 'They certainly weren't morose, but if a smile slips across David's face it's a fairly swift journey,' smiles Barclay. 'But he's a delightful person to work with simply because of his seriousness about being funny.'

Arguably the two titles the Renwick-Marshall partnership is remembered for are the satirical shows *Whoops Apocalypse* and *Hot Metal*, both produced by Barclay at London Weekend Television. The former ran for six episodes in 1982 and boasted a stellar cast, including Geoffrey Palmer, John Cleese, Barry Morse, John Barron, Alexei Sayle and Peter Jones. Spotlighting international politics, Renwick admits the programme was never going to reach a second series. 'It was a very wacky show with a limited life because it was all destined to end with World War III, when the entire planet would go up. It was written at the time of the troubles in Afghanistan, so it was a very jittery period. The show was a political soap opera, really – very mad yet still more realistic than anything else we'd done.'

Humphrey Barclay regards it as 'one of the most inspired and original pieces of comedic television you can imagine'. The show's sheer boldness and vision earned immediate plaudits, with its visionary message pulling no punches, as Barclay recalls. 'When, in Episode One, you're inside the Oval Office and outside a window a student is being crucified, you know what

you're in for. Later, when you reach the point where John Cleese's character, Lacrobat, smuggles an atom bomb across a Middle Eastern desert by transporting it on a trailer disguised as a twelve-foot erect penis, you know anything is possible.'

Andrew Marshall explains that they wanted to see whether it was possible to compile a World War III story. 'We knew the Pythons had been working on the same subject but had given up because they couldn't find a way to make it work. I think we found a way by reducing it down into lots of vignettes in various power centres.'

A big-screen version, which saw Richard Wilson team up with Renwick for the first time, playing Nigel Lipman, the foreign secretary who ends up being nailed to a cross, was screened five years later, by which time Renwick and Marshall were in between series of *Hot Metal*, inspired partly by the duo's irritation with tabloid newspapers' trivialisation of events, which the public cheerfully accepted. Set in a world familiar to Renwick's – the newspaper industry – the show followed events at the *Daily Crucible*, a tabloid which undergoes a facelift courtesy of Terence 'Twiggy' Rathbone, an infamous press baron. Just like *Whoops Apocalypse*, *Hot Metal* had been rejected by the BBC and initially looked like it would receive the thumbs down from Humphrey Barclay at LWT, too. 'I read it and at first didn't think much of it,' he says. 'I started to write the letter explaining I didn't think it was very good but ground to a halt. Although my instinct was to reject it, I suddenly couldn't think of a clear reason to do so. I decided to re-read the script and immediately changed my mind.'

With a cast including Robert Hardy, Geoffrey Palmer and, again, Richard Wilson, the series was similar in style to *Whoops*, being topical and satirical, and was screened on Sunday evenings at 10 p.m., the slot formerly occupied by *Spitting Image*. But although it attracted a regular audience, the figures weren't quite substantial enough and the series was cancelled after just two seasons.

Both writers have enjoyed their fair share of success since treading separate comedy paths. Asked why Renwick has achieved so much in his solo career, Marshall says:

'One of his greatest skills is his ability to edit. He has the extraordinary desire to keep on editing until he's completely sure it's right, which can be very wearying if you're not used to it. When we wrote together, we'd apparently decide all kinds of things, and I'd just be getting my head around this version when, next day, David would say things like, "I'm not getting a green light

Marshall and Renwick conceived a new series for Alexei Sayle while filming *Whoops Apocalypse* in Miami, in 1986.

on this, I'm getting a sort of amber!" I then knew we were in for more changes because he still wasn't happy.'

During the final days of 1988, following the cancellation of *Hot Metal* at London Weekend Television, their fruitful writing partnership reached a natural end. Marshall sold the pilot episode for his first solo sitcom, *Sob Sisters*, to Central Television, and when

a series was later commissioned, Renwick told his partner to grasp the opportunity. But the series, spotlighting the adventures of two sisters, played by Gwen Taylor and Polly Adams, was shortlived, surviving just seven episodes. Marshall admits it was a 'dreadful' show, but by the time the project was over, Renwick was already engrossed in *One Foot*. 'Stretching out in front of him was this enormous timetable involving *One Foot in the Grave*. I thought I'd start something else and wait for him to finish, so started *2Point4Children* and ended up with an enormous timetable myself. I guess after that it was too late to go back, although I'd never rule out working together again.'

Renwick says the demise of their partnership was 'just as informal as getting together'. The last project they worked on jointly was the BBC sketch show *Alexei Sayle's Stuff*, and with solo work keeping them busy, a parting of the ways was inevitable. However, it was more than just individual projects that necessitated a change in their working practices, as Renwick explains. 'I think our writing styles were diverging more than converging, to the point where I felt less comfortable about editing someone else's work, which is what I felt myself doing . . . Maybe I was just getting more and more rigorous about our material, to the point where I was becoming more brutal in my judgement. That applied to my work and Andrew's, so I found myself sending stuff back more and more. It's OK for me to say: "Everything I've done for the last week I'm going to throw away and write again." But it became increasingly awkward to say this to Andrew. At the end of the day, maybe it's better that one only deals with one's own material, and doesn't sit in judgement on someone else's.'

Renwick believes both have benefited from working solo. 'It's raised our game. Andrew has written his own series and I think the quality shows. Since we stopped writing together I don't think he's ever been without a project on the air, so it's all worked out well for both of us.'

Although they had written independently throughout the course of their partnership, venturing out alone was a significant step. What they didn't realise, of course, was that both were on the threshold of success and critical acclaim; within a short period of time, they would be immersed in sitcoms that would take over their lives.

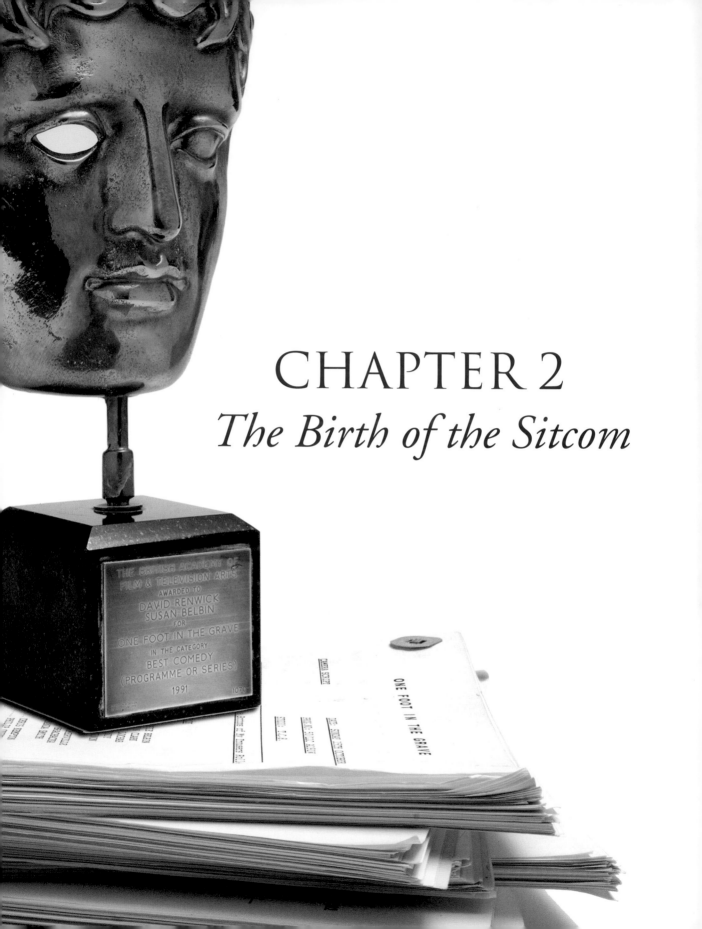

CHAPTER 2
The Birth of the Sitcom

Like all good writers, David Renwick is economical: ideas don't come cheaply and if a scene has to be cut from a script, he won't simply discard it but store it away inside his memory bank in a filing cabinet labelled 'could be useful one day'. And if he crafts a character in whom he spots potential, he'll try to revisit them, which is how his greatest small-screen character to date, Victor Meldrew, was born.

In 1988, as the year drew to a close, Renwick found himself with time on his hands. *Hot Metal* had been read the last rites and while his former partner, Andrew Marshall, was busy writing *Sob Sisters* for Central Television, Renwick filled his time with several assignments, some speculative, others commissioned, including instalments of *Agatha Christie's Poirot* and the feature film *Wilt*, starring Griff Rhys Jones as Henry Wilt, an incompetent teacher who fantasises about murdering his domineering wife. Renwick had even toyed with the idea of developing a feature-length thriller, but as he brushed off the tinsel in preparation for the festive period, his mind drifted back to the genre of comedy. He says: 'An irascible character I'd first developed for a comedy series at Thames in 1978 began to interest me again, and the shape of a half-hour domestic sitcom started to form in my mind.' A madcap scene quickly materialised, with a man trying out a conjuror's guillotine on his wife's best friend. 'It amused me, and within a short time I'd hatched enough funny ideas and scenes to patch together some kind of half hour.' Regarding it as little more than a writing exercise to prove he could write a sitcom on his own, Renwick set to work on a script. 'The premise was minimal: a man in his late fifties who'd been forced into early retirement, which is something that happened to my father when he quit his job as a milkman.' The character was christened Victor Meldrew, the Christian name being chosen with calculated irony because Renwick saw him as a loser. A flick through old notes relating to scripts for thrillers he tried writing for the big screen revealed he'd once given the name Meldrew to a female character.

Victor Meldrew was based on a character called Godfrey Above, whom he'd conceived for a sitcom titled *God Above*. A script had been written for the late Philip Jones, then head of light entertainment at Thames Television, during an exclusivity deal. It was intended as a year-long contract, but Renwick dropped out of the arrangement after just six months, by which time he'd completed a sketch show and two sitcom scripts, including *God Above*, none of which saw the light of day. Although he always believed there was mileage in Godfrey, Renwick realises now why the sitcom was never given the green light, classing it as 'far too mad'. He says: 'A lot of it was funny but overall just too wacky – more so than *One Foot in the Grave*. Also, I don't think my writing had maturity at that time.' This belief is shared by producer Humphrey Barclay. In the early 1980s, some years after Thames had rejected *God Above*, the writer offered it to Barclay at London Weekend Television. But just like Philip Jones, Barclay turned it down. He says: 'I can still see the script for *God Above* sitting in my cupboard at LWT; I didn't buy it, metaphorically or literally. I couldn't see it working. So, if you like, I missed *One Foot in the Grave* because I didn't see the potential of it in its early form.'

As well as Godfrey Above, the antecedents of Victor Meldrew are traced back to two characters created by prolific American playwright Neil Simon. Subliminal memories played their part when Renwick sat down to flesh out Victor for his initial half-hour script. 'Victor was partly inspired by a character in the play *The Plaza Suite*. I'll never forget the scene where this grouchy guy's daughter is supposed to be getting married but locks herself in the bathroom. The whole sequence is about him trying to get her out so she can get married, but his real obsession is that he's going to have to pay off the caterers. It's always made me laugh; it's Neil Simon at his wittiest.' The character in question was named Roy Hubley, portrayed by Walter Matthau when, in 1971, the play was turned into a Golden Globe-nominated film. Renwick didn't realise just how much Simon had influenced his small-screen character until, a couple of years ago, he watched another of his plays, *The Prisoner of Second Avenue*. Delivering the lines on the London stage was Richard Dreyfuss, playing Mel Edison. 'I suddenly thought to myself, "This is Victor." Edison was struggling to cope in a high-rise New York apartment, suffocating in the heat of summer, and everything was getting on top of him. It was twenty-four-carat Victor.'

Despite intending to write a script only to prove he could survive without long-term writing partner Andrew Marshall, once complete, Renwick began wondering whether he could sell it. Fortuitously, he bumped into Jim Moir, then BBC's head of light

> *But I guess it wasn't so much that I regretted that particular title, it's that I didn't have any confidence in it – I have very little confidence in anything.*
>
> DAVID RENWICK

entertainment, during a party at Barry Cryer's house. Taking a break from social chit-chat, both found themselves in Cryer's back garden, leaning against the garden fence. Moir had known Renwick for years, ever since his sketch-writing days, when he supplied material for *The Mike Yarwood Show*, which Moir produced in the late 1970s. 'David's a very gifted writer,' says Moir, 'and I'd always known about him. He produced brilliant sketch material, so we got him working on the *Yarwood Show*, where his work was of a high standard. At that time he was the luminary of Luton, and I watched his talents grow.' As far as Moir is concerned, it was always clear that Renwick was 'extraordinarily gifted'. He says: 'His ability to craft popular drama and comedy, and above all his ability to pick characters which have luminosity on the screen, who'll impress the public, is astonishing.'

On that mild evening in December 1988, in Barry Cryer's garden in Hatch End, Middlesex, Renwick and Moir conversed, discussing old times. Moir recalls: 'The usual conversation took place, and I remember asking: "How's it all going?" David explained he needed a bit of help because he had a script and didn't think he was going to make any headway, so I said: "Whatever you've got, give it to me. I'll look after it."'

Although he'd earned many admirers for his writing on *Alexei Sayle's Stuff*, Renwick had become somewhat

disillusioned with the BBC after seeing two of his situation comedies rejected, before eventually selling them to London Weekend Television. 'Although I'd worked a lot at the BBC on *The Two Ronnies* and other shows, Andrew and I had never managed to get our own show accepted. We sent *Whoops Apocalypse* to John Howard Davies and *Hot Metal* to Gareth Gwenlan and both were turned down. We then took them to Humphrey Barclay at LWT and made them there, but it formed a bit of a pattern that we'd never get anything on at the BBC.' And that was the channel Renwick wanted to work for. 'In those days, the BBC had this great wealth of production talent, an infrastructure that included expertise in every aspect of programme-making. The corporation's output was so polished it was where everyone wanted to place their material.'

Moir's offer helped lift the cloud of pessimism that had descended upon Renwick, and he applied the finishing touches to his script. 'It was about a man who was laid off from his job, which was basically a device to give him a lot of spare time to worry about everyday events, and to allow me to go anywhere with my plots.' By the time the script was posted to Jim Moir, in the middle of January 1989, Renwick had selected the title, *One Foot in the Grave* – a decision he quickly regretted. 'It was the first thing I came up with and I remember being very amused when I thought of it because it seemed to be piling adversity and indignities on the character, which was the object of the exercise in the scripts; so giving the show that title was half-sentencing him to death anyway. In the end, I had to be persuaded to go with it.' He submitted the second script under the title *Senior Citizen*, but admits it sounded drab. 'I found it safer, I suppose, not particularly daring in any way,' says Renwick, who realises the importance of programme titles. Over the years, the norm for situation comedies had been to choose a popular phrase or cliché. 'Maybe that was the reason for my initial reservation, that I was just following a rather boring trend. But I guess it wasn't so much that I regretted that particular title, it's that I didn't have any confidence in it – I have very little confidence in anything. You depend upon the input from lots of people whose judgement you respect. And Susie [Belbin] was one of them of course, telling me it was a good title, and that it would work. That kind of allayed my fears and, of course, at that point I had so much else to worry about, like writing the scripts and who was going to play the parts, so it wasn't my biggest headache. Interestingly, I remember toying with a quote from T. S. Eliot, taken from *The Love Song of J Alfred Prufrock*. I can't remember whether I tried putting it through as a programme title, but I certainly tried using it as the title for the first episode. Unfortunately we couldn't clear it with the Eliot Estate and it quickly died a death.'

On Monday, 23 January 1989, Renwick was sitting at his office desk when the phone rang. An enthusiastic Jim Moir wanted to give his verdict on the script. Moir had 'laughed a lot'[i] and had passed it with a strong recommendation to Gareth Gwenlan, then head of comedy at the BBC. Once a few pages of Renwick's pristine script had been turned, Moir had spotted its potential. 'David revealed his gift of imagination and skills in crafting a script. It also showed his ability to shake the kaleidoscope of life and reinterpret the pieces as they fell into patterns others had not seen.' One of the show's strengths which Moir had noticed was the finely drawn characters. 'They were true to themselves in a variety of extraordinarily inventive situations. But David wasn't just going for comedy, he was putting his finger on the pulse of the way life is lived. The reason we found *One Foot* so funny is that our own human condition was being reflected back to us by David Renwick's characters.'

Although he didn't broach the subject with Renwick, Jim Moir was uncertain about his choice of actor to play the leading character. 'When I read the first script I couldn't quite see Richard Wilson in the role as a security guard. But once the series moved along and got into its stride, you couldn't imagine anyone else playing it.' Moir wouldn't have tried persuading Renwick to reconsider, though. 'I wouldn't have quarrelled with a writer I respected like David,' he says. 'You have to put yourself in the writer's head, and if he wanted to express himself through the talents of Richard Wilson, you had to allow that to happen.'

It wasn't just Jim Moir, however, who couldn't initially envisage Scottish-born actor Wilson playing the lead: Gareth Gwenlan had doubts, too. 'I wasn't as convinced about the leading man as Susie Belbin [whom Gwenlan asked to produce and direct the series] was, but that was simply because I'd seen him do a dreadful thing about the end of a pier for the BBC; I wasn't familiar with his work and having only seen him in small roles, I just needed some convincing.' The show Gwenlan saw was a pilot titled *Walking the Planks*, which the BBC had aired in August 1985 before passing up the option to commission a full series. Written by the experienced team of Michael Knowles and Harold Snoad, who also produced and directed the episode, it featured Michael Elphick as Ron Archer, who decides to

Third time lucky: after two major sitcom rejections at the BBC, Renwick struck gold there with Victor Meldrew.

Tired and weary: the actors get some last-minute notes from Renwick and director Christine Gernon.

buy a dilapidated pier in the fictitious town of Mid-bourne, and Richard Wilson as Mr Talbot, manager of the National United Bank. When the BBC decided not to take the idea further, Snoad and Knowles sold it to Yorkshire Television, who, in 1987, transmitted seven episodes under the new title *High and Dry*, with Wilson reprising his role alongside Bernard Cribbins, who replaced Elphick.

Despite reservations about casting Wilson in the lead role, Gwenlan wanted to commission a series, even though he'd received a script titled *Waiting for God* a couple of months previously. Written by Michael Aitkens, the sitcom – which Gwenlan chose to produce and direct – was set at the Bayview Retirement Village and spawned forty-seven episodes during its four-year life. Although he felt both Aitkens' and Renwick's scripts would be playing to similar audiences, he didn't foresee that as a stumbling block, convinced both would succeed in their own right. '*One Foot in the Grave* was an excellent idea, an area that hadn't really been explored before. When you get a heavily drawn

character like that, with tremendous personality, there is no doubting exactly where he stands on almost anything; it was the basis of very fine comedy.'

A month after informing Renwick that he liked the pilot script and wanted to talk, Gwenlan called to discuss the project. It was Friday, 24 February 1989, and the BBC's Head of Comedy classed *One Foot* as a 'very strong piece with an excellent leading part'[ii]. Renwick reflected on the rest of the conversation in his journal, recording that 'he [Gwenlan] disagrees with my choice of Richard Wilson for Victor, saying he isn't a lead. Of course everyone used to say that back in the seventies about David Jason ("He's a great feed for Ronnie Barker"), so I shall probably take no notice.'

And he didn't. As far as Renwick was concerned, Wilson was the man for the job; he'd written the script with the actor in mind, after having worked with him on the big-screen version of *Whoops Apocalypse* and *Hot Metal*. 'He was wonderful to write for,' says Renwick, 'because fundamentally he's funny. That's something you can't define or quantify – he's just funny saying the lines. In addition, he has the ability to be very edgy, with great resonance to his delivery. And, of course, he has all the technical acuity in terms of timing, with all those wonderful slow burns and double takes. It's the whole repertoire of comic tradition that you depend upon in an actor to make comedy work. You can guide people so far, but at the end of the day you're totally reliant upon their intuition in front of the camera.'

Regarding Gwenlan not seeing Wilson as a lead, Renwick says: 'People in those jobs have funny ideas sometimes about the qualities required to play a lead role. I don't know if I ever considered a "lead" actor as such. What is a lead, anyway? I wasn't thinking along those lines, about seeing Richard as a star of the future. My one concern was who would make it work. Yes, you could cast a big name, someone who'd bring in a decent audience, but that doesn't mean they would be in sympathy with the material.'

The uncertainties and insecurities that have shadowed Renwick throughout his career came to the fore as he awaited a commission for a series. In his journal on Sunday, 30 April, he wrote: 'Head incredibly thick all morning, the old dizziness starting to kick back in. Went out for the papers and then came back and depressed myself by re-reading this sitcom pilot *One Foot in the Grave*. A fluently funny piece of work; looking back at it now I can't quite figure out where it all came from. But full of certainty I could never write another five as good.'

He was forced to try when the BBC commissioned a further episode in June 1989, to prove the idea extended beyond the pilot script. It was an exploration for Renwick, who wrote on Friday, 9 June . . . trying to play down the more obvious comic mechanisms in favour of more lateral, quirkier and character-based devices. I'm still very much feeling my way around though. There are no certainties.' But by mid-June, the second script was winging its way to Gareth Gwenlan, with Renwick delighted that he'd proven to himself that there was life beyond the pilot. Describing it as a 'rich script, balanced this time with a little pathos'[iii], he hoped it would result in an invitation to complete the rest of the series. Nearly a month later, however, a despondent Renwick called his agent, Brian Codd, complaining that he was still awaiting the BBC's verdict. Later that week he recorded, 'Andrew [Marshall] is on his third *Sob Sisters* of Series Two, and

I'm sitting here with nothing confirmed of any kind – it's a sobering thought after fifteen years of uninterrupted full employment.' The interminable wait was beginning to take its toll on Renwick, who considered taking the scripts to London Weekend Television, with whom he'd worked successfully in the past, but after discussing his dismay with Andrew Marshall, he decided to give the BBC more time. By the following Monday, however, Renwick was feeling melancholy about his work; the agonising wait for a decision on the sitcom meant he couldn't concentrate on other assignments. Unable to wait any longer, he plucked up courage and called Gareth Gwenlan. He recorded details of the conversation on 10 July: '"Oh yes, I'd love to commission another four scripts," he said. Music to my ears! . . . Of course he's put it out to tender within the department, which raises the spectre of some totally inappropriate producer becoming attached to it and miscasting the whole thing.'

Although Renwick was informed the show had been put out to tender, Gwenlan had Susan Belbin in mind as producer and director. An experienced member of the comedy team, Belbin was a Glaswegian who'd harboured dreams of working in the theatre since childhood. Aged nine, she attended part-time drama classes, but by the time she'd left school she knew that stage management was where her true interest lay, and enrolled on a full-time course for a year. Upon graduating she worked at Glasgow's Citizens' Theatre for twelve months before turning freelance and working at various venues until the opportunity arose to work, albeit temporarily, at BBC Scotland. Before long, a permanent contract was offered and she was promoted to assistant floor manager. During her twenty-eight-year career in the BBC, she spent four years based at Television Centre in Scotland and the rest in London, beginning with a three-year spell on the *Morecambe and Wise Show* in 1973. By 1976, she was working with veteran producer-director David Croft, and during seven years assigned to his office worked on, among others, *Dad's Army*; *It Ain't Half Hot, Mum*; *Hi-de-Hi!* and *'Allo 'Allo!*, which she helped direct. During the 1980s she directed shows such as *Bread* and the fourth series of *Only Fools and Horses*, and produced-directed *Life Without George* and *Sitting Pretty*.

Belbin was enjoying a few days' leave when the phone rang at her London home. Gareth Gwenlan explained he'd received a script he wanted her to read. 'He biked it round immediately, so I knew it had to be good.' Within the hour the script arrived and Belbin sat in her bay window in Chiswick relaxing as she opened the envelope. As the warming rays of the summer sun streamed through the window, Belbin was enamoured of the script. In her opinion a series should be pursued forthwith, even if, initially, she was uncertain whether she'd be working on this or *Waiting for God*, which was given the nod simultaneously. 'I'd been working with Michael Aitkens, who wrote *Waiting for God*, and he brought me his first script. I liked it and took it into Gareth, who enjoyed it as well.'

Key to the sitcom's success: producer/director Susan Belbin, with PA Amita Lochab and first series cameraman Keith Burton.

With two scripts to choose from, Gwenlan chose *Waiting for God* for himself.

He says: 'As head of department, I had the choice. I felt *One Foot in the Grave* was less my kind of comedy. Objectively, I could see that they were both great comedy scripts, but when you choose which one you're actually going to make, it becomes subjective and I thought I'd be much more at home with *Waiting for God*, and it was the right decision. Over the years I'd worked with a lot of women, including Felicity Kendall and Wendy Craig, and this gave me the opportunity to work with Stephanie Cole, whom I admired greatly. I think I work well with women, particularly when they're playing gutsy characters. That appeals to me more, in a sense, than working with a man playing a gutsy character.'

So Belbin was assigned to *One Foot* and soon after reading the second script, decided it was time to introduce herself to Renwick. When she phoned on Wednesday, 12 July, Renwick had been racking his brains all morning trying to dream up ideas for the third script in the series. The process had been arduous,

and he noted that he wasn't at his 'most confident'[iv] when Belbin called. Later that day, he recorded in his journal: 'She began by lavishing her praises on the material, saying One was "funny" but Two was "really funny", and suggesting I might think about inserting more black humour into the first script. My own feeling is that I'll be lucky enough to produce another four that are even half as funny as those two.'[v]

From the moment Belbin had read the first script, she knew it would be a winner. 'I had no doubts, and when I later spoke to Richard Wilson, I told him it would eventually be a BAFTA winner. It wasn't a glib remark; I meant it.' The script had many facets and, refreshingly, didn't follow the more traditional linear path. 'It weaved in and out, went off on tangents before resolving these off-shoots later down the line. I also liked the subject matter. At the time, I was in my late thirties and wasn't thinking of retiring or being made redundant, but it struck a chord because that's what happens to people and could have happened to me. But first and foremost, it was funny and felt fresh. I liked Victor's subversiveness and Margaret's loyalty.'

Belbin didn't share Gareth Gwenlan's concerns about Richard Wilson being offered the lead role. 'When David told me he had Richard in mind, I said: "I can't believe you're saying that because I'm a huge admirer of Richard Wilson." I'd worked with him at Glasgow's Citizens' Theatre, although that was a drama, and I could hear Richard's voice when I read the script. He has a very distinctive style: he bites words and spits them out, which is very attractive in comedy.'

Plans were afoot to begin location filming in October, leaving Renwick only three months to deliver the four scripts required to complete the series. With summer at its height, and temperatures touching the eighties, his thinking time was largely spent in the garden of his three-bedroom home in Kingsdown Avenue, Luton. Gathering ideas and assembling them into an orderly manner usually followed a particular pattern, as he explains. 'I'd think up as many funny lines as possible, then see if I could bring them together in a completely different order than originally planned, which is how I get the tangents working; it's the way I've always worked, with all these disparate ideas – not that I set out to think of them as unconnected. My main objective is to pack the shows with as much comic invention as possible, then try to legitimise it all, finding a way to pull it all together.' Like any perfectionist, Renwick is rarely completely satisfied with his work. 'I'm always worrying about things, but that's not to say that when I've completed a script I don't mostly feel: "Yes, that's as good as it will get." I'm not one for tampering around after that because nine times out of ten things suffer as a result. By the time I've signed them off to the producer/director, I'm feeling that by and large that's how it should be.'

Between mid-July and mid-August, Renwick beavered away at the remaining scripts, detailing in his journal the twists and turns, the highs and lows as he began the tortuous process of formulating ideas and weaving them into a workable script.

TUESDAY, 25 JULY 1989
Back here from a day at Andrew's to find Susan Belbin had left a message saying Show Three was so funny her mascara had run while she was reading it.

WEDNESDAY, 26 JULY
A morning spent desperately trying to write the opening scene in the old folks' home. I had a draft done by dinnertime but then decided I really haven't thought the whole show through properly yet, and I've got a complex about how good the others are, particularly Three, and I wonder how I'm ever going to achieve a similar standard.

THURSDAY, 27 JULY
Up and working by 8 a.m., and I developed a few more thoughts and some better permutations of existing ones as I plodded through the morning. Once I felt things were clicking again this afternoon I jotted down a new running order and then stopped. I knew that I could hardly expect all the shows to snap into place within three days in the way the first couple did. This fourth episode is proving a real headache and I still don't know if I'm actually in a position to proceed or not.

FRIDAY, 28 JULY
Moving forward a little more smoothly now, writing up the opening bees sequence and the dialogue in the bedroom afterwards. Now convinced that - despite all the endless hassle in getting it to come out right - this sequence is working at long last.

SATURDAY, 31 JULY

I'm convinced the business with Victor making various
"political" statements at the old people's home is all
wrong. But loath to lose some funny dialogue. I think
I can transplant a lot of their blethering into the eye
clinic waiting room. All of a sudden this - together with
the idea that the M. R. Loony candidate was himself
dressed as a bee - gave the events a kind of spurious
interconnectedness. As a result I then fell asleep.
Definitely feeling the strain and getting very tired now.

While Renwick concentrated on his scripts, Susan Belbin's priority was securing the services of Richard Wilson, whose television career had started back in 1965, playing a stonemason with a bad back in an episode of *Dr Finlay's Casebook*. Son of a shipyard timekeeper, Wilson was born in Greenock, Renfrewshire, in 1936, and discovered his ability to make people laugh while still at school. Although he harboured dreams of becoming an actor, he was dissuaded by one of his school teachers who shattered his fragile confidence. 'I was a very shy child, and one day she asked: "What are you going to do, Wilson?" I remember swallowing hard and being very nervous as I stumbled over my words as I replied: "Please, I would like to be an actor." She said: "Don't be silly, boy, you can't speak." Nowadays, I always find it extraordinary, perhaps because of that, when people say things like I've got a beautiful voice. I always think, "No, you're wrong, it can't be possible."' With an acting career seemingly unlikely, he contemplated working in farming – his father's wish – and a life on the ocean wave with the merchant navy, before finally training as a laboratory technician at a Glasgow hospital.

When, two years later, Wilson moved to the Gateside Hospital back in Greenock, spending less time commuting meant he could dedicate more hours to amateur dramatics. In 1956 he was called up for two years' national service, joining the Royal Army Medical Corps, but by the time he sailed home from the Far East, he was determined to pursue his dream of becoming a professional actor. Soon after demob he headed for London, securing a job at the Paddington General Hospital. Meanwhile, he enrolled in acting classes at the City Literature Institute, but in 1963 decided to give up his job and enrol at RADA to try his luck at full-time acting.

Graduating from RADA in 1965, Wilson's fleeting appearance on *Dr Finlay's Casebook* was followed by a stint in repertory theatre, beginning at Worcester. By the end of the decade he was appearing in one-off roles on television, including an episode of *The First Lady*. As the 1970s dawned, he continued working on the stage while his television roles became more frequent. His small-screen credits during this period include *Not on Your Nellie*, *The Sweeney*, *Some Mothers Do 'Ave 'Em*, *Crown Court*, *A Sharp Intake of Breath* and, in 1979, a more regular role as Dr Thorpe in Eric

Belbin never gave up in her quest to secure Richard Wilson for the role of Victor Meldrew.

Chappell's hospital sitcom, *Only When I Laugh*. The 1980s established Wilson as an adroit supporting actor and saw him work with Renwick in the big-screen version of *Whoops Apocalypse* and his sitcom, *Hot Metal*, but his other significant role during the decade was Eddie Clockerty in 1987's *Tutti Frutti*.

As far as Renwick and Belbin were concerned, Richard Wilson was the only name in the frame to play Victor – after all, the show had been written for the Scottish actor. With Gareth Gwenlan about to head off on holiday, Belbin visited his fourth-floor office at Television Centre to provide a progress report on *One Foot in the Grave*. When she confirmed they wanted Wilson, Gwenlan still wasn't keen on the idea.

The day after Gwenlan had left for foreign shores, Belbin suffered a blow that almost brought the *One Foot in the Grave* project crashing down around her. The first two scripts had been despatched to Wilson with an offer letter. Believing he'd spot the potential in playing Victor Meldrew, she was devastated when the phone rang in her office on the morning of Monday, 31 July. After exchanging pleasantries with Wilson's agent, he broke the news that his client had declined the chance to play Victor. As Belbin recalls: 'Richard felt he was too young.' Belbin, however, feels there was another reason he rejected the role. 'I don't think he thought Episode One was all that great; first instalments are always a nightmare to do because you have to introduce the characters and make them likeable so that the viewers want them in their sitting room the following week. It also has to be funny and tell a story – a lot to get over in thirty minutes.'

Belbin's attempts to persuade Wilson failed, leaving the director, still reeling from the shock, with the unenviable task of informing David Renwick. 'He was upset, although not overtly because he's a pessimist, always looking on the black side, because then you're not disappointed if anything doesn't go to plan.'

Renwick confirms Belbin's assessment of his mood on that Black Monday. 'Yes, it was a major shock, but then again it didn't surprise me; in some respects I share Victor's sceptical, negative view of the world. I'm never surprised when something like that happens because beforehand I'd have been thinking: "What's the worst thing that could happen here? Richard will turn it down. That's not going to happen, though, is it? After all, he's worked with me before. Why would he turn us down?" After going through that kind of thought process, it means I wasn't overly shocked when it happened.'

> *He was upset, although not overtly because he's a pessimist, always looking on the black side, because then you're not disappointed if anything doesn't go to plan.*
>
> SUSAN BELBIN

When Wilson received the offer to play Victor he was planning a holiday, but upon hearing that David Renwick, with whom he'd worked the previous year, wanted him to read a couple of scripts for a possible new series, he agreed. As soon as they arrived at his London home, he poured himself a coffee and settled down to read, but it didn't take long before he realised Victor Meldrew wasn't right for him. 'Victor was sixty, and I didn't feel ready to play older men. I also didn't take to the idea particularly: the character seemed too angry all the time. There were other aspects I didn't like, such as bits not being particularly believable, so I sent the scripts back, saying: "No, thank you very much." Then I had a further call from my agent, saying it had been written specially for me; it's typical of David that he'd go ahead and write something for you but not tell you about it,' smiles Wilson, who pointed out to his agent that he was 'very touched' but was planning a break and the answer was still 'no'.

With Wilson ruling himself out of the running, Belbin and Renwick were forced to return to the drawing board. At first Renwick could only envisage one possible alternative: Les Dawson, for whom he'd written earlier in his career. 'Two things I admired about him were how quickly he learnt his lines and that wonderful lugubrious diction. People were probably surprised that he was my second choice and, yes, he wasn't the actor Richard is, but nevertheless, returning to my overall imperative about being funny, he

I didn't give a very good interview . . . It did the programme some favours because you couldn't have got anyone better than Richard Wilson to do it.

ANDREW SACHS

certainly would have got the laughs. On the other hand, the series would never have had the same depth and reality if Les Dawson had played the role.'

Dawson, however, was tied up with *Blankety Blank* as Renwick discovered when he called Susan Belbin on the afternoon of 1 August to discuss alternatives. His frustrations were reflected in his journal entry that day. 'Called Ms Belbin this afternoon and to my tentative casting ideas she responds with "Ohh come on!" (I think we can aim higher than that). She said the schedule was now locked in because they'd got some transmission dates in the autumn. The usual cavalier BBC attitude of let's make it whether the right people are available or not. I mentioned Timothy West as another possible Victor and she said he was probably doing more *Brasses*. John Thaw isn't available . . . She is suggesting Eric Idle, but of course he isn't right either. I put the phone down in a tetchy frame of mind, but the sun is now peeping through in fresh, windy fashion, and it's silly for me to get this antsy over a sitcom. Episode Four is virtually home and dry, so I must just get my head down and be done with it.'[vi]

The search for their leading actor saw Belbin meeting Andrew Sachs, who'll for ever be remembered for his delightful portrayal of Manuel, the Spanish waiter in *Fawlty Towers*. She advised Renwick not to dismiss him and arranged a further meeting at her office on Monday, 7 August. Renwick left his Luton home that afternoon for his first face-to-face meeting with the show's producer-director. They'd chatted on the phone on several occasions, but never met. Renwick later noted: 'She was less intimidating in person, slimmer and more restrained than I'd imagined, and in the event we seemed to connect fairly effortlessly.'[vii]

Andrew Sachs had become the strongest contender to play Victor, although Renwick admits he didn't think he was right when his name was first mooted. 'Susie said she'd seen him and liked him; she didn't think I should rule him out and arranged for him to come back and meet me.' Renwick recalled: 'Andrew Sachs arrived and his remarks were a mixture of compliments about the material and reservations about where he thought the writing was basically too exaggerated, like the character of Nick in Episode One, and the girl who makes up the woman in a coma. Paradoxically he said he had showed the scripts to his thirty-five-year-old son who had laughed out loud and said as far as he was concerned they were fine. But it hadn't changed his father's mind. He said he was fifty-nine now, and he liked to play comedy with pace, and I said how angry did he think Victor should get, and he said "very angry". But somehow I wondered if there was enough fire in him to make it work. He said he most definitely wanted to play the part – "I think Susie wants me to do it – and I hope you want me to do it." Talk about putting you on the spot! Then, going through the dialogue he pointed out speeches that were "too wordy", viz Margaret's line about being "horribly crushed to death in a horrific road accident". He had bracketed the words "horribly" and "horrific", saying it worked just as well without them.'[viii] To a writer like Renwick, who deliberated over every sentence in his scripts, each word was essential to the success of the scene. As he recorded, the 'over-statement here was quite deliberate; it was funny to me that a housewife would pepper the conversation with those words, and generally I found myself equivocating as he left us, bound for Budapest tomorrow.'[ix]

Reflecting on the meeting, some sixteen years later, Andrew Sachs admits: 'I didn't give a very good interview or felt I said the right things; I wasn't on form and didn't do myself any favours. On the other hand, it did the programme some favours because you couldn't have got anyone better than Richard Wilson to do it.' Securing the services of Wilson, though, was some way away.

After the interview, Renwick felt 'relieved'[x] when Belbin, sensing his doubts, decided they must continue their search. After spending forty-five minutes flipping through the casting directory, *Spotlight*, for inspiration, they called it a day and headed home. The following day, Renwick suggested actor Ken Jones, but Belbin, establishing that Michael Gambon might be available, had mailed copies of the scripts for him to read. Although Gambon liked the scripts, their density meant it would be too much work to undertake alongside his theatre commitments. It was becoming increasingly difficult to find someone to replace Richard Wilson. Whenever they considered alternatives, it wasn't long before their minds drifted

Working together again – eventually . . . Renwick and Wilson filming the first series, September 1989.

back to Wilson's attributes, including his ability to imbue the character with the degree of wit and realism Renwick had envisaged when he began writing the script. 'You try eliminating the strengths Richard Wilson has as an actor from your mind; you try looking for another interpretation or the same interpretation but with another actor,' explains Belbin. 'But you can't because there is only one Richard Wilson. Whatever it was we wanted, Richard had it. His enunciation, the biting of his words and spitting out and, of course, the Scottish accent helped enormously. Being a Scot, it was music to my ears and worked for me.' Realising they were never going to find an alternative, Belbin turned to Renwick, announcing: 'This is ridiculous. There's only one man to play this and that's Richard Wilson: you wrote it for him. He should play it." So I went with the begging bowl to his agent.'

Realistically they thought their chance of attracting Wilson had gone. Belbin and Renwick had exhorted the actor to rethink, so they felt utter relief when he not only decided to read another two scripts, but upon reading them and realising what Renwick was looking for, agreed to discuss the project. Although there was still work to be done, it was the breakthrough Renwick and Belbin had craved. 'By the time Richard saw the other scripts, the character was developing,' says Belbin. 'There were more situations, more things happening to Victor, and Richard could see that.' Wilson, who was directing a play in the West End, called Belbin's office, expressing his appreciation of the additional scripts he'd been sent, but said he wanted to reread the first two and would give an answer within a few days.

It was an agonising wait, during which time Jim Broadbent's name was suggested as a possible Victor, but it wasn't taken further because it was felt that he was the wrong age;

meanwhile, Renwick was inching his way towards completing the final two scripts. The finishing line was excruciatingly close now, but his confidence suffered a blow when Belbin, upon reading Show Five ('The Eternal Quadrangle'), called. Renwick jotted in his journal, 'Susie called and shattered my spirits for the day by saying the stuff in Show Five with Victor putting razor blades in his mouth at the supermarket check-out was all too dodgy, and she had guessed the pay-off with the Valentine cards, which was a shame when usually she found all my writing so unpredictable. She was very decent about it, and of course spot-on with her comments, but the result was that I felt just emotionally sledge-hammered for a few hours.'[xi] A couple of days earlier, he'd written: 'I seem to be feeling a bit more comfortable with Susie now, less apprehensive about her directional judgement.'[xii]

It was the start of a long friendship and working relationship, the coming together of equally strong-willed individuals. Susan Belbin says: 'We started working together as a partnership, which I hope David agrees with. Yes, it did get me down at times, and was occasionally exhausting – I can't deny that, but the end product was always worth the effort.'

As the clock ticked on, Renwick reported 'another day of creeping depression in the BBC sweatbox interviewing actors'[xiii] on Tuesday, 29 August. The day worsened, as far as he was concerned, when Richard Wilson popped in for an hour. Over sandwiches in Belbin's office, they discussed the show but still no commitment was forthcoming. His unwillingness to commit was fuelled by the fact that after spending an exhausting year directing not only a film for television but the stage play, *Prin*, he'd promised himself a holiday. Therefore, he didn't feel ready to give the nod to a series that would undoubtedly be a strain on his energies. Although he expressed reservations that the character had to be likeable, and that he wasn't confident he could inject the London-based ordinariness he felt was present in the scripts, he did, however, acknowledge that the scripts got 'stronger, funnier and more anarchic'[xiv] as they went along.

Overall, though, the news was disheartening for Renwick who concluded, 'The whole prospect of this series going down the pan big time is now looming large.'[xv]

But as August drew to a close, the phone rang in Belbin's office at the BBC, bringing news that had seemed increasingly unlikely: Richard Wilson had

> *The whole prospect of this series going down the pan big time is now looming large.*
>
> DAVID RENWICK

accepted the role. Everyone was finally able to breathe a huge sigh of relief: their worries dissipated immediately. 'David and I were absolutely thrilled,' says Belbin, who also recalls breaking the news to her boss, Gareth Gwenlan. 'When he returned from his trip, he phoned and asked how I was getting on. He was interested to know who I'd cast as Victor. When I told him Richard Wilson, all he said was: "On your head be it!" before putting the phone down. That cheered me up no end,' says Belbin, who's remained friends with Gwenlan. 'In many ways, though, it was like a red rag to a bull. Because there's nothing I like better than a challenge, I decided I was going to show this man. It ended up as a joke between us, because every time we got another comedy award, I'd always say to him, tongue-in-cheek, "On your head be it!"'

Gwenlan, though, was quite content to leave Belbin to get on with making the programme as she saw fit. 'If you had producers whose talents you appreciated, and by and large that was the case because you tended not to employ people you didn't rate, you let them get on with it. One would only interfere or make suggestions if you thought it was absolutely vital. Susie had a very good track record and was an extremely talented producer and went on to make a huge success of the show.'

CHAPTER 3
Casting the Net

By the time the protracted discussions with Richard Wilson had finally reached a fruitful end, Susan Belbin and David Renwick were busy casting the one-off roles frequenting early episodes of Series One. Casting is obviously a crucial component for any programme: make a mistake in the selection and a characterisation, a scene, a strand of comedy can be ruined. As far as Belbin is concerned, casting minor roles can often be more taxing than regular characters. 'They can blow it and take the reality out of the scene completely.' *One Foot* was not only about comedy: a degree of gravitas permeated the script and, at times, it was best described as a comedy drama, therefore performances had to be truthful. 'If the performer suddenly thinks they're in a comedy and starts being funny, it becomes a nightmare. Because these small roles are an integral part of the show, it's imperative you get the right person.'

Renwick felt Annette Crosbie would bring a 'truthful intensity' to the part of Margaret.

The views are echoed by David Renwick, who placed such importance on securing the right people that he sat through every casting session. For some writers, it's too time-consuming a procedure to get wrapped up in and thus it's left to the director to resolve. Others, meanwhile, feel a need to be involved every step of the way; few are present when the minor roles passing through their fictional world are cast. It can be a dispiriting experience, observing quietly while a host of performers – many of whom are swiftly recognised as unsuitable – do the script an injustice with a lacklustre reading. As Renwick recorded on 29 August 1989, after another gruelling day: 'Various people for various parts, some more useless than others. It's so hard not to believe your material is shit when it's given a shit performance.'[i]

But the process continued with Belbin and Renwick focusing on someone to play Margaret Meldrew. Just as he'd set his sights on Wilson playing the male lead, Renwick knew who he wanted as the female lead – Annette Crosbie. Having watched her performance as Liz in Tony Marchant's three-part drama *Take Me Home* for the BBC, which had aired earlier in 1989, he knew she possessed the qualities he wanted for Margaret. 'Seeing her in *Take Me Home* I just got a sense of a truthfulness and intensity that would lift all this above the level of the conventional sitcom. It wasn't that I found her funny as such, but intuitively I just think she could bring incredible weight to the show.'[ii]

Auditioning for the role of Margaret began in earnest on Thursday, 31 August, just eighteen days before filming was due to begin. There wasn't much time to find the right woman. As well as Crosbie, a string of actresses was seen that day, including Marjorie Yates, then appearing in *The Plantagenets* at the Barbican, and Anne Stallybrass. But for Renwick there was only one choice, and as soon as she read for the part, Susan Belbin was convinced, too.

Born in Gorebridge, near Edinburgh, in 1934, Crosbie was the daughter of an insurance agent. Her mother was gifted musically and wanted her to fulfil her own dreams by becoming a piano tutor. 'My mother couldn't exploit her talent because there wasn't the money – and if there had been my father would have drunk it all.' Crosbie, however, admits that she simply didn't have her mother's talent. When she was eleven, her mother tried a different avenue and entered her into singing classes at the local Edinburgh Competition Festival. Her parents were 'terribly shocked and appalled' when it became apparent that she wouldn't become either a piano teacher or an opera singer. Her future was assured, however, when, thanks to her piano tutor, she discovered it was possible to obtain a bursary from the Edinburgh Corporation to study drama. By the early 1950s she was training at the Bristol Old Vic Theatre School. During the final year of her two-year course, Crosbie was cast in a minor role in the original production of Arthur Miller's play *The Crucible* in Bristol. She was subsequently transferred to the London Old Vic for a year before working for three months in an Alastair Sim-produced play at London's Aldwych Theatre.

Her first experience of the big screen came with an appearance as a waitress in the 1959 picture *The Bridal Path*, concerning a Hebridean islander, played by Bill Travers, who travels to the mainland to find a wife. Her first job on television quickly followed, while she was working at Glasgow's Citizens' Theatre. After nearly three years she returned south and worked at various venues, including the Royal Court. During the 1960s and 1970s, Crosbie was in demand for all media, particularly theatre, while on the small screen during this period she was seen in, among others, *Callan*, *Thirty-Minute Theatre*, *Menace*, *Shadows of Fear*, *Special Branch* and *The Edwardians*. She was also regularly cast in regal roles, playing Catherine of Aragon in the 1970 mini-series *The Six Wives of Henry VIII*, Duchess of York in *The Tragedy of Richard III* and, most notably, Queen Victoria in the 1975 mini-series, *Edward the King*.

Annette Crosbie had established a reputation for being forthright and not one to suffer fools gladly; her frankness and at times frosty demeanour frequently conveyed the wrong signals, something the actress is painfully aware of. 'Even during my teens when I got to know someone, they'd admit that they had been afraid of me, which isn't a comforting thing to know; in fact,

> *If you've the kind of face that in relaxed mode just falls into a Greek mask, there's nothing you can do about it.*
>
> ANNETTE CROSBIE

it upset me a lot. I could never understand it, but as you get older you realise what they meant: if you're brusque and don't have many social graces, like phoning someone up and cutting to the quick rather than going through all the accepted overtures before asking them something, it does disconcert people. It's something I've just had to get used to.' Ironically, as Crosbie points out, she's often cast as vulnerable people, the kind who 'wouldn't say boo to a goose'. She cites this part of her make-up as a drawback. 'My mother was just the same, so it's either in the genes or I've picked it up as a behavioural trait and stuck with it. Occasionally, while minding my own business, strangers would come up to me and say: "Cheer up, it might never happen!" If you've the kind of face that in relaxed mode just falls into a Greek mask, there's nothing you can do about it. When I used to meet directors, I was so aware of this forbidding exterior that I'd go in, saying to myself: "For God's sake, Annette, try and charm them – be nice, polite and friendly." I'd do my best and perhaps get the job, but later find out that I'd put the fear of God into them as soon as I walked in the room.'

And that's what she did when she turned up for the meeting at the BBC with Belbin and Renwick, who noted that 'you could feel the room ice over the minute she entered, looking cold, stern and threatening. After the usual business of chatting round the houses, Susie courageously went for it and asked if she'd mind reading for us, and immediately I just wanted to be swallowed up to the earth's core.'[iii] As Renwick expected, though,

Crosbie was a big fan of Renwick's writing from the start . . . and the admiration was mutual.

Crosbie put in a good performance: his assessment reveals just how satisfied he was with her reading. 'It was brilliantly funny. She managed to mine even the in-between lines for humour, not just the more obvious "jokes". And my intuition proved to be correct: through sheer depth and honesty in her performance she made you believe in the character, believe in her attitudes, relate to those attitudes, and laugh at them.'[iv]

Believing they'd found their Margaret, Belbin and Renwick lunched with Richard Wilson at Rules, arguably London's oldest restaurant, in Covent Garden. While discussing aspects of the upcoming show, including the scripts, Wilson explained he didn't feel the first was up to the standard of the others, something Renwick agreed with. He also felt that socially the Meldrews were placed in the upper-working category – again, something with which Renwick concurred. Belbin and Renwick were stunned, however, when it was clear Wilson wasn't convinced Crosbie was right for the role of Margaret. Belbin says: 'When I told Richard I noticed a bit of hesitation; I guessed something wasn't sitting comfortably with him. I asked if he had a problem with it. I don't think he saw Annette in the

role the way he envisaged Margaret. Perhaps he saw her in one of the roles she was famous for, such as Queen Victoria – a very stern but admirable performance. I guess it was quite a big leap to then imagine her as a housewife in suburbia, living with a man like Victor.'

Wilson suggested to Belbin that perhaps they hadn't seen all the actresses they could have and, to be certain, they should see a few more. Belbin didn't want to rock the boat as far as Wilson was concerned. 'We didn't want Richard going anywhere and, at that stage, he probably wasn't even signed up. I didn't think for a minute that he was going to jump ship, but you had to do things right.'

Wilson points out that he had nothing against Crosbie, and although he didn't know her personally, regarded her as a 'very good actress'. Any initial hesitations resulted from his desire for another thespian, Rosemary Martin, whose lengthy list of credits included playing Verna Johnson in the wartime drama *Tenko*, to be given the part. He says: 'Rosemary was a very good friend with whom I'd worked in several workshops, back in the 1970s. I knew she was very funny and was keen for her to do it.'

Although they couldn't envisage finding anyone better suited to the role than Crosbie, they agreed to see other actresses. In addition to Rosemary Martin, a wide range of talented actresses was invited to read for the part, including Sheila Reid, Hilda Braid and Anna Cropper. Dilys Laye, who's recently played running characters in *Coronation Street* and *EastEnders*, but whose long career has seen her appear in four *Carry On* films, was invited back to read for a second time, while scripts were sent to Jean Alexander, who later declined to read. Belbin even tried her best to pitch the idea to Geraldine McEwan's agent, but however hard they looked, they couldn't see beyond Annette Crosbie. 'They were all fine actresses, but David and I weren't convinced,' explains Belbin. 'Maybe if it wasn't such an edgy piece there would have been three or four we could have cast, but it just wouldn't have been the same; it would have ended up comfortable and cosy. We wouldn't have got that extra mile that Annette gave. We just saw Annette and Richard as an ideal married couple for television: all we had to do was convince Richard of that, and time was running out.'

Wilson was disappointed when he heard Rosemary Martin hadn't convinced Belbin and Renwick and suggested they read together, so on Thursday, 7 September, just under two weeks before filming was due to begin, everyone gathered at Television Centre to see if the chemistry between actor and actress was such that Martin would shoot to the top of the wanted list. David Renwick dodged the late summer showers as he made his way to the BBC to meet Susan Belbin, prior to Wilson and Martin's arrival. A potentially tense meeting transpired to be nothing more than a friendly chat, aided by the friendship of Renwick and Wilson, which had been cultivated during their time on *Hot Metal*. Everyone felt at ease as Wilson began reading two-handed scenes from Episode Two ['The Big Sleep']. Here, for the first time, Renwick was afforded the chance to hear Victor come alive. Ultimately, however, despite encouragement and guidance from Belbin, Renwick still wasn't convinced by Martin's reading, recording, 'The simple reality was that she didn't really make me laugh.'[v] Renwick says: 'By that stage, it's not only a case of "Is this person worthy of consideration?" but "Is this person better than Annette Crosbie?" And no one was.'

As the days passed, and no decision was taken regarding Margaret, an increasingly nervous Renwick admits his defeatist tendencies came to the fore again. He assumed that Crosbie was out of the equation, not realising that the tenacious Susan Belbin was still on the case. It was now the eleventh hour, just days before filming was due to start, and Belbin was on a recce, checking out locations in the Bournemouth area, where the series was filmed. Despite every effort, no one had been found to match Annette Crosbie in the director's eyes and she decided it was time to explain the predicament to Richard Wilson. 'I phoned him and said: "I'm very concerned; it's now Thursday and we start shooting next week. You have to trust me on this one – I really think it has to be Annette Crosbie. She's

perfect for the part. She complements you as a character and you need that. I believe in you as a married couple." Richard replied: "I trust you, Susie."'

Casting the two main roles in *One Foot in the Grave* had been a wearisome affair but, albeit worryingly close to the off, Belbin and Renwick had their dream pairing. In most double-acts there is the funny man and the stooge, simply acting as a feed or a focus for their partner's quips, and this was one of Margaret's responsibilities. Although providing a counterpoint for the volatile Victor, the character was multi-layered, possessing a sense of humour which, in line with the sitcom's style, was portrayed within a scenario rooted largely in reality. Reflecting on Crosbie's performance in the show, Renwick says: 'People are either funny or they're not; funny is something that is resident in you as a person. You can't teach it to anyone – it's not even a talent, it's just a certain quality that you have as an individual. Oddly enough, though, Annette is a bit of a special case. She's not what I would call an inherently "funny" actress, but she has the ability to complement the humour through the intensity of her reactions. I once had a discussion with her about this whole issue. She felt that if her approach was too severe, it would stop you laughing. I know what she means, but sometimes the reverse is true and the sheer passion of her performance does actually underscore the comedy. I adored the way she could convey so much by saying so little.' With just a glance, a flick of the head, a withering stare or simply the way she holds herself, Crosbie has been gifted with an array of tools to enhance her performance, and she used them adroitly. Casting a more blatant comic actress as Margaret would have altered the entire complexion of the show, even with Wilson's presence, and with Renwick's drive for equal measures of comedy and reality, Crosbie's manner and style undoubtedly helped steer the show in the right direction, embellishing it with a touch of class and maturity.

Two other characters who debuted in the opening episode of Series One were Jean Warboys and Nick Swainey, played by Doreen Mantle and Owen Brenman respectively. While Mrs Warboys would appear in two further episodes in the first season, Swainey's was a one-off appearance. Both, however, would become regulars

All smiles for the camera . . . though for some reason Margaret doesn't seem very amused.

in the show, providing characters for Victor and Margaret to play off, but also affording David Renwick extra vehicles through which to express his comedy.

The rather batty Mrs Warboys – a name Renwick adopted after standing behind a real-life Mrs Warboys in the queue at a Luton post office – was a friend of the Meldrews, though tended to gravitate towards Margaret, whom she frequently drove up the wall. It was from her naïvety and maladroitness that her appeal as a character flowed. Despite her frustrating tendencies and irritating gullibility, she was liked by Margaret and they looked out for each other. The character was initially viewed by Renwick as a device for the first scene he ever dreamt up: the neighbour being guillotined by Victor. Throughout the six series and numerous Christmas Specials, a number of mishaps befell the hapless Mrs Warboys, which helped cement her value to the production as a whole. Any misfortunes devised by Renwick needed a victim, and

invariably it was Mrs Warboys who would deliver maximum impact in terms of humour. 'In the guillotine scene, it wouldn't have been funny if it happened to Margaret, just as in 'Starbound' [the 1996 Christmas Special] it wouldn't have been funny if Margaret had been trussed up in a sack, thrown down a hill and mounted by an Alsatian.' Why it wouldn't be as amusing is something which intrigues Renwick. 'These are the things I find fascinating and unanswerable, and it's why comedy defies too much analysis. Going back to the scene in 'Starbound', if it had been Margaret, the dog scene would have just died on the screen and you'd be thinking: "My God, what a terrible thing to happen to someone." But with Mrs Warboys you laugh. It's largely to do with the character, but also because it's Doreen playing her.'

South African-born Doreen Mantle impressed Renwick and Belbin from the moment she began reading for the part on Wednesday, 6 September 1989. It had been the usual mix of thespians, some impressive, others disappointing, but Mantle outshone her rivals. Recording in his journal, Renwick noted: 'We were very impressed by a rather conservative-looking actress named Doreen Mantle who gave a weighty, truthful reading, and was amusing in a subtler way than I'd envisaged, like a classy version of Doris Hare.'*vi*

When just six weeks old, Mantle left Johannesburg with her parents and spent the next five years in England before returning to South Africa. While studying social studies at university, with the aim of becoming a social worker, she began acting in her spare time for the South African Broadcasting Corporation and various stage productions. In her early twenties, Mantle found herself becoming increasingly uneasy with the state of politics in the country, so headed to England with her husband. 'We were young and poor, and needed to earn some money. I decided with the wonderful ignorance and arrogance of youth to earn a living by acting – and, luckily, I did.'

She began working in repertory theatre before taking an eleven-year break while raising a family, afterwards resuming her career in the theatre, working for, among others, the Royal Shakespeare Company. During a lean

Off-camera, Mantle and Wilson shared a great passion for the theatre.

spell she worked as a London tourist guide until, in 1972, she agreed to appear in the William Trevor play *Going Home* at London's King's Head Theatre. The play's success helped launch a career which, although predominantly in the theatre, included screen work, such as episodes of *Special Branch*, *Strange Report*, *Secret Army* and the running character of Mrs Catchpole in the 1970s period drama, *Duchess of Duke Street*, while on the big screen she'd appeared in such films as 1967's *Privilege*, *Black Jack*, *Yentl* and *Mountains of the Moon*.

Busy working in the theatre when she attended the *One Foot* audition, Mantle didn't expect the role to become a landmark in her life. 'It began in a very minor way, but I remember how beautifully the episode was written, right from the beginning.' Regarding Mrs Warboys as her favourite screen character, Mantle says: 'She always wanted to help and meant well all the time; it's just that she was tactless and not very bright, although occasionally she'd have these strange streaks of knowledge, like the time she knew all the answers while playing Trivial Pursuit.'

During the life of the sitcom, Mrs Warboys, like most of the secondary characters, was seen, on average, in three episodes per series. Such was the enjoyment she received from playing Jean, Doreen Mantle wishes she'd appeared more often. 'In the last series she's only in two episodes – both wonderful episodes, mind you. But David used to say: "I can't manufacture situations for each character."'

Deciding when to use Mrs Warboys or any of the other oft-seen characters wasn't something Renwick consciously thought about: for him, every episode is a new journey. 'If I think of an idea which will be great for Mrs Warboys, then I put her in. I don't think: "She's already been in three episodes this series; there's no way I can have her in a fourth." More often than not, it's the reverse: I suddenly reached Episode Six and Mrs Warboys had only been in one, so I tried to move heaven and earth to get her in.'

When you work with a performer who delivers the goods, most directors and writers are understandably keen to re-use their talents at the earliest moment. When it came to casting Nick Swainey, who was originally expected to make just one appearance as a character who dedicated his time to helping the elderly at the local care homes, Renwick earmarked Brenman, with whom he'd worked on *Alexei Sayle's Stuff* and held in high regard. Although he only made a fleeting appearance in the opening episode, Renwick's appreciation of the actor's work led him to revive the character in Series Two, when he joined Mrs Warboys as the show's only other semi-regular at that point.

Nick Swainey cut a forlorn figure. You didn't have to scratch too far below the sunny, ebullient, forever-smiling exterior to find a feckless individual full of deep insecurity, pain and sadness – areas of his make-up that were occasionally explored via Renwick's astute character observations. For me, Swainey is one of the show's gems, a character who works on more than one level. Primarily he's a comedy character, and the catalyst for numerous laughs, but there's a degree of sorrow which is exploited within the darker elements of Renwick's writing, such as the fear of loneliness, so beautifully examined in the penultimate episode, 'The Dawn of Man', from November 2000. Upon spotting all-action television presenter Skip Hoberman on a television documentary, Margaret notices that he bears an uncanny resemblance to Nick Swainey, so she passes the tape to her neighbour. Watching the courageous

taunting me with a glimpse of the man I should have been. It's hard to imagine Skip Hoberman living at home with his mother for forty years, running tombolas like an overgrown boy scout.

MARGARET: Life isn't just about ambition, Mr Swainey. Just earning the respect of others as a decent and gentle human being is enough for anyone to be proud of.

NICK: Oh, yeah, I've certainly wheeled a lot of old ladies about, Mrs Meldrew. But who's going to wheel me about?

Like all the semi-regulars, Renwick's economical writing meant Nick Swainey was never over-used. 'It conforms to this overall philosophy I have that I want to ration people,' he says. 'I never wanted to create a group of characters who were there all the time, even if they didn't have much to do in a given week. The actors would probably disagree because they get paid for their appearances, but from an artistic perspective I'm sure they'd agree that if their characters are going to be in the show, I should give them something decent to do, a meaningful function within the main plot. That way you don't get fed up with them – and above all you want to avoid predictable.'

Owen Brenman remembers reading to Susan Belbin, but knowing that she was seeing him on Renwick's recommendation, felt he stood a good chance of securing the role. When offered the part, it didn't take him long to understand his character, especially after spotting similarities with a teacher from his North London school. 'This teacher was always very enthusiastic about everything. Even when other people were taking the piss out of him, he somehow carried on relentlessly, oblivious to it all. I didn't consciously say, "I'm going to play the character like him", but having thought about it since, I see the parallels.'

> *Nick's funny and people like him, but I don't know if he opens doors for other work: because he's quite an extreme, odd character, there aren't many other parts that naturally follow.*
>
> OWEN BRENMAN

Hoberman risking his life in the line of duty while reporting from one of the world's troublespots has a profound effect on Swainey, as Margaret soon realises when she finds herself rendering advice and support.

NICK: Bit of a shock to the system, something like that, as if . . . I dunno, someone was

Brenman, son of a doctor, was born in London in 1956. His first taste of acting was at the age of twelve, attending a local drama class, where he discovered an ability to make people laugh. 'I never did much on Saturdays so began going to these drama classes that a woman organised in her front room. A school friend of mine went along too, and we'd do some improvisation or sketches. I was rather reluctant to attend at first, but when I found I could make all these older girls laugh, I thought, "I quite like this", and carried on with it. People like Emma Thompson and her sister, Sophie, used to go at the same time, although in a different class. This woman, Sheila Sachs, was very good and was the inspiration behind a few people who went on and succeeded in acting, but it was never intended as stage school training – just imaginative, creative fun.'

After graduating from university, where he'd studied drama, he completed a one-year postgraduate course in 1980 before enduring several months out of work. He secured his Equity card via a performance at Alan Ayckbourn's Stephen Joseph Theatre, Scarborough, and other stage work quickly followed, punctuated by the occasional screen credit. He'd only made a handful of screen appearances before joining the cast of *One Foot*, beginning in the early 1980s with a live appearance on BBC's comedy programme *The Oxford Road Show* and including episodes of sitcoms such as *No Place Like Home* and *'Allo, 'Allo!* as well as playing a policeman in 1983's *The Jigsaw Man*.

Playing Nick in *One Foot* was the highest-profile job he'd secured at that point in his career, but he's unsure whether it can be regarded as his big break. 'I've never really discovered the "big break", when a job opens all these doors. I think it's more a series of little breaks that you get. Probably meeting David Renwick through the *Alexei Sayle* series was important because that did lead to other work. My agent couldn't get me seen for the series, so on one of the few times I did something and didn't just sit there, I sent a tape in and fortunately was invited to meet Marcus Mortimer, who produced and directed the series. Then I met David and Andrew Marshall. I read these sketches and they were all

laughing. Then they cast me in a sketch, but I only had about two lines. But they must have thought I did well because I was invited back. In the end I appeared in the rest of this series and the others. So that brief meeting and that tiny little part in the sketch led to all the work I've done with David.'

Brenman, who most recently worked with Renwick in his comedy-drama *Love Soup*, regards Nick Swainey as one of his favourite roles, although it has become a double-edged sword. 'I sometimes think that because he is so off-the-wall, some people aren't sure what to make of him, or me! Nick's funny and people like him, but I don't know if he opens doors for other work: because he's quite an extreme, odd character, there aren't many other parts that naturally follow.'

Brenman found the character challenging to play, technically, with Renwick presenting him almost in the form of a monologue. 'It read like a comedy sketch. I'd come on and have to bring my own energy to it, which was slightly removed from what might already be happening. Normally, when you're in a scene with other people, there's a two-way relationship going on – a sense of give and take. The way he wrote Nick, he almost had to come in like a steamroller: he does his thing, regardless of what anyone else is doing, then disappears. So you have to psych yourself up and get your energy bubbling at the right level, which made it quite lonely in a way. I had to be completely self-motivated.' Swainey with his ultra-sunny manner was hard work at times, particularly on location. 'When you're filming you don't get any rehearsal, and when we were starting a new series, it might have been twelve months since I last played him. I'd be turning up in Bournemouth at 9 a.m. to play someone who has to be going 100 miles an hour from the minute he opens his mouth. It's "Morning, Margaret" and you're off from a standing start. I found it difficult at times to do that.' A challenge it might have been, but Brenman certainly rose to the occasion, bringing to life one of the most memorable supporting characters of the series.

CHAPTER 4
Getting the Show on the Road

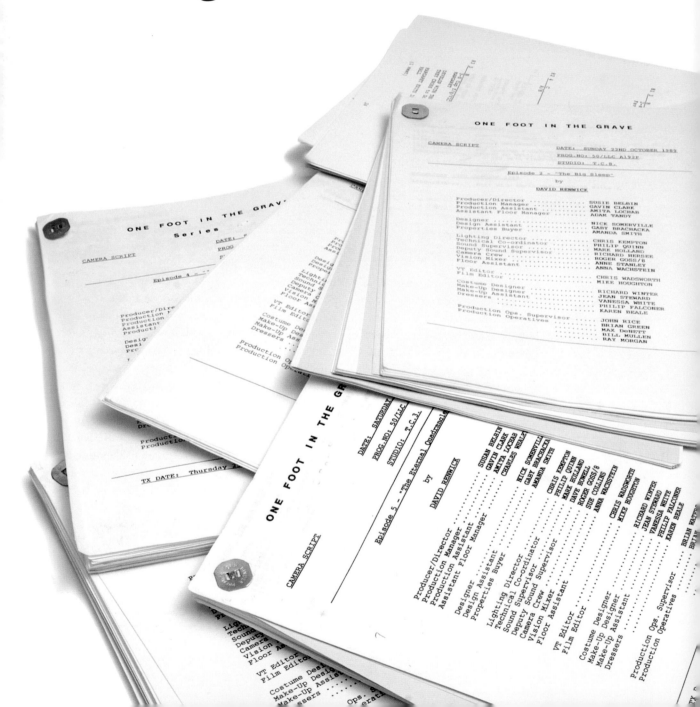

One of the requisites of being a producer-director is the ability to juggle a million balls at the same time. After assembling the necessary individuals to form her production team for the first series, duties were assigned as preparations for *One Foot* gained momentum. The sitcom's setting was kept deliberately vague, and although placing it in the north wouldn't automatically alienate southern viewers, Renwick wanted to avoid regionalising the programme too much, and, besides, didn't see the need for declaring where the Meldrews lived.

Thus with no specific locality required, the two principal considerations were, firstly, finding somewhere that boasted a favourable climate and, secondly, an area easily reached from the BBC in London, where the crew was based. The Bournemouth area, with its relatively mild and stable climate, fitted the bill perfectly and production manager Gavin Clark, a member of Belbin's team for the first two series, and production designer Nick Somerville, who worked on the first and fourth series as well as the 1993 Christmas Special, headed for Dorset to find suitable locations, beginning with a house for the Meldrews. It was no easy task, particularly as Renwick had provided a very specific description about how the house should look. Clark, who couldn't drive, usually hired a car and driver from a local firm. 'Each day, I'd tell the driver the areas I wanted to explore and we'd simply drive around the streets.' Clark had filmed in the Bournemouth area years earlier, so knew its benefits over London in terms of filming. 'Filming in the capital is difficult and, of course, the BBC didn't want to spend too much. If you start hiring houses or closing off roads in the capital, it costs a lot more. Also, it's much more practical to go off somewhere as a team for a couple of weeks to get things sorted in one go, rather than everyone driving each day to a location in or around London and getting lost.'

After scouring the streets of Bournemouth, Clark, Somerville and assistant floor manager Adam Tandy

Waiting for the weather: filming snow scenes for 'The Wisdom of the Witch' was often held up due to too much sunshine.

were driven to the district of Boscombe, where they happened upon the perfect property for the Meldrews' home. Clark spotted the house: number twenty-eight, a 1920s semi-detached property standing on the corner of Warnford Road and Corhampton Road. He alighted from the vehicle and strolled along the pavement. The owner, Carol Rowbrey, will never forget the day the BBC came calling. 'I looked a mess because I'd been gardening,' she says, smiling. 'I'd just dragged a massive bag of weeds up the garden when this man came through the side gate and said: "Excuse me, I'm from the BBC."' Clark explained that he'd been looking at her property and considered it ideal for a new BBC comedy series. 'He asked if I'd let them film outside, using the garden, so I invited him in and we had a chat,' says Carol, a widow, who was happy to give her consent. 'The only thing I didn't want was everyone treading all over the house, particularly as I worked all day. It was an exciting experience, though, and they always told me not to worry about cooking meals for myself because I could use their catering van.'

Like most aspects of the production, finding the right property wasn't easy, as Nick Somerville explains. Reflecting on the three-week search, he says: 'The brief,

Exterior scenes were filmed in and around Bournemouth throughout the eleven year run.

took to the air. She recalls, 'I was at work, but my son and his wife watched the filming one day. They sat indoors while Richard Wilson prepared for a scene where he got angry with children throwing rubbish over his fence. He was walking backwards and forwards, psyching himself up. As soon as he heard "Action!" he opened the door and walked out in his angry state. Just as he started to talk, a small aircraft flew over, so filming stopped. He started psyching himself up again, but as he went outside for the second time, a flock of swans flew over, so filming stopped once more. I think even Richard found that funny.' Another occasion highlighting the problems of filming within residential areas involved a neighbour. 'They were doing a scene in the garden and every time you heard the word "Action!", this man across the road started sweeping his yard with a broom,' says Carol. 'As soon as the director said, "Cut!" he'd stop. In the end, she whispered: "I'm going to say 'Action!' very quietly so he can't hear." Eventually they managed to film this little bit without him knowing they were doing it – it must have been irritating, though.'

With the house sorted, Nick Somerville rushed back to London and began creating the interior of the Meldrews' home, bringing alive their tastes and styles. Unless the requirements are detailed within the script, it's down to the designer to try and interpret the world the writer has formed in his mind, either by asking questions or rereading the scripts for little clues. 'I thought about what jobs they've had, what they've done with their lives, how much they earn – those kinds of things. I felt the Meldrews had lived in the house for a long time, which determined the slightly older look to the decor and style of furniture.'

While Somerville concentrated on dressing the Meldrews' home, costume designer Richard Winter, who worked on five series and five Christmas Specials, was busy dressing the characters themselves. When Winter, who'd first worked with producer-director Susan Belbin on *Only Fools and Horses*, sat down to create the image of Victor and Margaret, he drew inspiration from his parents. 'The mac was David's idea, but when we got onto other items of clothing it

as far as I recall, was that it had to be like a Victorian terraced house in Finsbury Park [London]. And finding one of those near Bournemouth wasn't going to be an easy task.' Once they'd found some possibilities, Susan Belbin was invited to cast her eye over them. 'I read the first four scripts and there was no indication of Finsbury Park; therefore, assuming that this was just to give us a feel for the kind of property required, we ignored that and concentrated solely on finding a Victorian terraced house.' There were, however, other physical aspects to be considered. Somerville recalls: 'In one episode Victor came out a side door and could see the garage. It was also important to have an end wall because in the first episode there was graffiti on it but, of course, you couldn't have one if it was a terraced house. I remember making several trips back and forth because we were struggling to find the house as it was written; David had obviously created this property in his head and subconsciously put the architecture of his own house into the one he wanted for *One Foot*.'

Everyone was relieved when Belbin checked out Warnford Road and gave the nod, and owner Carol Rowbrey supplied her consent for the house to be used. She doesn't know, however, if the BBC was aware of the small airport situated a few miles away at Hurn, which caused the occasional problem for the sound department, especially when the local flying school was very much like my father, whereas Margaret was dressed in the kind of styles I'd expect my mother to have worn,' says Winter, who bought most of the characters' clothes from Marks and Spencer. The cap, meanwhile, was based on the one Wilson was wearing himself at the time, but he soon switched to a baseball cap in real life, partly because he regarded them as 'cooler' and because the flat cap was becoming too closely associated with Victor Meldrew.

Winter says: 'I saw the Meldrews as fairly middle-class, not down-trodden or anything, so created a smart yet friendly style.' As for dressing the other characters, he recalls picking clothes that were slightly too tight for Nick Swainey, to project a childish look, and will never forget working with Doreen Mantle. He says: 'She used to make me laugh. Occasionally I'd say: "We want you to wear this," and she'd reply: "Oh no, I can't wear that, I would never wear that." So I'd say: "You wouldn't wear that, but it

Cameraman Ian Jackson lines up a shot for the riverbank scene in 'The Dawn of Man'.

isn't for you, it's for the character!" She was fine, though, and just wanted to look nice on the box.' Richard Winter enjoyed working on the show and feels it's a compliment that he was left to his own devices when designing the

> *I saw the Meldrews as fairly middle-class, not downtrodden or anything, so created a smart yet friendly style.*
>
> RICHARD WINTER

outfits. 'David [Renwick] and I just clicked – he was fantastic. He never poked his nose in, leaving everything to me.'

Renwick only gets involved when the need arises and was delighted with Winter's work. 'I don't think I ever had any concerns. It's the greatest compliment I can pay Richard that I never had to say: "Why is she wearing that?" It was all about real people in the real world and he dressed the characters accordingly.' Aiding Renwick's drive for realism, we saw the characters wearing the same clothes again and again. 'I thought that was all spot on,' enthuses Renwick. 'They had a rack of clothes for all the main characters, and so you'd see the same cardigan, shirt or skirt popping up later on in another episode. It wasn't like they had access to some limitless costume-department budget. Richard Wilson used to make a joke of it, although I'm sure he bristled a bit internally. He'd say to the studio audience "Look at this everyone, do you know how much this shirt cost? Ten pounds from Marks and Spencer!" It was a far cry from his own Jermyn Street wardrobe.'

Important elements in any programme are its theme tune and opening and closing titles; so many memorable programmes kick off with a sequence representative of the show's style and content. Think of *Hancock's Half Hour*: the sound of the tuba symbolised

A four-second sequence of Victor being showered with grass cuttings could take hours to set up and shoot.

reflect on the way things have worked out for me. The fact that I can sit in my house in Luton imagining all these famous, gifted people working on my shows, and then a few months go by and it becomes reality, like getting Eric Idle to sing the signature song for us.'

Idle's credentials as a composer were, of course, already impressive: most memorably he had penned the classic closing number from *Life of Brian*, 'Always Look on the Bright Side of Life'. And so, unfazed by Renwick's ambitious suggestion, Susan Belbin decided to test the water. She put the proposal to Idle's agent, and to everyone's great surprise Idle jumped at the opportunity. From Renwick's diary of 4 September 1989: 'Before I left, Eric Idle rang the office and Susie put me on to explain the basic feel of the show and guide him on the title song he's writing for us. He hasn't read the scripts and I said he probably didn't need to; I just felt it would be deliciously subversive to have him singing something very jaunty . . . He said he'd already got the opening line: "They say I might as well face the truth, that I am just too long in the tooth." I got the impression he was going to enjoy himself on this one.'[ii]

Filming in Bournemouth had already begun by the time a demo tape of Idle's song arrived a fortnight later. While driving to the day's location with Susan Belbin and Amita Lochab, the production assistant on Series One, Renwick switched on the cassette and initially at least was slightly disappointed, commenting at the time, 'It seemed more simplistic and middle-of-the-road than I was expecting, lacking that characteristic *Python* edge.'[iii] But as the days passed he began warming to the tune's 'perky melody'[iv]. It was a catchy song and soon became a favourite with viewers, spawning a single in 1994, in which Eric Idle was joined by Richard Wilson on backing vocals. The record may not have set the music world alight, peaking at a lowly number fifty in the charts, but it was indicative of the show's appeal that a sitcom's theme song could ever enter the charts.

From the moment Susan Belbin took charge, she had an immutable faith in the show's future, bravely splashing out £2,000 to acquire the rights to Idle's song on behalf of the BBC. She says: 'It was a lot of money for a theme tune in those days. No one, of course, knew how long the show was going to last, so if it stopped

the pomposity of Anthony Aloysius St John Hancock perfectly, while the authentic, period-feel of the Bud Flanagan vocals on 'Who Do You Think You Are Kidding, Mr Hitler?' is apposite for the wartime sitcom *Dad's Army*. Then there's the jaunty, saloon-bar sound of John Sullivan singing on *Only Fools and Horses*, which was fundamental to the whole tone of the programme that followed.

In deciding on a title sequence for *One Foot in the Grave*, David Renwick felt a jolly, upbeat feel would serve as an ironic counterpoint to the 'dark and disastrous events in the life of the main character'[i]. As an ardent fan of *Monty Python* he became excited about the idea of getting Eric Idle involved with the music, although never holding out much hope of success. Even now, with all the success he's achieved, Renwick remains self-effacing. 'Sometimes I have to pinch myself when I after the first series, it would have seemed an awful lot to spend on just a few notes at the beginning and end of six episodes. I don't know where my faith came from, but I just knew the programme would be a winner.' Not everyone thought buying the rights was a good move,

suggested using images of an animal associated with longevity — so a giant tortoise seemed appropriate. It was probably one of the simplest title themes ever, and meant there was more money to spend on the rest of the show.' Production manager Gavin Clark headed to BBC Bristol, home of the Natural History Unit, where he raided the archives for any footage involving giant tortoises; once he'd gathered sufficient examples, the material was passed to Chris Wadsworth, the video editor on the first four series. On Friday, 17 November he sat down with Belbin and Renwick in the editing suite to begin work. Eventually, they settled on trims that had never been broadcast, showing giant tortoises fumbling and picking their way through the undergrowth. 'The shots were then squeezed into a box against a black background and cut to Idle's music, with the fortuitous image of one tortoise slightly losing its footing serving as a nice little punctuation mark on the final lyric,' says Renwick. After a four-hour session,

Initially, Richard Wilson had serious doubts about the role of Victor.

though. 'I got my knuckles rapped by someone for that,' laughs Belbin. 'I can't remember by whom — probably Gareth Gwenlan, because I was always getting told off by him. I can imagine him saying: "This isn't what we do. You should know better because you've been around long enough!"' As it transpired, Belbin saved the BBC a lot of money in residuals.

With the theme tune organised, attention shifted to the opening and closing titles. While he relaxed in his hotel room after filming early one afternoon in September, four months before the first episode would be transmitted on BBC1, Renwick found himself mulling over various ideas. 'I decided it might be nice to avoid the convention of a series of sugary stills of the main characters and maybe go for something more symbolic. Because the show is partly about old age, I

the title sequence was complete, meaning one more piece of the production jigsaw had been set in place.

Other members of Belbin's production team included Christine Gernon, who joined as a twenty-six-year-old production secretary but would eventually direct the 1997 Christmas Special and the sixth and final series in 2000. Back in 1989 she was working on Radio 4 when, deciding to broaden her horizons, she asked for a secondment to television. Offered a nine-month contract as a production secretary, the first series she was assigned to was *One Foot in the Grave*, where her long association with Susan Belbin began. Her recollections of those first few days are of sitting opposite Belbin in her office, reading Renwick's scripts. 'My first month was brilliant because I thought it would be all typing letters and making cups of tea — and, yes, I did some of that, but I remember us reading bits of the scripts out loud, making each other laugh.

Even though I'd applied for the secondment, I wasn't entirely sure I wanted to work in television, but loved it from my very first moment.'

Belbin had built a reputation for nurturing new talent and Gernon became one of her protégées. 'I got on very well with Susie, who was fantastic to me throughout my career.' As well as Gernon, the core of Belbin's team consisted of a production assistant, initially Amita Lochab, the production manager Gavin Clark, and assistant floor manager Adam Tandy. The faces changed as the years passed, but the positions formed the nucleus of her regular team. As it was a small unit, Gernon was afforded a chance to experience

Mel Smith sitcom *Colin's Sandwich*, was originally pencilled in to work on another series of *Dear John . . .* before squeezing into Room A405A in Centre House, near BBC Television Centre, which became the show's production headquarters. Belbin's starkly decorated office, which she deemed to be the 'shabbiest in the world', was certainly a confined space, as Tandy explains: 'It was an extraordinarily compact working environment, to say the least. We often spilled out into the corridor because we didn't have room in the office.'

Despite the inconvenience, Susan Belbin worked hard cultivating a team spirit. Establishing comfortable working relationships is crucial because setting the right mood can reflect on the end product. Perhaps the most important relationship was between Belbin and Renwick; frequently writers supply the scripts before stepping back into the shadows, leaving the director to get on with the job of making the programme. They believe it's not their role to get involved in the mechanics of putting the show together. Some writers, meanwhile, act like silent partners: they're visible but not active. David Renwick didn't fall into either camp.

> *A lot of the reasons I'm a director are because of Susie. . . She was good at bringing people on, although there were times when she could be terrifying!*
>
> CHRISTINE GERNON

various aspects of programme-making. 'When we went filming, I'd become the runner. On the first series, people like Richard Wilson wouldn't have his own caravan, and every lunchtime he would have a quick nap in his car. One of my jobs was to knock on his window and wake him up.'

After the first series, Gernon worked as production secretary on *Don't Wait Up* before beginning her climb up the career ladder. The next time she worked on the show was on 'One Foot in the Algarve' as a production assistant. Now a director with several years' experience, Gernon realises she owes much to Belbin's support. 'A lot of the reasons I'm a director are because of Susie, who always claimed she saw potential in me, which is nice to know. She pushed me from day one, as she did other people, like Angie [de Chastelai Smith] and Nick [Wood]. She was good at bringing people on, although there were times when she could be terrifying!' smiles Gernon.

Adam Tandy, who'd just finished working on the

His inimitable style of working, involving himself closely in every stage of the production process, was something Susan Belbin hadn't experienced before. An intense man with a tendency to frown and worry over every detail, he occasionally caused friction within the ranks, particularly in the early days when everyone was finding their feet. He realised, however, that this was inevitable if he was to help steer the show creatively. Let's not forget, this was his 'baby' and, like any proud and anxious parent, he wanted the best for his offspring.

In his mind's eye, Renwick knew what he wanted to achieve visually, although, at times, translating it into the practical world of television wasn't easy. Susan Belbin, who admits she might not have been so accommodating regarding the writer's heavy involvement had she not admired Renwick so much, says: 'David had a lot of experience in television – and film to some degree. What

It might look hot and sunny, but the weather for filming was invariably freezing.

good as it could be.' When given the opportunity to work closely with Renwick, Belbin invited him into the fold with open arms, despite learning later that deferring to the writer was regarded by many as unusual. 'Some people in the production team found it a little difficult at first because they were conditioned to the mentality of "one singer, one voice". I worked in collaboration with David because he knew what he wanted and interpretations can get muddled along the way. So I told everyone that I was happy for them to deal directly with him, if necessary.'

It's fortunate Renwick had a director like Susan Belbin, who was not weighed down by an ego as a director. She tried her utmost to reach Renwick's wavelength, even if it meant swotting up on Edward De Bono. 'David's a lateral thinker, so to try and understand him and to reach a point where I could second-guess him or at least feel an equal, I read plenty of De Bono's books on the subject. Latterly, it got to be a game, inasmuch as I'd read the scripts and say: "I knew that was coming," and he'd be worried about it, so I'd have to reassure him that nobody else would.'

he hadn't grasped, which I did find irritating on occasions, were the technicalities of the actual filming. I remember one scene involving a little girl where the script called for a close-up of her face reacting. To get a really nice shot, I loved using the end of the lens. So you'd take the camera back, and use a long lens to produce a big close-up while diffusing the background. David said to me: "This is supposed to be a close-up." I told him to look down the lens and, of course, there was a big close-up and he was happy. But the cameraman was very unhappy that a writer should look down the camera; only the cameraman and director were ever allowed to look down the old box, as we called it. I ended up doing a lot of pacifying during moments like that.'

Initially, Belbin had to secure the crew's trust in allowing Renwick access to every stage of the production. 'I don't know if anyone saw it as a weakness in me, having David around so much,' suggests Belbin, 'but I had very genuine reasons for allowing him to be there full-time, and that was to make the product as

Belbin wanted to ensure she transferred everything from the page and in Renwick's mind to the screen; some directors compliment the writer on their script and proceed to alter it to fit their style, but not Belbin. 'It's an old-school belief that the writer delivered the scripts and then the director took over and made the programme. There are probably a number of writers up and down the country, even to this day, crying in their beers, saying: "What have they done to my script?" I don't believe that two people can think identically, although by working together you can get very close, so in tune that you hardly have to speak to one another. That doesn't happen very often, though. But with David being such an exact person, and having spent a long time getting his script absolutely right, it was now up to my team to complement what he'd done.'

David Renwick recognised that in Susan Belbin he had a producer-director who shared his aims. 'The strength of my collaboration with Susie was that we both wanted the same things.' He acknowledges that he's had relationships with other directors who haven't had the same vision, leading to fundamental disagreements about how the product should look. 'Susie would never favour the obvious sitcom approach. Like me, she preferred to come at things more indirectly – while never sacrificing the essential focus required to get the laugh she knew it was possible to achieve a kind of truthful elegance.' Waters don't always run smoothly, though, and as in any relationship there were moments when they didn't see eye-to-eye. 'In the early days, when we were getting the measure of each other, Susie sometimes managed to wind me up,' admits Renwick, smiling. 'She was, at times, aggressively complimentary about what I was doing, and about how low I set my sights, and occasionally there was friction in those areas.' But he's quick to point out that,

countless other considerations. She says: 'I had to worry about the budget, timings, staffing, my head of department, the delivery date – and when it all goes wrong, I had to pick up the pieces. David was marvellous, though, and on occasions where we had a problem, I'd go to him and say: "Look, I have a problem here, can we resolve it?" He'd always be helpful because he understood that problems occur; he also appreciated it when he could see people putting in one hundred per cent effort for the good of his show.'

Renwick's presence on location as writer was unusual. 'The crew found it difficult because they thought it was a bit committee-orientated: the committee being myself and David,' says Belbin. 'Personally, I actually liked working with him in that way. It was bloody hard work, a nightmare at times, but the whole point was to get it right, so why not have the man there, rather than picking up the phone every two minutes, or misinterpreting what he'd written?'

At times, the actors also found the regular consultations between Belbin and Renwick frustrating. Richard Wilson says: 'What used to annoy me a lot, usually when filming, was we'd do a shot and David and Susie would get into a huddle, which you weren't privy to – even though you were in the shot. Depending on how serious it was, Susie might come over and explain what the problem was, but if it was *really* serious they'd both come over. I used to think: "Why can't we discuss this together?" I was always complaining slightly that I wasn't being valued, and I know Annette felt the same at times.'

> *David's a lateral thinker, so to try and understand him and to reach a point where I could second-guess him or at least feel an equal, I read plenty of De Bono's books on the subject.*
>
> SUSAN BELBIN

technically, she was spot on. 'I can't think of anyone I'd rather have made the series with. Attitudes and relationships develop over the course of the years, and ours became more instinctive, collaborative and competent.' In all the years they worked together, Renwick can't recall a moment where they had a serious disagreement over the way something should be executed. 'Even during the more fractious moments it was still about getting the best for the show.'

Susan Belbin believes implicitly that Renwick's significant contribution to the mechanics of the programme-making was fundamental to the show's glittering success, although accepts the decision could have backfired. 'The writer only has one focus – quite rightly – and that's to make the programme as good as possible.' The director-producer, meanwhile, has

The coming together of so many people, even when they are chasing a common goal, undoubtedly leads to intermittent problems, especially if you're making a television programme within a restrictive timeframe. Everyone's efforts, though, would eventually pay dividends with *One Foot* becoming one of the BBC's top-rated shows.

CHAPTER 5
The First Show

CAMERA SCRIPT

ONE FOOT IN THE GRAVE

Series 'A'

DATE: SUNDAY 15TH OCTOBER 1989

PROG.NO: 50/LJC.A191N

STUDIO: T.C.8.

Episode 1 - "I Shall Wear the Bottoms of My Trousers Rolled"

by

DAVID RENWICK

Producer/Director .... SUSIE BELBIN
Production Manager .... GAVIN CLARK
Production Assistant .... AMITA LOCHAB
Production Floor Manager .... ADAM PANDY
Assistant Floor Manager .... CHRIS GERNON
..... Secretary .... NICK SOMERVILLE
.... GABY BRACHACKA
....TH

A heavy bank of foreboding cloud was creeping across the September sky as the cast and crew began arriving at Ferndown, near Bournemouth, in preparation for filming location scenes in Series One. It was Monday, 18 September 1989, and everyone was gathering in the reception of the Coach House Motel, chatting over drinks. Belbin and Renwick were joined by Richard Wilson and Annette Crosbie and, after exchanging pleasantries, they repaired to a local Greek restaurant to celebrate the birth of a new sitcom. It was an important juncture because for the first time Renwick was in the company of both leading performers. Over dinner, conversations soon turned to *One Foot*, as Renwick noted: 'Richard, much lubricated by the wine, began floating a host of reservations about the show: if Victor appeared to be a miserable chauvinist we would never sympathise with him; and why did he never display tenderness towards Margaret? I suppose I should have responded in defence of these charges but am never comfortable addressing a whole table of listeners, so I privately filed it all away for later. Annette, for her part, didn't seem to be fazed by these worries at all, and I got the feeling she will be able to make it all work instinctively. Susie contributed with much diplomatic professional prattle, and afterwards observed that the

Richard has a very strong sense of reality about what he does, yet there is still a comedy broadness about him.

DAVID RENWICK

two of them looked and behaved wonderfully together. And I agree, I think it's great chemistry.'[i]

From that first evening together, toasting their new project, Renwick and Belbin knew their initial instincts concerning casting were correct, and that it was worth enduring the circuitous journey undertaken to secure their first-choice performers. 'I felt incredibly privileged to have Richard and Annette in the show,' says Renwick. 'Richard has a very strong sense of reality about what he

does, yet there is still a comedy broadness about him. That isn't a criticism of any kind – it's the same quality that David Jason has as Del Boy. It's what makes him more loved than Nicholas Lyndhurst, who, it's probably true to say, gives the subtler performance. One of the things that makes *Only Fools* great is the confluence of those two styles of acting, and that's what we had with Richard and Annette.'

The first series opened with 'Alive and Buried', which established the premise for the show: a sixty-year-old man who's made redundant after twenty-six years working for Watson-Mycroft Associates as a security guard. Adjusting to what is now an empty life is hard, leaving an inordinate amount of time to begin fretting about the plethora of ills which, to Victor, are blighting not just his own life, but society as a whole.

If it had been humanly possible, David Renwick would probably have made *One Foot* single-handedly, because that would have ensured that the end product was exactly how he imagined it when he first committed words to paper. Once you're relying on others, however skilled they are at their job, you run the risk of seeing your creation taking on a new shape, or your intentions being misinterpreted when it comes to bringing the scenes alive in front of the camera. Such frustrations surfaced on the first day of filming at the Abbey Insurance office block in Holderness Road, Bournemouth. In the opening scene we see Victor Meldrew's desk being demolished by workmen, symbolising the brutality of the decision that has thrown Victor onto the unemployment scrapheap. When Renwick arrived in the lobby, he noticed only a straightforward free-standing desk had been supplied instead of something more substantial. Some writers wouldn't have worried, but for Renwick it undermined the effect he was seeking. He noted later that it was 'the usual business of damage limitation'[ii] and suggested a way of rescuing the situation, but that afternoon there was also a clash of minds on how to shoot a scene showing Victor underneath a road sign warning drivers to look out for elderly people. While cameraman Keith Burton felt that cutting to a tight shot of the sign would be more powerful, Renwick wanted a wide shot showing Victor standing beneath the sign. He felt the alternative was a 'classic sitcom approach – not only are you hammering the joke too much, you lose the essential character comedy of the moment, the relationship between the man and the sign, all in the same picture.'[iii]

Renwick had worked with Keith Burton on *Alexei Sayle's Stuff* and admired his work. Other than a few discussions about shots and framing, they got on well. However, the general aura that seemed to surround film cameramen was something that grated with Renwick. 'Directors of photography are essentially there to service the vision of the director,' he says. 'But I felt that Susie, even with her strength of character, often accorded them more reverence than was helpful. To most people on a film set the science of lighting and cinematography is such a closed book that no one ever dares to interfere or question what's going on and why. And so, frequently, they'll be given too much latitude when time is at a premium, and enjoy the kind of luxury and flexibility that are denied to other areas of production. For me, the best DoPs are sensitive enough to say: "Well, that shadow on the wall wasn't as good as I'd have liked, but you got a good performance from the actor, so let's buy it and move on."'

Something else in Episode One that concerned Renwick was the fit and sprightly supporting artists who were supposed to be at death's door. In the scene where Nick Swainey is driving a group of elderly women around in his car, Renwick's script called for 'frail little old ladies'. And when a bunch of incredibly agile extras arrived, one of them in a leopardskin coat, it was a case of making the best of a bad job. 'One lady who was slightly dumpy-looking was the closest match to the kind of characters I had envisaged, so we framed the shot to favour her. But the others still looked like middle-aged women in perfect health who, of course, would never need ferrying around by Nick Swainey. Discrepancies like this occurred all the time.'

The first location scene with Mrs Warboys, filmed on Wednesday, 20 September at Warnford Road, didn't start well. Actress Doreen Mantle nearly didn't make it on time, as Chris Gernon, assigned to collect her from the railway station, explains. 'Doreen had to be rushed to the location. The trouble was, I got completely lost in Bournemouth. She was needed around 2 p.m., but we didn't get there until about 2.30 because we were driving round and round, getting more and more tense, with Doreen saying: "I'm sure we've been around this roundabout before!" Luckily, although we were late, they were behind with filming, so weren't ready for her anyway.'

And if that wasn't enough for one day, there was the problem of Victor's car, which fortunately Renwick and Belbin weren't aware of. The script stipulated a crimson-coloured Avenger: the right model was delivered, but the wrong colour, as Adam Tandy recalls. 'The car that turned up was green. I don't think anyone noticed, except me. The prop buyer turned to me and said: "There's Victor's car." I replied: "That's fine, but it's the wrong colour."' The prop buyer looked pallid but, miraculously, was able to get the car sprayed within hours. 'It wasn't ideal because the paint kept coming off every time anyone touched it, but we managed.'

The opening script for any programme is, arguably, the most difficult to write. Renwick had spent a lot of time reworking it, taking on board Richard Wilson's initial concerns about his character appearing too irate. After reaching for his red editing pen, it was the first scene with Victor preparing for a job that he'll soon discover no longer exists, which received most streamlining. Says Renwick: 'There was a moment when Victor got in such a rage because he couldn't find anything, and in his frustration because Margaret kept moving everything around, he grabbed a hammer and nail from a nearby toolbox and nailed a slice of toast to the breadboard, saying: "Right, now I'll know where it is!" It wasn't something that came naturally to Richard, and when he did it in the studio, he tapped the nail into the toast in such a delicate fashion that the whole effect was rather limp. In retrospect, of course, it was excessive in terms of the characterisation. But, let's remember, these were early days and I was still finding my way around.'

A scene that was cut completely from the finished shooting script saw Victor being offered a new job cleaning out toilets, while believing he is being interviewed for more security work. After the meeting is over, the personnel director shakes his hand and hands him a bucket and lavatory brush. It was decided the scene didn't work and it was deleted, affording more time for Victor to wander aimlessly around the house, trying to fill in time, accentuating the predicament in which he now found himself. Richard Wilson says: 'I was always telling David to write less because there would be so much material that we'd start cutting bits here and there. The writing wasn't allowed to breathe. The breathing was things like watching bread being buttered, just doing simple things like that. David's lines are very funny, very rich and very clever, but I used to love filming Victor walking along a street – I don't know why, but I found that exciting. I guess it was a bit like silent comedy: trying to understand the man through his body language.'

Focusing on the minutiae, to reflect real life, was something Renwick enjoyed, too, and he increasingly employed the technique as the series progressed, mixing observation with absurdity. 'Margaret might have been hoovering crumbs out of the bread bin, and people would ask whether anyone really did that. Yes, of course they do, and I think most people related to those kinds of things. Annette has a line in an episode where she's preparing

Belbin and production manager Murray Peterson discuss one of Renwick's more elaborate comic images.

to some comedy later on, but we all enjoyed lines like that. Richard loved it when we showed the rhythms of real life, whether it be settling down in a chair or just reading a newspaper – you can see in his behaviour what it means to him.'

But Renwick was always ready to slot in an absurd sight gag, one of the best being the appearance of a Citroen 2CV in a rubbish skip he's hired. 'I felt at the time that we could afford to take even more risks with the comedy. So although there were some ambitiously absurd ideas in the show, the challenge was to ground them in reality and say: "Look, someone has put a 2CV in a rubbish skip: that is utterly ridiculous, but I think it's a funny idea." In order to make it work, you have to imagine that it's happening in real life, and decide how everyone would actually respond in that situation. Providing they behave honestly, with suitable incredulity, it will work. Hence Victor's constant

I guess it was a bit like silent comedy: trying to understand the man through his body language.

RICHARD WILSON

some toast and says: "Do you want fresh bread or shall we finish up the stale?" It's not a joke or particularly funny, but I laugh at that – it's reality to me. It's a stepping-stone utterance, "I don't believe it!" If the character's reaction is in any way knowing, or "comic", the whole thing is rendered implausible.'

Renwick accepts the fact that much of his material is improbable but says it's the tightrope he chooses to walk, even to this day, because it's what makes his scripts more interesting. His love of the absurd is rooted in his admiration of *Monty Python*. 'I adore the fact that you can just have this guy living a perfectly ordinary life, in a world we all recognise as real – as opposed to the cartoon universe of the traditional comedy show – and then something utterly bizarre or silly occurs, and it's so much funnier because you've gone to all that trouble to put it in the right context. The more naturalistic the environment, the more unexpected it becomes, and that contrast, between the mundane and macabre, is what makes me laugh.'

As the series progressed, so the characters developed and the performers gradually became more comfortable with their screen roles. Early episodes were about

> *I adore the fact that you can just have this guy living a perfectly ordinary life, in a world we all recognise as real – as opposed to the cartoon universe of the traditional comedy show – and then something utterly bizarre or silly occurs.*
>
> DAVID RENWICK

establishing the programme, presenting interpretations of the people existing in the scripts and allowing viewers to become acquainted with the characters. Even for seasoned pros like Annette Crosbie, Richard Wilson, Owen Brenman and Doreen Mantle it took time to settle into their parts. When Crosbie spoke her first line of dialogue, Renwick and Belbin were alarmed to hear her using a broad cockney accent, something director Susan Belbin feels responsible for. 'It was irresponsible on my part,' she says, 'or more of an oversight. When Annette came to read that day, David and I knew she was the one for us. However, it didn't occur to me to tell her to play it naturally. When it came to the first scene, which we hadn't rehearsed, we noticed she was trying to put on a cockney accent. I should have told her to use her own voice, but because she'd been so good in the reading and hadn't used an accent, I assumed that's

'A collision of the macabre and the mundane' – Renwick's favourite formula for comedy.

what she'd do on the day.'

For Crosbie, playing Margaret Meldrew posed the occasional difficulty. 'With Richard's character being so very over the top in

Crosbie had enough time during lighting changes to read the complete works of Dostoevsky.

theatrical terms, it was sometimes difficult to hang on to a complete orderliness from Margaret. She didn't hit him or leave home, and the first thing I'm asked by people who watch the show is, "How did she put up with him?" Margaret losing her temper is only something that crept in towards the end. I had to find some kind of reality between the two characters, although it was pretty difficult getting hold of this woman who was prepared to put up with so much.'

Crosbie enjoyed working alongside Richard Wilson, but does, in my opinion, underestimate the impact her character made on the show's success. She says in a matter-of-fact manner: 'I realised that my function was to be a feed, and I tried very hard to do just that. Working together is all about chemistry and Richard and I got on well, although I admit to embarrassing him at times because I'm tactless and assertive. Early on, I sensed that he wasn't happy or perhaps relaxed with me, and I was unaccustomed to that when I work with people. There was a reserve that made me feel uncomfortable. During one rehearsal I got fed up. Susie sensed it and kept us back after rehearsals to ask what was going on. After knowing it wasn't a problem to do with her, she left us alone and I told Richard that I was trying hard but didn't feel I was getting anything back in return. Richard, bless his heart, realised and after that we were fine. He's very professional and I have huge respect for people who are; he didn't mess about, got on with the job and didn't complain – except when he had good reason.'

Susan Belbin believes Crosbie's performance was probably underrated. 'She was a great foil for Richard to play off, and was excellent in the role.' Crosbie sets high standards for herself and is disappointed if she feels she hasn't reached the required level. 'I'd catch her at rehearsals and she'd maybe fluff a word – one in a whole week. I'd tell her it didn't matter, but she'd scold herself, saying things like, "Stupid woman, get it right."'

Richard Wilson, meanwhile, doesn't recall thinking about how he was going to play Victor. Instead, it was a process of osmosis combined with wonderful scripts that showed him the way. 'David is such a good writer you rely on him to give you the signposts. You read the text and things happen, although often you're not aware of the decisions you make. I think there was a lot of David in Victor, and probably a lot of his father, too, and although my father was a quiet man, there was some of him as well. Of course, there was no doubt a lot of me in Victor. Thinking about it, the fact David wrote it for me isn't a great compliment in a sense!'

With all the filming inserts in the can, the production moved on to the studio to prepare for the recording of Episode One. The read-throughs began on

10 October 1989 at the BBC's rehearsal centre in Victoria Street, North Acton. The venue was a purpose-built block of rehearsal rooms, replicating the size of the studios, affectionately known within the BBC as the Acton Hilton. By the time Renwick finally pulled into the car park after crawling along in the North Circular traffic, he was an hour late and the cast had to reread the first episode for him. Finding the early scenes 'totally flat and unfunny'[iv], he swiftly edited them down upon learning that the first show was over-running by nine minutes. The following day, however, Susan Belbin called Renwick to tell him the performers felt his cuts had eliminated much of the material which focused on the relationship between the central characters. Belbin suggested a series of adjustments which, to Renwick, 'seemed very constructive'[v]. It was another sign of the trust and friendship forming between director and writer.

Each episode was allocated six days from the read-through until the recording in front of the studio audience, beginning – in the case of *One Foot* – on a Tuesday. The first day involved the read-through and blocking, whereby the set is represented by marking tape on the rehearsal room floor and the actors begin synchronising their moves to the dialogue. It was an aspect of sitcom-making new to Renwick, who found it an effective exercise. 'In the scripts I'd obviously defined a lot of the business, but there are many other physical aspects that I hadn't. So we would then fine-tune all the stage directions for each actor: "When you say that line, you could be walking over to the sideboard and picking up that can of furniture polish, which you can take to the kitchen as you finish speaking." And so on. It was a very useful way of working, to get the actions locked in before the interpretation. It allowed you to marry the visual rhythms to the verbal ones, and it meant Susie would also know exactly where all her shots would go.'

Blocking the entire choreography of the show in this way wasn't something uniquely adopted by Belbin; it was a practice used over the years by many directors in situation comedy. It was a crucial step towards producing a crisp, polished programme. Renwick has also witnessed the result of not following this systematic approach. 'Actors come onto the set or location and don't know what they're going to do, where they'll be standing or what they'll be doing physically at any particular moment. So they start busking, ad-libbing as they deliver the lines, drifting around on instinct. And, of course,

I think there was a lot of David in Victor, and probably a lot of his father, too . . . Of course, there was no doubt a lot of me in Victor.

RICHARD WILSON

then you end up with no focus or comic timing.'

Within the weekly production cycle, Wednesday and Thursday involved rehearsals with the cast, leaving Friday for a technical run with the camera and sound crews present, enabling them to mark out their positions within the set. On Saturday morning, rehearsal time would be determined by how well the cast was progressing, before Sunday when everyone would be working flat out until the recording in the evening. It was a pressurised time for all concerned. 'One of the hardest jobs for me was deciding how much to rehearse them and when to stop,' explains Susan Belbin. 'If I thought we were getting very close to the required performance when we met on Friday, I might only rehearse a tiny bit because if you over-rehearse, you'll kill the performance dead.'

Both Richard Wilson and Annette Crosbie were nervous when they began the week's studio work. 'I was also excited. Susie [Belbin] kept saying to me during Series One and Two: "Just you wait, you'll see, this will take off." I never envisaged it taking off the way it eventually did, though,' says Wilson, whose nerves weren't helped by the fact he was leading in a sitcom for the first time. Although no stranger to the genre –

audiences had delighted in his recent performances as Eddie Clockerty in 1987's *Tutti Frutti* and Eric Chappell's medical comedy *Only When I Laugh*, which saw him playing Doctor Thorpe in four series transmitted between 1979 and 1982 – he regarded himself, prior to Victor, as a 'middle-range player'. So this was an important juncture in his career.

As for Annette Crosbie, an actress with years of experience playing a host of stage and screen roles, she was embarking, surprisingly, on her first sitcom role, which brought a serious bout of nerves. As she arrived at Studio Eight on 15 October she felt, in some ways, like a green actress arriving for her first job. There were several reasons for the nerves, including the discovery that she'd be performing in front of a live audience. 'I knew I could do comedy because I'd done it in the theatre, but this was my first comedy series on tele-

Richard Wilson felt it was vital to 'bond' with the studio audience before a show.

vision, and working in front of an audience after only a week's preparation was frightening.' The exacting standards set by David Renwick didn't help the butterflies, either. 'David writes a lot of words, and nearly has a heart attack if you change anything, even a preposition – it has to be said exactly as he wrote it,' says Crosbie, smiling. 'I understand that totally and have never been one for approximating.' Crosbie learnt her trade, like Wilson, by always trying to get her performance word-perfect, but under such a tight turnaround within the studio, the pressure mounted. 'We'd go in on the Sunday at 10 a.m., work through for the cameras, so were constantly stopping, starting and repositioning, followed by a dress-run which never went smoothly. Then we only got a short break because Wardrobe wanted us back, by which time we were running on adrenalin. When I heard the audience arriving the nerves began to kick in again, and made me even more worried about my lines. I'd find myself saying: "What was that word? Has anyone got a script?"'

While Wilson started chatting with the audience prior to recording, Crosbie could be found standing

out of sight, fretting about her first set of lines, praying to God she'd get through the performance. Actors differ in their opinions about performing in front of a live audience for television sitcoms: some relish the anticipation and expectations they can sense, while others find having people in front of them, whom they're expected to ignore, an unnecessary distraction. 'In the theatre it's so easy: you get a big laugh and there's a kind of unspoken agreement between you and the audience that you'll wait for only so long and then they have to stop – so you're in charge of the momentum of the play. On television, you're not allowed any kind of contact with the audience; you have to pretend they're not there, and with cameras lined up on you, you can't wander around the set waiting for them to pull themselves together. You're stuck there with whatever prop you have in your hand at the time. I agree there is a certain chemistry with a live audience but, personally, I found it difficult.' Despite such challenges, it didn't put Crosbie off television comedy. 'No, I'm a Scot, I love difficulties, and if there aren't any, I'll make them!' she says, again smiling. 'I love the discipline of getting it right and trying to do the best with David's scripts, because I think his writing is brilliant.'

While attempting to get the performance right, notes would occasionally be passed to the performers from either Belbin or Renwick. On the day of record-ing, the inevitable bout of nerves occasionally led to frayed tempers. As Annette Crosbie says: 'It might be that you hadn't said a word right, which you knew as soon as you said it, but it didn't help to be told it.'

Richard Wilson adds: 'David was around a lot, which used to drive me crazy at times. We were always working very close to the deadline of the audience coming in. Sometimes the dress rehearsal would finish and we'd have twenty minutes to grab a sandwich and cup of tea before going back to make-up ready for the off. It was a crazy system: you'd work all week and on the Sunday work the hardest, so by the time you actually did the show, you were exhausted. David was at his most prolific in note-giving at this stage because

he could see so many things. I was always saying: "David, I can't keep all this in my head. I'm going to lose my rhythm."'

No, I'm a Scot, I love difficulties, and if there aren't any, I'll make them!

ANNETTE CROSBIE

Renwick was fully aware that his passing of notes wasn't liked, and only once commented in his journal, 'My notes today all apparently taken seriously, with no friction.'[vi] However, he felt it essential to produce the best result. Richard Wilson acknowledges that Renwick was right to give notes: being a director himself, he does the same. 'But to do it so close to the recording was the problem. If I'm directing a play and we have a dress rehearsal close to the actual performance, I probably wouldn't do it, unless it was absolutely vital. David, though, is a champion worrier and his input, especially during filming, made me say to myself sometimes: "We wish you'd go away, David, and let us get on with it." I'm not decrying the nitpicking and checking on the details because that was everything to the show, it's just that often you know you've made mistakes because it's all done in a rush, particularly on the recording day, and some of those things would be ironed out, whether you had a note or not. He knew how I felt about this, though, and we used to joke about it.'

Infuriating it might have been for the actors at times, but Renwick's discerning eye rarely failed him, although even perfectionists have to draw the line at some point. It must, however, be frustrating when one can still see potential mileage and fear it's going to be missed. Renwick once wrote: 'Ultimately there's so much more to look for, in terms of timing, rhythms, thought processes, that can turn a very funny scene into something even funnier. With two really skilful performers that process of discovery can be joyous, but all too often nobody bothers because they don't know what they're looking for.'[vii]

However much additional pressure was caused by Belbin or Renwick, it culminated in a stronger and more successful show. Renwick admits that he always assumed that 'everyone resented my interference'. He says: 'I always felt terrible tension about it, but one hoped that the more I interfered the more successful the product became; there must be some correlation between those two things.'

Renwick found it fascinating watching the characters he'd created, Victor and Margaret Meldrew, being honed by Wilson and Crosbie as the week passed. Now it was the day of recording. Of that first Sunday he wrote: 'All day at TVC for the first recording, which was, I suppose, relatively painless. When I arrived the sets were literally still being built, but most of Susie's shots seemed about right. She basically seems to understand what we need to see at any given moment, although now and again I feel the framing may be too tight. The audience gallery only half full tonight but those who came obviously liked Richard and were incredibly generous throughout; you couldn't have wished for better. If anything I felt the laughter was too explosive and possibly intrusive here and there. Annette was a bit too big in the early scenes, but Richard seemed to find the right note from the word go, fluffing a few lines through nerves, but generally delivering Victor Meldrew as a flesh and blood character. On the night, the guillotine and escapology stuff worked well, miraculously, and the flat patches are really just the opening two scenes, as I always knew they would be.

I felt terrible after the first show, and remember waiting in my dressing room for Susie to pop in.

RICHARD WILSON

Up in the bar afterwards, Richard was depressed, claiming that he'd gone to pieces, but otherwise I think we were all very pleased to have got this one under our belt. So far I think I feel it's a perfectly competent, funnier-than-average sitcom and I've proved I can do it. It's not yet remarkable, elegant or stylish enough to

mark it out as something special, but given time hopefully it can grow.'[viii]

Actors are notoriously self-critical and Wilson remembers the first recording as a 'very nervous experience'. He says: 'It wasn't as if I hadn't done much sitcom before, but in that first episode I dried continually. My very first lines as Victor included "watch, fountain pen, cap, wallet, car keys" and I got through three of the words and then dried. I did it again but the same thing happened.'

Wilson regarded the first episode as 'fairly fraught' but assuages his views by reminding himself that it was only the first instalment and, therefore, expected to a certain degree. When the final scene was done and dusted, he retired, physically and emotionally drained, to his dressing room. His anxieties about the day worsened, though, when he never received a visit from either Susan Belbin or David Renwick. 'I felt terrible after the first show, and remember waiting in my dressing room for Susie to pop in. If I'm directing in the theatre, I find a seat near the door, and after the show, go straight to the actors. Television is, of course, different because of technical issues that have to be sorted, but I did expect Susie to come round. I eventually went to the bar and said: "I'm sorry, Susie, that was terrible." She replied: "Yes, but we'll get something out of it," instead of saying, "It wasn't that bad." My complaint, at times, was that she didn't understand the acting processes and didn't value the actors. Actors just want to be looked after, to be cuddled and encouraged, and want to know they're doing well. David, too, isn't very encouraging – but, then, he'd argue that he picks the right people and expects them to perform.

'Susie will deny this, I know, but she was always happier with the technicians. I remember once losing my rag a bit. We were filming in Tresillian Way [where the Meldrews' house was located from Series Two onwards] and Susie was shooting Pippa and Patrick's house. All I had to do was pull my curtain back and look out. I was sitting in this living room with a sparks [electrician] and we were chatting away. I did my bit and then sat down. After a while, I said: "This is a long break." So I pulled the curtain back and noticed the rest of them had gone, just walked off, while we were sitting there like nanas.'

Despite his occasional grumbles, though, he's quick to point out that he feels Susan Belbin was the right director for the show. 'She loved the script, understood comedy and knew how to put a show together. Although, as I said, I don't think she particularly understood actors, she knew what she wanted and didn't let go easily. She was a very good company woman, in terms of the big family. People wanted to work for her, she was very popular, and created, by and large, a good working environment. She was great fun, too, and also loved the show, which was important. She was particularly good at shooting, liking loose, medium two and three shots, rather than going in too close, which was probably her most important asset. She shot it brilliantly.'

'Alive and Buried' was transmitted on Thursday, 4 January 1990 at 9.30 p.m., attracting an audience just under 9.3 million. Eagerly awaiting its transmission, albeit rather apprehensively, was Renwick, who for the first time in his small-screen writing career didn't 'squirm with acute embarrassment'[ix] as the show was aired. His overall assessment of the opening, which was recorded in his journal, read: 'The title sequence had actually worked out rather well in the end: simple but elegant, and bolstered by music from someone with impeccable comedy credentials. And the revised opening actually pleased me – it was so much better than the original rough-cut – and I'm so relieved that we trimmed it down and re-shot it. Some of the incidental music sounded intrusive, and the garage scene still worried me, but this apart I found the BBC production standards and general maturity highly satisfying. As ballsy ground-breaking new comedy it was probably way off, and much of the early stuff was solemn and sad rather than funny, but on balance by the end of the evening I was not an unhappy man.'[x]

Reactions from the press over the following days were mixed. Peter Waymark in *The Times* thought that readers who'd admired Wilson's previous work would enjoy watching his 'skilled playing and ability to squeeze the last

> *She loved the script, understood comedy and knew how to put a show together. Although, as I said, I don't think she particularly understood actors, she knew what she wanted and didn't let go easily.*
>
> RICHARD WILSON

drop out of a line of dialogue'[xi]. As for the show, the critic wondered whether his readers would find it 'too near the truth to be funny'[xii]. Hilary Kingsley, meanwhile, writing in the *Daily Mirror*, didn't mince words, stating: 'Richard Wilson is so unlovable as the grumpy old codger . . . that you'd kick the other foot in given half a chance. It may be the strangulated Scottish accent. It may be the flat script. Perhaps it's the waste of Annette Crosbie as his stooge-wife.'[xiii] Stafford Hildred in the *Daily Star* joined in the condemnation, stating that the sitcom was 'as deathly as the title suggests. It should have been called *One Foot In The Bin*.'[xiv] John Russell in the *Sunday Express* was equally damning. 'Richard Wilson is one of our finest comedy actors but you never guess it from the dire new comedy about old age.'[xv] He acknowledged that there is an amusing series about growing old waiting to be written but felt *One Foot* wasn't it. He closed by passing on advice to his readers, saying: 'If you were fortunate enough to avoid the opening episode then take my advice: miss the whole series.'[xvi]

Jaci Stephen, meanwhile, writing for the *Evening Standard*, was much more upbeat about the sitcom's prospects, claiming that 'among the current crop of sitcoms, this is one of the few worth looking out for'[xvii]. Noting again that the show was helped along by a 'strong central performance from Wilson'[xviii], with approximately 'one in every three lines hitting the jackpot'[xix], she observed that this was one more than other offerings within the genre. Such positivity was echoed by James Saynor in the *Listener*, who commented that although *One Foot* 'stays heroically within the bounds of the carpet-slipper-comedy form, it's so lively and well-disciplined that it makes you think there might be hope for Britcom after all.'[xx] Admiring the way the central character, Victor, had been crafted, Saynor felt 'ironic abandon is coupled to a deep inner exhaustion, which gives the comedy a useful dramatic tension and three-dimensionality.'[xxi]

While Nancy Banks-Smith in the *Guardian* rated it as a 'good little situation comedy'[xxii], Christopher Dunkley, over at the *Financial Times*, was impressed because 'there were half a dozen good jokes in the opening episode'[xxiii]. And at the *Daily Mail*, Elizabeth Cowley, after having seen a preview tape prior to transmission, wrote about the 'first delicious chapter'[xxiv] in the new sitcom.

Keeping an eye out for the reviews made Renwick feel like he was enduring a rollercoaster ride. After a clutch of negative responses he wrote: 'I try to rationalise it all, forcing myself to dismiss what are essentially self-indulgences by the over-opinionated, but there's no denying how much it stings you to the core. The greatest concern is that they are reflecting a more widespread negativity, and that the whole thing will go down the pan.'[xxv] A couple of days later, however, noticing two positive assessments of his work, his spirits were lifted enough that he was able to write that he'd put his 'suicidal tendencies on hold for the moment.'[xxvi]

Although Renwick understood the industry well enough to know critics either laud one's efforts or tear them to shreds, it didn't make life any easier, especially for someone sensitive who didn't take his work lightly. But at least he could find solace from the critics who had already spotted the germ of longevity present in this opening instalment, boding well for its televisual future.

In 1990 it was hard to imagine Victor becoming a star, much less an entire constellation.

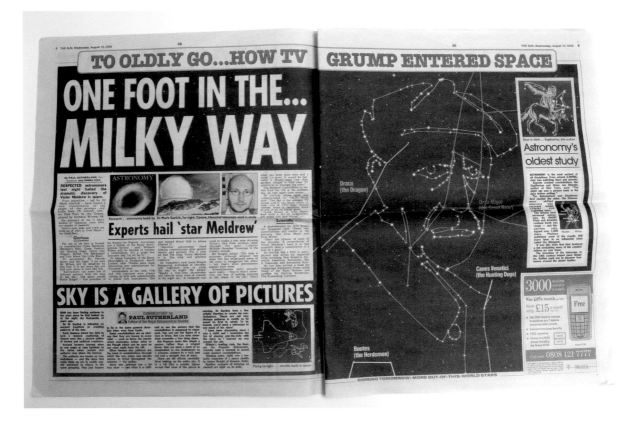

CHAPTER 6
*Completing
the Opening Series*

The opening episode of *One Foot*, attracting just over nine million viewers, may not have set the world on fire, but this modest start satisfied those associated with the show. It was hoped that the audience, having enjoyed their glimpse into the Meldrews' life, would be eager to pay another visit, while new faces would join them for the second instalment, 'The Big Sleep', when transmitted on Thursday, 11 January. Unfortunately it faced stiff competition from *Sherlock Holmes* over on ITV, and took a battering, losing nearly two million viewers from the

> *It's the same with Dickens – the memorable characters are always the two-dimensional eccentrics with peculiar mannerisms or tics.*
>
> DAVID RENWICK

previous week. While Conan Doyle's eccentric detective clocked up figures of ten million, *One Foot* was watched by just 7.5 million: it turned out to be the least watched episode not only in the first season but the entire six series. Such low figures saw the programme drop out of the BBC's top thirty, and did nothing for David Renwick's spirits. As it transpired, it was just a blip: the remaining four episodes in Series One recovered ground, pulling in audiences of just over nine million once again, with the third show, 'The Valley of Fear', toppling Holmes, much to everyone's delight.

'The Big Sleep' saw Victor still struggling to adjust, as he moped about the house and garden, miserably picking up the crisp packets and empty beer cans discarded by all and sundry. Forced to kick his heels while Margaret worked at the local florists, he dwelt on the news that his cousin, also sixty, had died of a heart attack. A touch of hypochondria soon set in and before long he believed he'd contracted every illness under the sun, leading to a visit by Dr Snellgrove (played by Helen Fraser), a character named after Renwick's former family GP. Even Margaret's idea of attending

keep-fit classes failed to help, especially when the instructor keeled over and died.

Over the coming weeks, Victor would regularly reveal the grouchy side of his personality, incessantly complaining about one thing or another, but Meldrew's sobriquet 'misery guts' belied a man of sentiment. This short-sighted view of his character, which was given plenty of mileage by the tabloid press, frustrated David Renwick, who felt that if people had taken time to analyse the show, they would have realised there was more depth to the man. 'It's the same with Dickens – the memorable characters are always the two-dimensional eccentrics with peculiar mannerisms or tics,' he says. 'The ones that are more realistic, with interesting shades of grey to them, never catch on with the public. So I suppose I shouldn't really complain – it's the two-dimensional view of Victor as a moaning old curmudgeon that's made him such an enduring and popular figure.'

Although Renwick has always been grateful for the success and adulation his character enjoyed, he regrets the way people dismissed Victor as an irascible old man. 'I was watching some coverage of the 2005 General Election and a journalist referred to the "Victor Meldrew Syndrome" of the Conservatives. What does that mean? Presumably that they were all very negative, complaining too much without offering any positive solutions, but that's not what Victor is about at all.

'Someone at the BBC once wanted to use him in a promotion about licence fees, in order to get people to cough up. They'd written a script in which Victor was moaning about having to pay for his TV licence. I said: "How do you know Victor would have complained? How do you know he's not an avid supporter of public service television? I happen to think he would probably pay his licence fee without hesitation. People seem to imagine Victor is mean-spirited. They don't remember the episode "Who's Listening?", where he gave up his Christmas Day to work in a soup kitchen.'

Reflecting on how he brought the character to life on screen, Richard Wilson says he never set out to play him grumpy. 'I couldn't play him grumpy all the time; there was no point. I saw him as a man upset about being made redundant, who didn't hold much hope for the future. To me, he was brighter than many and prepared to speak out. He wasn't a selfish man, but a lot of people wondered why Margaret stayed with him. It was simply because she loved him, and he loved her. It was clear that neither of them could have existed without the other.'

'The Big Sleep' was an episode that helped reveal there was more to Victor than his bemoaning – he had a tender side, too. He befriended a little robin in his garden, feeding it regularly until its life was snuffed out by a neighbour's cat. Instead of highlighting this poignant scene, or picking up on an endearing character trait, critics lampooned the poor little robin instead. It's fair to say it wasn't one of Colin Mapson's [visual effects designer on Series One] best props, and Margaret Forwood, writing in the *Daily Express*, felt that Renwick's new comedy deserved 'better than the stuffed robin which marred last week's episode'[i]. She added: 'This was a puny little object, obviously stuffed, nailed to the branch and singing by dint of some mechanical device. Couldn't they have slotted in some footage of a real robin?'[ii] She ended her stinging assessment of the under-developed feathery friend with the quip that perhaps it hadn't been killed by a cat, but 'put out of its misery by some BBC props man who couldn't stand the sight of it.'[iii]

If anyone had inflicted mortal wounds on the robin it's more likely to have been David Renwick, who hadn't been impressed the moment it arrived in the garden at Warnford Road, Boscombe. He knew it wouldn't fool anyone and prayed that shots focusing on the animatronic bird would be short and sweet. He felt 'the shape was all wrong and the movements, engineered by men behind the fence squeezing little rubber bulbs, were a joke.'[iv] It's said that time is a great healer, but the pain Renwick endures every time he sees the robin, even after seventeen years, is still intense. 'I still think

it's shit!' he exclaims. 'It's an embarrassment and I wonder why it was put on television. The second you look at it you know it's a mechanical robin.' For Renwick, one of the funniest moments in the programme – for all the wrong reasons – was when flapping wings were heard and Victor's eyes followed the bird's flight path, before the camera cut to this fragile creature on the bird table. 'There was, of course, no way we could show it flying,' he says. 'And unfortunately in that moment the whole fakery is cruelly exposed. I'm not blaming Susie, but if something like that happened now in one of my shows, I'd probably have the authority to say: "It doesn't work. We'll have to cut the scene."'

Mapson realises much of the blame for the robin landed on his shoulders, but it was suggested by his design manager that an external company should make the emaciated bird. 'In my head I had a vision of a big

fat robin but they made him too slim; I wish we'd kept it in-house now.'

The third episode, 'The Valley of Fear', took

A routine chat between Margaret and her mother about the perils of spontaneous combustion.

its title from a Sherlock Holmes novel and was a reference to the fear instilled in the community by the yob element at large, who were responsible for beating up Victor and daubing his house with obscenities. It also contained a brief storyline inspired by real events in Renwick's own house. A plumber, played by Christopher Ryan, visited the Meldrews' house and was forever berating his assistant. 'My own radiators were making a clanking noise,' says Renwick, 'and that gave me the idea for the old lady banging on the pipes. And the guy who came to fix them had this rather dim-witted young assistant whom he seemed to enjoy humiliating, so of course that whole relationship went straight into the script.'

After the experience of the robin, bees were next to cause Renwick headaches. In the fourth episode, 'I'll Retire to Bedlam' (a line from Ebenezer Scrooge in *A Christmas Carol*), Victor's days were going from bad to worse when he was trapped with Margaret inside his shed for three and a half hours as a swarm of bees descended on their garden. As Margaret commented, it was as though her

'Is there anyone else who wants to sleep in my bed? Mahatma Ghandi is just leaving!'

husband was 'soaking up every hideous disaster and piece of misery in the world like a giant sponge'. While preparing to film the scene, it soon became clear to Renwick that, in his view, there weren't enough bees to make the situation credible. When the bees were placed on the shed's window, they clustered round the edges and were barely visible. 'It was obvious that Victor and Margaret could have escaped quite easily, so that all the panicky dialogue between them became pointless.'

Renwick realises that it was another tricky situation for Susan Belbin. 'Did she think that the bees were wonderful? I doubt it, but she probably felt a bit insecure because the buck stops with her – she's the director and this was what she'd been lumbered with. She wasn't the one who'd ordered the bees and, of course, she was just after the same effect as me. The problem was, she had an incredibly disgruntled writer on the set radiating doom and gloom, and throwing up his hands, saying: "It's never going to work!" I tend to be so defeatist about everything, whereas she was

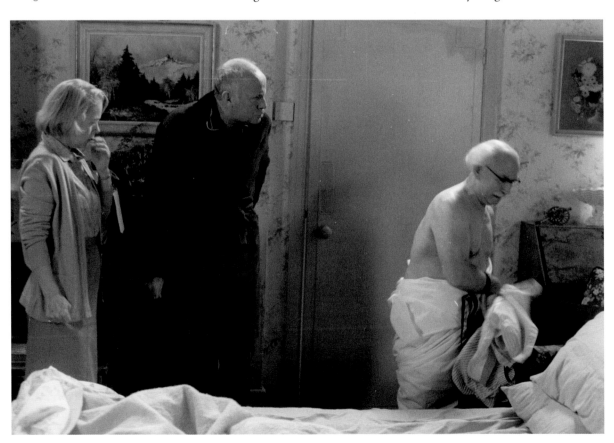

probably thinking: "Come on, I've got to shoot this bloody thing and at least go away with some footage and see what we can do with it".'

It was a warm late-September day when the scene was filmed in Bournemouth. A wall of the shed was removed and Wilson and Crosbie spent a considerable time within the confined space while the scenes were shot. Unfortunately, some bees escaped and were flying around. 'Only one person got stung – an electrician,' recalls Susan Belbin. 'He was bald and a bee landed on his head. He didn't know until he put his cap on and it stung him.'

When the show was transmitted on Thursday, 25 January, an audience of just under nine million tuned in. Renwick was in a confident mood afterwards, noting: 'The show looked really great tonight. I laughed a lot and thought, bloody hell, if they run this one down they clearly have no taste of any kind.'[v] Within a few days, though, he'd already noticed critics in the *News of the World* and the *Daily Express* were far from complimentary, with Peter Tory in the *Express* regarding the character as too whingey and negative for the comedy to work.

Such is David Renwick's sensitivity that every piece of bad press felt like a dagger being pushed deeper into his creative soul, and he admits he is constitutionally unsuitable for the cut-and-thrust industry of television. 'Sadly, I don't have the resilience you need to coast through this business. I'm incredibly wounded by adverse comments – many of which can be quite brutal.'

Renwick describes having a 'love-hate' relationship with the reviewers. 'I try to rationalise it all by saying, "Your work is never as bad as they say, or as good as they say – it's usually somewhere in between." Inevitably, you're nervous about reviews, but situation comedy is like real-life relationships: you have to get to know the characters, to become familiar with them before you're prepared to let them into your life. It's very hard because you're struggling with all of that, particularly during the first series, but the critics don't always take that into account.'

One Foot was in the vanguard of a new wave of situation comedy, where realism, pathos and a desire to push the boundaries of acceptance within the genre were of paramount importance to the writer. Reviewers and, to a degree, elements of the public failed at first to notice or appreciate what Renwick was trying to achieve with his show. He says: 'It's difficult for people to take on board a style that's slightly different. I remember sitting down to watch the first episode of *Fawlty Towers* and being slightly mystified by the first

> *Your work is never as bad as they say, or as good as they say – it's usually somewhere in between.*
>
> DAVID RENWICK

five or six scenes because nothing much happened – there certainly wasn't any overt comedy. It was all about setting up the environment, the pace and the characters in a way that was far more realistic than we were used to in a comedy show – it was quite groundbreaking in a way. As the episode progressed, the comic elements began to coalesce and by the end I was helpless with laughter, and a fan of the show from that day on. No question that I was hugely influenced by it, partly because it was such a rarity. Most situation comedies at that time still had a very obvious, broad feel to them, and if you tried to play that down and attempt something more muted it was natural for people to think it was dull.'

Renwick admits that *One Foot in the Grave* could never be regarded as a comedy show with warmth, which, he feels, is one reason it would never rival a show like *Only Fools and Horses* in the hearts of the nation. '*Only Fools* has what I would call the Queen Mother factor; you take it to your heart and welcome it into your home like an old friend. Watching Del Boy, I think, gives you a cheery, optimistic glow, whereas there is something a bit bleak and uncomfortable about Victor's world. It's more David Lynch than Laurel and Hardy, which means you never really feel safe.'

Another factor considered by critics and viewers alike when assessing a new show is the volume of laughter on the soundtrack. 'In certain scenes in the first series there was very little laughter, which I think will have deterred some people, subconsciously at least. It's not very common to see characters going about their business in an understated, low-key fashion, in complete silence. You find yourself asking: "Where's the comedy? Where are the jokes?" Well, at that particular moment there weren't any. That was the whole point – not every second of someone's life is a sitcom.'

Evaluating the feedback received from the press and public, Renwick feels Episode One did the show few favours; a tragic tone existed from the beginning, with Victor losing his job and his agonies played out against mournful incidental music. He says: 'There wasn't much of a feelgood factor in that episode.' He may not have intended to be overly melancholy, but moments of darkness regularly pervade the series, helping lift the sitcom above its contemporaries; when you watched *One Foot*

'We've had to freeze the kitty...' Not quite a traditional sitcom.

you knew you were entering a world not as safe as those occupied by other examples of the genre.

Some people argue that all publicity is good publicity – whether the critic is savaging the programme or not, at least it's being brought to the public's attention. In the case of *One Foot*, initial coverage across the newspapers wasn't overwhelming. 'In the early days, my wife, Ellie, and I used to complain that there was so little coverage in the press,' says Renwick, who understands the reasons. Not only was it a new series with no 'star' names in the cast, but it didn't fit into any easily recognised category. 'We didn't have that instantly accessible theatricality that the tabloids would pick up on, but nor did we court the so-called quality press by being in any way trendy, satirical or erudite. So we tended to miss both boats.'

The tide, however, was slowly turning. Writing

about 'I'll Retire to Bedlam', leading tabloid critic Hilary Kingsley admitted she was wrong with her assessment of *One Foot*. After almost writing off the sitcom's chances of long-term survival upon watching the first episode, she was now lauding its humour. She wrote: 'I was wrong about *One Foot in the Grave*... I'm now entirely on his side. The cat in the freezer [a scene in 'The Valley of Fear' which led to several complaints from disgusted viewers] the other week was hilarious. The rage on Thursday about perforations on loo paper and the scene as he was shaved for an operation by a whistling mental patient in a white coat gave me pains laughing . . . Victor has raised grumpiness to an art form.'[vi] Meanwhile, over at the *Daily Star*, a journalist was commending Annette Crosbie in her first comedy series, declaring that it was unlikely to be her last.

If events had turned out differently, actress Janine Duvitski, who later played semi-regular character Pippa and – along with her husband Patrick (played by Angus Deayton) – became the Meldrews' next-door neighbour, would have appeared in the sitcom much earlier. Before being offered Pippa, she was asked to play Iris, the Meldrews' niece, in 'I'll Retire to Bedlam'. She was invited to the BBC to read for the part on 4 September 1989, with Renwick remarking at the time that she was 'a bit eccentric as a possible Iris, but undoubtedly has a strong and individual presence'[vii], something that stood her in good stead when later cast as Pippa. Despite harbouring minor doubts about whether Duvitski's style was suitable for Iris, Belbin and Renwick were impressed enough to offer the one-scene role. She later declined the opportunity. When invited to read for the part, Duvitski was holidaying in France. 'When I heard they wanted to see me, I returned from France early. I hadn't seen the script because I'd been away, so when I arrived home, I thought: "God, this is a bit small. I wish I hadn't come back so quick." Anyway, I went along, read and was offered the job, which I turned down the following day.' With Duvitski out of the frame, the role was offered to Rebecca Stevens instead.

There were just two episodes remaining to complete Series One. A stage in the programme-making process that he'd particularly enjoyed was the read-through, which for Episode Five ['The Eternal Quadrangle'] and Six ['The Return of the Speckled Band'] took place on Monday, 16 October 1989, with just Richard Wilson, Annette Crosbie, Susan Belbin and Renwick present. Sitting at the table in the rehearsal room at Acton, the writer found both episodes funny. Impressed with the day's proceedings, he recorded that 'there were times when I was wiping the tears from my eyes'[viii]. He was delighted with both leading players, particularly Crosbie, noting 'she was quite brilliant at the table today and I went away assured that the strengths of this show are undeniably the two of them under the microscope'[ix].

Actors work differently, some jumping into the shoes of their characters from the moment they pick up the crisp, newly bound scripts on the rehearsal room table, while others play it straight, letting their interpretation develop as the week progresses. At the read-throughs, while Crosbie was, as Renwick once noted, 'as near to her final rendition as you could want'[x], Wilson fell into the latter category. 'I'm not sure it's deliberate,' says Renwick. 'He probably intends to give it his best shot at the table, but usually it's still very raw and erratic at that stage. I think it's a combination of not trying too hard too soon because he wants the performance to grow organically as he goes along. By the time you get to the recording, his interpretation is built upon a very solid foundation because the material and attitudes have all seeped in and had time to grow. That's the way Richard works, which I have no problem with. But it does mean you have to keep your nerve early on and take it on trust that the material will eventually ignite. It's a bit like watching a very rough diamond being gradually polished to perfection in front of your eyes.'

The atmosphere at read-throughs was conducive to some imaginative performances. Around a table, everyone felt relaxed and natural, with the lack of pressure often leading to moments of glorious comedy and comic performances that sometimes couldn't be recaptured for the recording. 'Owen Brenman is an interesting actor because his instincts are mostly spot on,' says Renwick. 'He's the kind of performer who commits himself whole-heartedly to the role with much soul-searching and self-critical analysis, and of course his great strength is his spontaneity. I've found over the years that the funniest moments at a read-through can almost never be recreated when you shoot it. Comedy is so delicate, ineffable and fragile, you really don't know half the time what it is that's making it work or

It's a bit like watching a very rough diamond being gradually polished to perfection in front of your eyes

DAVID RENWICK

fail. You just know when it kicks in and when it doesn't, and trying to reproduce certain glorious nuances to order is impossible. So in general it's quite important for people not to peak too early.'

Just as a moment of magic or inspiration can be lost between the various phases in the studio, the same happens while on location, filming. 'All too often there is an indefinable element of the chemistry that fails when you put it on film,' says Renwick, pointing out that exchanges between actors can lack fluidity because they have been spliced together from different takes. 'Sometimes the light, organic quality that existed when those two people were talking to each other is lost when it's all chopped up in the cutting room. You might, for instance, be using one line from Victor that was shot on 13 August and then Margaret's reply from 1 September when we went back to the location for some pick-ups. Sometimes it still works, but often the way the shots are cut together is dictated by continuity, at the expense of the natural pacing and timing.'

Renwick's influence on the shape and direction of the situation comedy increased as *One Foot* progressed. Everyone realised that alterations would have to be made if he wasn't entirely happy with the look and feel of a scene, which is what happened in the studio during rehearsals for Series One. His diary revealed a series of concerns that he had to address. On Sunday, 22 October, the dress run, in his eyes, wasn't encouraging. He noted: 'I'm afraid there were lots of notes from me, and it was one of those occasions I just feel like throwing in the towel – absolutely nothing seemed to be working.'[xi] The following week, before the recording of Episode Three, Renwick found himself addressing the cast after the dress run, explaining how the performances could be improved. And prior to recording Episode Four on Saturday, 4 November, he recorded in his journal: 'I realised – too late – that it was a mistake to stay away from rehearsals all week. Even Richard was saying he wished I'd been there on Friday. A lot of the performances were all over the place: the delicacies of the eye clinic conversation, the bedroom chats and the hospital scene had all gone haywire.'[xii]

Renwick respected the role of the director, though, and his concerns were always routed through the chair. Susan Belbin says: 'I found it tricky initially, but I'm quite adaptable. I think I can read a situation fairly well and go with it. David knew what he'd written and what he wanted. He also understood the character Victor better than anyone so it was difficult for me to say, "Victor would do something" or "Victor wouldn't say something like that" or "I want him standing up",

Crucified by the critics: the show was far from an instant hit.

when David would have a very good reason for him sitting down. But he was very diplomatic and would always go through me: he wouldn't dream of going up to an actor and saying: "Do it like this." He'd say to me: "I don't think he's quite got the grasp of it." And it was me who gave him the lead, inasmuch as I'd tell him to speak to the performers because there's no point in it coming second hand.'

The problem for a perfectionist like David Renwick is knowing when to stop. He always felt that, given sufficient time, performances could be enhanced. Frustratingly, time constraints normally dictated when he had to let go. During the read-through and blocking for 'The Eternal Quadrangle', he stated: 'I would clearly have liked to get more immersed in all the nuances. I feel there's so much you can actually do with it, so much funnier it can become if you really apply yourself.'[xiii]

Renwick enjoyed his direct involvement with

actors, and even while preparations were being made to begin recording 'The Eternal Quadrangle', he was taking Annette Crosbie aside for a 'final reminder that the confrontation in the kitchen needs as much intensity as she can give it'[xiv]. Some thespians didn't always welcome such advice, particularly at the eleventh hour. Crosbie, of course, would have made her feelings known if she'd felt this way, but overall she welcomed Renwick's advice and involvement. She particularly enjoyed him being around for the early episodes when, recording in front of a live television audience for the first time, she was on unfamiliar territory. She says: 'I remember being awfully glad he was there to talk to.'

Renwick recalls conversing with the actress in the early stages of the series, and feels her initial nervousness reflected in her performance in the opening episodes. 'Her portrayal of the character was bigger in those early episodes than it needed to be. She said she found it difficult playing in front of an audience with all the cameramen around. I replied: "This is sitcom – you mustn't play to the audience. You're playing to people at home. Yes, you're aware of the audience, and a part of your brain should be picking up their reaction because it can be helpful to your timing."'

A growing number of critics were appreciating the acting talent of Crosbie, with a journalist in *City Limits* commenting: 'Annette Crosbie puts in an equally good performance as grouchy Victor's long-suffering wife.'[xv] But the media response to the final two episodes, culminating in 'The Return of the Speckled Band', which saw the Meldrews heading off on their holidays with an extra passenger in their suitcase, was, again, mixed. Tony Pratt in the *Daily Mirror* initially thought the show's title 'could apply to some of the jokes, which are past their sell-by date'[xvi] but felt Richard Wilson saved the day with his skills at 'edge-of-madness comedy'[xvii]. But by the penultimate episode he was praising Renwick's 'extraordinarily savage comedy'[xviii] and regarding it as 'rum stuff'[xix]. While Liz Atherton, writing in the now defunct *Today*, was sad to see the end of the series, and Margaret Forwood, in the *Daily Express*, was predicting a second series of a show in which she thought Richard Wilson had 'at last found a comedy role worthy of his wonderful whining voice'[xx], Garry Bushell in the *Sun* regarded the show as one of the 'brightest new sitcom hopes'[xxi].

Not everyone was complimentary, with Mark Wareham in the *Independent* reporting on the 'last episode of a bafflingly unfunny sitcom'[xxii]. He joined a small band of journalists who weren't struck on the programme, including Christopher Tookey in the *Daily Telegraph* who, in response to an earlier instalment of the series, was trying to understand why he'd taken 'such a dislike'[xxiii] to it. While he thought the setting was 'all too recognisably BBC sitcom-land'[xxiv], and criticised Renwick for allowing his own political views to enter the scripts – meaning lines about Norman Fowler and Kenneth Clarke – he also felt the programme offered 'in general, a distorted and depressingly old-fashioned view of old age'[xxv]. I think Tookey missed the point behind the show: it wasn't meant to be a portrait of old age, more a study of a man whose life is thrown into chaos when kicked out of his job prematurely, and he's left with plenty of time to examine the inanities of the world around him. Yes, Victor was approaching retirement age, but this wasn't the driving factor behind the show.

Renwick realised that his deliberate attempt to establish realistic pacing within the scripts, affording the time to undertake real-life events like opening doors, crossing the room and walking down the road, which other writers might class as superfluous to the overall plot, might lead some critics to regard the show as downbeat. Unperturbed, though, he wasn't going to slip into the trap of injecting the 'artificial energy level that sitcom characters always seem to adopt when they want to be funny'[xxvi]. Realism was an integral part of the show's fabric and would remain so.

Over the coming days, further journalists carried reviews of the closing episode, but by the time the last had reached the news stands, David Renwick had already been given the good news: the BBC wanted a second series.

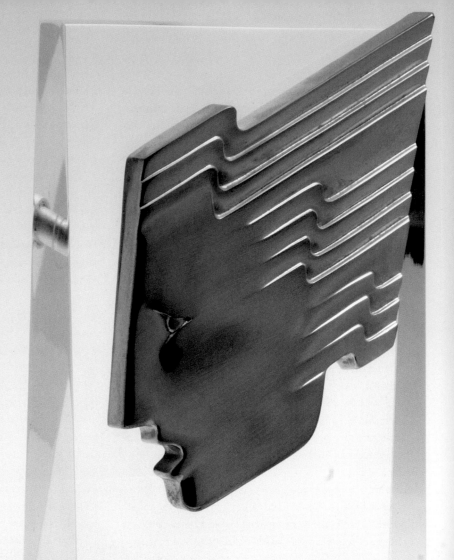

CHAPTER 7
Preparations for Another Run

ROYAL TELEVISION
SOCIETY

PROGRAMME AWARDS 1992

SITUATION COMEDY

BBC TELEVISION

As February 1990 dawned, David Renwick was glowing after confirmation from Susan Belbin that the BBC wanted a second series, to be transmitted during the autumn. However, for a time it looked as if thoughts of another season of *One Foot* would have to be put on ice. Days after receiving the green light, a speculative project Renwick had been working on bubbled to the surface, much to Belbin's chagrin.

British film producer John Goldstone, whose credits include such titles as *Monty Python and the Holy Grail*, *Life of Brian* and *The Meaning of Life*, had been approached by Paramount Pictures Corporation, which owned the rights to the famous Bing Crosby/Bob Hope/Dorothy Lamour *Road to . . .* movies. Seven pictures were released between 1940 and 1962, beginning with *Road to Singapore* and ending with *Road to Hong Kong*. An eighth title, provisionally called *Road to the Fountain of Youth*, was due to be filmed in 1978, but Crosby's sudden death from a heart attack scuppered plans. Paramount wanted to revisit the series, with two new faces stepping into the lead roles. *Carry On* director Gerald Thomas was drafted in to direct the picture, and Marshall and Renwick attended various meetings to discuss the concept, which spotlighted the central characters' adventures when they headed to Moscow to make their fortunes from the raft of business opportunities emerging in the former Soviet Union.

Goldstone contacted Renwick on 8 February, suggesting a recce to Transylvania in March, to explore the writers' idea of casting Gene Wilder and John Candy, and seeing them rerouted via Transylvania. The offer was inviting but the timing couldn't have been worse. Realising he had to inform the BBC, he called later that day. With Belbin unavailable, he informed production manager Gavin Clark that *One Foot* might have to be put on hold – news that didn't please Belbin when she returned from her meeting. In his journal, Renwick remarked on her subsequent phone call: 'Susie came on the phone, arguing that "we had an agreement, don't let me down like this" and so on, as if my loyalty to the series was in some way in doubt.'[i] They resumed their conversation the following day, by which time

Belbin had managed to agree a new schedule for the second series, with filming in July and studio recordings in August. Crucially though, Renwick had to decide whether he could deliver the scripts in time – and Belbin wanted a decision by the end of the working day. A

Almost every movie project we embarked on had, for whatever reason, ended up going nowhere. I started thinking that this idea had the kiss of death about it, too.

DAVID RENWICK

commitment that afternoon was out of the question, as far as Renwick was concerned, because the proposed film remained in the balance. Finding the pressure to commit unhelpful, Renwick confirmed that if pressed, he'd have to pull out of the second series. He later recorded his exasperation: 'I have to stop myself getting very angry because I don't need any more sourness in a relationship I have to preserve.'[ii] Belbin finally agreed to give Renwick eight days to decide what he wanted to do. Ten days later, though, when he met with Belbin and Richard Wilson at the French restaurant L'Escargot in London's Greek Street, he still hadn't made a decision regarding the film, but was convinced he'd be able to deliver the scripts for *One Foot* in time.

Before long, though, Renwick and Marshall pulled out of discussions regarding writing a screenplay for *Road to Moscow*. Renwick explains: 'It was looking very positive, as if it was going to happen, but at the back of my mind I was becoming more nervous about it.' Previous experience of trying to write for the medium had somewhat tainted Renwick's views. 'Almost every movie project we embarked on had, for whatever reason, ended up going nowhere. I started thinking that this idea had the kiss of death about it, too.' Assailed by increasing doubts, and unable to see the project materialising, Renwick didn't want to spend a lengthy period on a script that would never see the light of day. 'We just pulled out. Other writers were approached but, as I predicted, nothing ever came of it. Andrew and I could have spent a year on that film, and although it would have been nice to visit Romania on a Paramount expense account, I preferred to start thinking about the second television series – a project that was real, and that would definitely happen.'

Over lunch at L'Escargot, on that cold February day, discussions centred on the second series of *One Foot*. Wilson, who was in an ebullient mood, informed Renwick and Belbin that he'd never received so many letters from the public, complimenting him on his fine performance, with some stating that they were 'in pain from laughing at the show'[iii]. Wilson took the opportunity to express, once again, his wishes that Renwick would refrain from cramming the scripts with relentless comic plotting, so that the characters could breathe more freely. But packing each script with lots of ideas, Renwick admits, was a result of insecurity. 'The trouble is I get nervous if I don't feel we're delivering enough invention.'[iv] Wilson was also keen that Victor was seen as kind and not always crotchety, but Renwick thought the actor was wrong to think of the character as a bigot simply because he didn't wholly share his own liberal ideology.

With less than five months before location filming started, Renwick settled down to complete the scripts. The first series had closed with the Meldrews jetting off to Athens for a holiday, and when he began mulling over ideas of how he could open the second season, he toyed with thoughts of Victor and Margaret returning to find their house blown up by a bomb, but instantly dismissed it for fear of some real disaster occurring just before transmission. However, the image of Victor's house being razed to the ground still appealed, so he swapped the bomb for a fire, and threw in the effects of a freak hurricane for good measure.

After enduring a protracted search to find the house used in the opening series, production manager Gavin Clark had to start the hunt all over again. His brief this time, however, was even more complicated because of two factors: firstly, he also had to find a demolished building to act as the remains of the gutted house and, secondly, there was a plot twist in which Victor mistook a neighbour's home for his own, so Clark had to look for a row of completely identical houses.

Clark struck lucky upon discovering that a house in Northcote Road, Bournemouth, was due for demolition, but finding the Meldrews' new property was more difficult, as Susan Belbin explains. 'It was a nightmare location to find. Most houses in a terrace seem to be built so the front doors are mirrored, next to each other. If you entered the front door, one would have rooms coming off the hallway on the left, while next door they'd be on the right.' But in Renwick's script the layout of the houses had to be identical or the mix-up wouldn't work.

Accompanying Gavin Clark on many of his house-hunting trips was John Asbridge, the new production designer. 'For me, of course, it also had to be a

Cameraman John Record lines up a classic 'I don't believe it' shot.

84

(Above) Victor's new house was found near Christchurch, Dorset. (Right) Nick Swainey finds it hard to express his feelings to Nurse Tania (Anita Chellamah).

house for which I could create a convincing interior for the studio sets. But as with many of David's scripts there were several requirements that made it far from straightforward to find. It had to be, above all, ordinary and easily mistaken for other houses in the road, for storyline reasons. It required a back garden gate leading to an alleyway that a tortoise could escape down to a road on which white lines could be painted. It also required neighbouring houses, and to one side a variety of opening fence panels for Nick Swainey to appear through.'

When Carol Rowbrey, whose house had been used for the first series, heard that her property was no longer required, she was disappointed. 'I was a little upset because I hoped they'd carry on.' However, references in the opening script of Series Two to children causing the house fire by pushing fireworks through the letterbox annoyed Carol, who put her

concerns in writing. 'I wrote to the BBC saying it wasn't a very nice thing to do because so many people around where I lived knew my house had been used, and I'd hate youngsters to think, "Let's go and put something through the letterbox." I said that if anything like that happened, I'd blame the BBC!' Fortunately it never did.

The houses used for the Meldrews, Nick Swainey and Pippa and Patrick were found in Tresillian Way, Walkford, near Christchurch in Dorset. Victor and Margaret's property was owned by the Southgates. 'Gavin Clark knocked on our door and said he worked for the BBC and was interested in using our house for the new series. It didn't take long for us to agree because we thought it would be fun,' recalls Kelly, who doesn't regret letting the BBC film at her house, despite the inevitable inconveniences. 'To start with it was great fun, but you tend to get a bit blasé after a while. My husband is retired, so was here throughout the filming. Admittedly they only filmed for about eight or nine days at a time, but that was long enough because I don't think we could have coped if it had been longer. You wouldn't believe the number of people we had in our garden, and it's not a very big area! But everybody who came was considerate and friendly – you couldn't have asked for better.'

Next-door, Mike Lewis, whose house was used for Nick Swainey, recalls the day he saw strangers armed with cameras wandering up and down the street. 'One or two of us in the street went out and asked what they were doing,' says Mike. 'Being a fairly close-knit community, we were a little suspicious when they began taking pictures of several houses. They said they were considering using the site for filming, although initially we weren't aware for which programme.' Mike has happy memories of the filming, too, although one particular memory is etched permanently on his mind. 'It must have been about 1991, because it was the same time as my wife, Anne, who has since died, was diagnosed with cancer. As soon as the crew got wind of that, they arranged a lovely bouquet of flowers and brought it in for her – a very kind gesture.'

While Gavin Clark made the arrangements to secure the three houses in Tresillian Way, David Renwick was completing the final scripts, a task that remained as exacting as ever, with all the insecurities that befall writers. His journal entries covering this period reveal moments of elation as a sequence or idea came to fruition, and times of despair as he wrestled with his thoughts, such as 'head like glue all morning, in a terrible state verging on nausea with all the old tension'[v] and 'I came close to outright panic today as this plot just refused to fall into place.'[vi]

Just what he always wanted: a cursed scorpion.

This was the series that marked the arrival of two new regular characters, in the shape of neighbours Patrick and Pippa Trench, played by Angus Deayton and Janine Duvitski, and the promotion from being a one-off character to regular for likeable Nick Swainey. Whenever Owen Brenman is recognised it's often his voice, which became a feature of his screen character, that gives him away. It wasn't, however, something Brenman consciously adopted for the show. 'When people spot me in the street, they often say: "I thought it was you, but when I heard your voice I knew it was." I just think it's my own voice, really. It's a bit sing-songy, and I can reach that slightly higher register, but I don't consciously work on it.' Reading the script enables an actor to gradually formulate in his mind the personality traits of his character, and this is what happened to Brenman. 'I could hear the voice in my head – slightly earnest, sing-songy, relentlessly cheerful but underneath it all, quite sad.' The voice typified the character, a guy whose life was, despite all the pretence, empty and disconsolate; it's what appealed to Brenman. 'Here was this very cheerful guy living with his mum, whom you never see, and doesn't have a girlfriend. The flipside of the image he presents is that his life is probably miserable and dark.'

Brenman enjoyed working with the rest of the team. 'The casting of Annette was spot on and inspired. I don't think she had done a sitcom before and, therefore, probably wouldn't have been on most casting directors' lists, which is the depressing reality of the frequently unimaginative and conservative casting process. Thankfully, David Renwick and Sue Belbin bravely stuck with their gut feelings and cast Annette, who brings real weight and depth to the constraints of a sitcom, making it all the better. Richard is also very

good to work with – a fantastic team leader. He's exemplary: he'd do all the things I'd find difficult, like remembering everybody's name on the crew. He was very generous and would buy bottles of champagne at the end of the series, and take people out for a meal. He's an object lesson in how you should behave. Whether it's because his success came later on in his career, I don't know, but he didn't take anything for granted, and was always nice and supportive. As well as acting, he directs as well, but you wouldn't have known because on *One Foot* he remained an actor and didn't try to direct anyone or anything.'

Susan Belbin concurs with Brenman, adding that she never felt inhibited by Wilson's other career as a director. 'Richard is the nicest chap in the world, and has the ability to divide the two roles: when he's an actor, he acts and you direct him, and he's very easy to direct, too. Like everyone, if he believes firmly in something he'll tell you, which is fair enough, and there were one or two instances of that while making *One Foot*, but I find it remarkable that he's able to divide the two responsibilities so easily.'

Nick Swainey was the one character who was never wound up by Victor. While everyone else whose path crossed Mr Meldrew's found themselves pulling their hair out, a phlegmatic Swainey was never riled. 'It's probably because Nick treated him as a joke and always laughed at him. Nick Swainey was very self-contained and, let's be honest, slightly bonkers, so it didn't affect him like others.' says Brenman. Swainey lived in a world of his own, which saw the character stand out from the crowd, highlighting his humour and strengths. The downside, however, was that occasionally Brenman appeared to be acting in isolation. 'It would have been nice if he'd been less isolated, I guess, but then he may not have been so successful,' he muses.

Brenman enjoyed teaming up with David Renwick again, having worked for him regularly on *Alexei Sayle's Stuff.* He remembers the read-throughs for the genuine

laughter ringing around the rehearsal room as the cast sat down and began studying the scripts. 'People laughed out loud quite spontaneously – it wasn't forced, as often happens on comedies; the scripts were genuinely funny. When you have a humorous script, the only thing you can do is mess it up. I realised *One Foot* was extremely well written and wanted to ensure I did it justice. Sometimes when you work on comedies, the scripts are OK or not

Supporting characters were used sparingly, but memorably, in Renwick's scripts.

Annette Crosbie was always uncomfortable about scenes involving animals.

later they were the neighbours who were heading off on a month's holiday the day they arrived at their new home. Duvitski found the scene funny. 'I'm terrible at remembering faces, so that scene was plausible to me, but it was a funny idea – as was the script.'

Born in the Lancashire seaside resort of Morecambe, Duvitski says she's often been cast as 'dim' characters, although regards Pippa as a little less so. 'I liked her ordinariness. She was like any normal, average person, just trying to get on with life but getting irritated by her husband, who'd become obsessed with the neighbours.'

Arriving in London at the age of sixteen, Duvitski attended the East 15 Acting School for three years. While still at drama school, she appeared in one-off episodes of *Z Cars* and *Man About the House*; upon graduating in 1973, she spent two years in rep at Derby and Manchester before in 1975 playing the lead role, Diane Weaver, in *Diane*, an instalment from the *Play for Today* series. Her early career was equally divided between theatre, including a spell with the Royal Shakespeare Company, and the screen. On television her credits prior to *One Foot* included *Brush Stokes, Alas Smith and Jones, The Georgian House, Citizen Smith* and a running part as Muriel Bailey in the 1980 series *Cowboys*, while on the big screen she was seen in, among others, *The First Great Train Robbery, Dracula, Breaking Glass* and *The Missionary*.

One of Duvitski's highest-profile jobs, and the one that put her name on the map, was the 1977 *Play for Today* production *Abigail's Party*, written and directed by Mike Leigh, and based on the earlier Hampstead Theatre production. 'That's what most people knew me from, and it meant that everyone saw me as doing comedy from then on.' By the time she joined *One Foot*, she'd also started another sitcom for the BBC: *Waiting for God*, playing Jane Edwards. It marked a busy period in her career. 'I was also having children around that time,' she says. 'I was pregnant during some of the *One Foots*, and was very pregnant at one point in *Waiting for God* but did my best to disguise it.'

very good and you find yourself thinking: "How do I make this funnier?" We didn't have to do that.'

Owen Brenman respects Renwick's talents and his relentless drive for perfection; while he accepts some people, particularly those not used to the writer's style, might find his presence on location and in the studio claustrophobic at times, Brenman enjoyed having Renwick there. 'I appeared in the first series of his recent programme, *Love Soup*, and he wasn't there for all the filming, and I missed him being around. He's the quality control: he knows the subtle nuances and knows what you're capable and not capable of doing.'

Appearing for the first time in Episode Four, 'Who Will Buy?', Patrick and Pippa Trench became an integral part of the show's success, playing the Meldrews' neighbours at their new abode in Riverbank. Having earlier declined the part of Victor and Margaret's niece, Iris, Duvitski accepted the role of Pippa, knowing the character was a neighbour of the Meldrews' and could, therefore, be required for more episodes. In 'Who Will Buy?', Patrick and Pippa's arrival on the Meldrews' doorstep led to inevitable confusion because Victor and Margaret couldn't remember clapping eyes on them before, only to realise

Janine Duvitski formed a valuable screen relationship with Angus Deayton, with whom she enjoyed working. It was a pairing that pleased the writer, too, who expressed his delight in his journal after watching them in action on location: 'Something undeniably magical about the pairing of Angus and Janine Duvitski tonight . . . you can't in any way quantify it; there's just something definitive about the two of them together that's funnier than the sum of the comic parts. Probably the implicit incongruity of Janine with her trademark gawkiness and Angus, currently enjoying the tabloid label "Mr Sex". I made a mental note that they were well worth bringing back, possibly in the Christmas Special.'[vii]

In answer to questions about the characters' development, David Renwick told me: 'Janine has undeniable comic qualities. She basically made a living from being the slightly goofy girlfriend, so I imagine she was grateful to be given a normal character to play. She was simultaneously playing yet another rather dippy part in *Waiting for God* and sometimes I had to drag her back out of that when she came to *One Foot in the Grave*. I'd worked with Angus on the *Alexei* shows and thought he'd be fantastic for the part of Patrick. He was becoming well known as a bit of a heart-throb, so to put Janine with him I thought was quite brave; it certainly created an amusing dynamic. Of course, I'm not committed to using any of the characters apart from Victor and Margaret. Everyone is dispensable if I don't really feel it's working. But as a result of that fourth episode, I wrote Patrick and Pippa into the Christmas Special and from then on there was no question but that they should be running characters.'

In addition to the valuable dynamic between Patrick and Pippa, the interplay between them provided a rich vein of humour. 'I always felt in the early days that Angus was a younger version of John Cleese,' says Renwick, who noted the similarities in his delivery and intonation. 'He certainly wasn't trying to be, but I think it's partly born of the whole Oxbridge revue culture because Angus, of course, attended Oxford. And it suited my purpose to have someone in the cast with that immaculate comedy technique, who could handle slightly more baroque dialogue with fluency and precision. I never claimed the dynamic between Victor and Patrick was terribly original: it probably has its roots in something like *Bewitched*, where the neighbour is always peering through the curtains, watching something bizarre going on across the road, and then as soon as she calls her husband over it's all stopped and he misses it and thinks she's mad.' The formula in *One Foot*, however, was that the audience understood what was going on behind every apparently madcap event witnessed by Victor's neighbours. 'Patrick and Pippa only saw the tip of the iceberg, as it were,' explains Renwick, 'a peculiar event or piece of behaviour which in isolation convinced them Victor was insane. We knew exactly why Victor had a lawnmower and a rake in his front room: because he'd just carried it in from the front garden and the grass cuttings had blown through the window. But to Patrick, Victor is to all intents and purposes mowing the carpet. Eventually it reaches a point where nothing surprises him any more. A police dog apparently digging up human bones in Victor's back garden, for instance, is almost par for the course by the final series.'

Director Susan Belbin was equally enamoured of the talents Duvitski and Deayton brought to the show. 'They both played their roles beautifully. As far as

> *I liked her ordinariness. She was like any normal, average person, just trying to get on with life but getting irritated by her husband, who'd become obsessed with the neighbours.*
>
> JANINE DUVITSKI

Angus is concerned, I just like his stiffness and awkwardness, which sat very nicely with the character.'

Deayton, who's probably best known for the years spent hosting the topical satirical quiz show *Have I Got News For You*, which started as he began playing Patrick, had, in the early 1980s, made appearances in shows such as *Radio Active* on Radio Four, *Rowan Atkinson's Stage Show* and *The Black Adder* before moving on to appear in *KYTV* and work with Renwick on *Alexei Sayle's Stuff*. Also a writer on radio and television, Deayton admits Renwick and himself had been mutual admirers. 'We have similar senses of humour and find the same things funny. David's writing is very verbal and *One Foot* could almost have been a radio show, which is where his background is. It's cleverly written, cleverly phrased and very precise – each word is important.' As for playing the role of Patrick, Deayton admits that for once it was a relief not to be involved in the writing. 'Most things I'd been in I'd written as well, which meant feeling the pressure of responsibility if something wasn't working. So to be in a show where someone else looked after the writing was a relief. That's one of the things I enjoyed: it was more like play than work. If it wasn't funny you could think:

"It's his fault, he wrote it."'

From day one, Deayton and Renwick worked on the same wavelength, which was beneficial, particularly as the launch of *Have I Got News For You* meant Deayton wasn't available for every read-through. However, he made up for any absences by being spot-on with his performance when he rejoined the team, a job, he feels, made easier by the calibre of the scripts. 'The character was there from day one, really, because it was all in the writing. All the characterisation and personality were clearly defined, so it wasn't as if I had to invent anything particularly alien to my own character in order to make him work.'

Deayton was happy with how the role of Patrick developed. 'I like the way he gradually resembled Victor – in fact, towards the end of the show, he morphed into Victor as he looked in the mirror, which was very funny. As Patrick got grumpier, David realised that the characters were becoming closer together – Patrick was almost a younger version of Victor.'

Reflecting on the years spent on the show, he recalls the friendly environment, particularly at read-throughs and rehearsals. 'They were great fun, and Susie Belbin was fantastic as the producer-director, making everyone feel at

home. Rehearsals were like a well-oiled machine, and I don't remember reading through an episode and thinking: "My God, this isn't working, how am I going to make this funny?" It was always funny: the writing was good, the performances came from very seasoned professionals who knew their way round a script and how to make a line work. In other projects, very often you have to think about ways to make it work, but I don't remember having to do that with *One Foot* – it was about as effortless as it gets.'

With the Meldrews now living at 19 Riverbank, a completely different styled house to that used in Series One, an entirely new set had to be designed and constructed. Assigned to the series was designer John Asbridge, who subsequently worked on three Christmas Specials and two other Renwick-scripted shows, *Jonathan Creek* and, most recently, *Love Soup*. Thinking about the challenges he faced when designing the interior of the Meldrews' house, Asbridge says: 'It not only had to be believable, echoing the feel, period and architecture of the exterior, but it had to work for an audience watching the action, lights lighting the action and the cameras and sound booms recording it.' He admits that the interior of the Meldrews' house is probably the most watched of any he's designed, although, on the surface, it was deliberately one of the least remarkable, too. 'It was very important that the extraordinary things that happened to Victor occurred in a home that was in itself very ordinary, thus often helping the comedy to be so extreme and bizarre.' The set, as far as Asbridge was concerned, needed to remain inconsequential in the overall canvas. 'The set wasn't the star of the show. It wasn't a gothic mansion to be viewed with wonder, nor a kitsch assembly of wacky wallpaper and funny props. It had to be a low-profile foil for the action and, therefore, rarely noticed.'

When it came to the décor, Asbridge's ideas didn't immediately match with what Renwick was expecting, as the designer explains. 'The style of the décor, I felt, could be reasonably good taste, and just because Victor

was retired I saw no reason why they should be surrounded with 1940s furniture and bamboo wallpaper. Sometimes influenced by the taste of my own parents, I used a palette of creams and browns, blue and white, brass and wood. However, David on the first recording wanted me to bring the feel of it down a bit and for it not to be quite so smart. I recall having to audition floral sofas in the studio! Some less coordinated curtains, more ordinary lamps and, I think, even a bit of teak got introduced. I often think it was in order to change the furnishings further that David wrote in a burglary in a subsequent episode, though I've never quizzed him on this.'

Renwick's journal entry, upon seeing the set for the first time when the production moved into the studio for the pre-recording of Episode One, reveals the worries he

had over the feel and look of the set. 'I was rather concerned by the opulent look of the Meldrews' new home: a huge, plush cream three-piece suite, long polished dining table with six chairs, wooden chandeliers, and repro antique furniture and nice elegant curtains with tie-backs. As Susie and I discussed the logic behind it all with our designer on the floor I could feel my patience wearing wafer-thin. I

Director Susan Belbin liked the 'stiffness and awkwardness' that Deayton injected into his character.

CHAPTER 8
Series Two

Margaret's arrival from Greece marked a radical departure in her appearance.

attitudes to the characters, and sometimes it's not terribly helpful. I can understand, to a point, why they do it; I bring my own personality and attitudes to my characters – they become extensions of me, but that's different. There are many aspects of Annette's personality that wouldn't sit comfortably with Margaret at all. And I couldn't believe that Margaret would have her hair cut on holiday by some scissor-happy Greek barber. But even that wasn't the point; it was more to do with the rather severe style, which I didn't feel fitted the character.'

Renwick says there wasn't an exchange of views between writer and performer. 'It was a matter of Susie and me muttering dispiritedly on the sidelines, thinking: "How can we make this work?" I think in truth that Annette is a much more modern woman than Margaret Meldrew, and I don't mean to make Margaret out as some antiquated fuddy-duddy, because she isn't. But there is something fundamentally more everyday and conventional about her than Annette. You would never, for instance, find Annette wearing the clothes that Richard Winter put her into as Margaret. And also remember that the hairstyle in the first series wasn't some twee thing we dreamed up and imposed upon the

It was Tuesday, 26 June 1990, and the day was warming up to be another scorcher as David Renwick arrived at the BBC's rehearsal centre at North Acton, London. The read-through for Series Two was on the agenda and the brilliance of the summer weather meant spirits were high, but as he strolled through the canteen and caught sight of Annette Crosbie sitting at a table sipping coffee, his 'heart sank [i]. Seven months had passed since the cast had last assembled to record the closing instalment of Series One, so you wouldn't think having a haircut would cause such a stir, but in the eyes of Renwick it was a disaster for continuity reasons. Gone was the mid-length bob that had become associated with Margaret's character, replaced instead by a much shorter cut. Even now, Crosbie can't understand what all the fuss was about. 'It wasn't as though we were picking up from where we left off at the end of Series One because I was supposed to have been away on holiday.'

For Renwick, though, it was an issue. 'There are moments when actors bring their own personality and

> *There are moments when actors bring their own personality and attitudes to the characters, and sometimes it's not terribly helpful.*
>
> DAVID RENWICK

character – it was Annette's own hairstyle at the time. So I did feel we were presented with a bit of a fait accompli.'

'If you're in a series and have your hair cut a certain way, when you turn up for a new season you should make sure, in the main, that it's the same,' says Susan Belbin. 'When we saw Annette in the rehearsal room canteen, David and I looked at each other aghast. Bear in mind there was plenty of time for her to inform us that she looked completely different: as an actress she should have done that. I appreciate *One Foot* wasn't the only job she ever did, so her hair could have been cut short for another part, but from a professional point of view she should have told us.'

The only solution, as far as Renwick and Belbin were concerned, was to have a wig made. Time was tight, though, because within a week they would be heading to Bournemouth for location filming with one of the first scheduled scenes involving the Meldrews inspecting the remains of their gutted house. It was the responsibility of Jean Steward, make-up designer for the first four series and two Christmas Specials, to organise a wig for Crosbie. Fortunately, in the end, it was only used for the opening scenes of Episode One, where Mrs Warboys meets the Meldrews at the airport on their return from Athens, and the night scene with Margaret and Victor picking through the rubble at 37 Wyngate Drive, all that was left of the house Victor christened the birds' mess capital of Europe. A time lapse in the story found us next visiting the Meldrews six months later, by which time they were settled at their new home, 19 Riverbank. Because the wig had looked so poor, Renwick had no alternative but to let Annette Crosbie wear her own hair for the remainder of the show.

As make-up designer, Steward had already made her customary call to the principal artists prior to the read-through. 'During the conversation with Annette she mentioned having had a trim, not a total restyle. Knowing Annette, I believe she thought the show would be a success and have a long run, so had no intention of spending the rest of her private life walking around with what she considered to be an unflattering, ageing bob! Her new haircut was a nice short style. It was much more flattering and wasn't extreme – something my mother would have worn. No one said anything at the read-through, so I assumed David and Susie were OK about it. After all, lots of sixty-year-old women have short hair." Later that day she received a phone call in her office. 'I was told David wanted her hair returned to the style of the first series.' With only a few days to make a wig before

filming began, Steward was extremely concerned how it would turn out. 'Ideally, you need around two weeks: to take head measurements, mix the hair for colour and arrange a foundation fitting and return for a final fitting. We didn't have enough time, so after the initial measurements were taken the next time we saw the wig was when it was couriered from the wig maker in London, and we were standing in the street in Bournemouth an hour before shooting the scene.' As soon as she opened the box, Steward knew it was far from ideal. 'It wasn't good so I asked David whether I really had to put it on.' Trying to dream up alternatives to avoid using the wig, she suggested that during the airport scene, Mrs Warboys could comment on her haircut, thereby intimating that it had been done on holiday but Renwick said 'no'.

Knowing how Renwick felt about the wig – he later described it as a 'disaster' *[ii]* – Steward thought her advice may have resolved the matter more satisfactorily. 'No make-up artist, given the choice, would put a full wig on a leading lady – and certainly not one made in a rush! The filming was a relatively brief night shot with limited lighting. But when we got back to the studio under more stringent lighting, the wig looked even worse, so we ended up with Annette wearing it for only two scenes before she suddenly appeared with a new short haircut and no explanation – it would have made more sense to me if she'd come back from Greece with a new hairdo.' Steward feels the situation highlights Renwick's occasional 'stubbornness'. She says: 'As a writer working in isolation, what you create in your mind and commit to paper you can do what you like with, but when you're working within practical and technical limits, you sometimes have to compromise and accept someone else's expertise.'

Steward admits that sometimes designers can get carried away, treating a show as a tool to demonstrate their own individual craft and talent, but that wasn't her style. 'If you're doing historical material, where you have to consider historical accuracy, you're there to guide and be creative, but for a sitcom, it's basically producing whatever is required by production as quickly as possible and within budget.' Steward admits there were occasions when she didn't agree with Renwick, but nothing became an issue. 'You never had words with David. You might shrug and turn away, but philosophically you know that you're really there to provide what the director, writer and actor wants.'

Despite rare differences of opinion, an inevitability on most productions, Steward, who left the BBC in

As a writer working in isolation, what you create in your mind and commit to paper you can do what you like with, but when you're working within practical and technical limits, you sometimes have to compromise and accept someone else's expertise.

JEAN STEWARD, make up designer

1995 and divides her time between homes in England and America, enjoyed working on *One Foot*. 'It was a real treat to be asked to do each series. Susie Belbin was a heavyweight BBC producer and what Belbin wanted, Belbin got.' She also enjoyed working with Richard Wilson and Annette Crosbie. 'They were lovely. Neither of them was like their characters, particularly Annette. Margaret is very long-suffering, but Annette is a very independent woman: outspoken, upfront and extremely assertive. She's the most fantastic actress and it was a joy working with her.

'The first time we worked together was in *Paying Guests*, a period drama. I obviously knew her as a well-respected and established actress. She had to wear a wig and at the fitting she just sat there, hands folded in her lap. I tried discussing what she wanted, within the confines of the period research I had done. This can often lead to the actress effectively saying: "I want to look as good as possible, and like myself!" You can end up fighting every inch of the way for what the director wants or to create the period look. But Annette sat there, absolutely motionless. Every time I asked her

something, she'd reply: "Umm, whatever." I thought: "She's going to phone the producer and say, 'That make-up girl is hopeless – get her off the show.'" But that didn't happen, and the wig looked fine. Years later on *One Foot*, I said to her one day: "You frightened the life out of me that day, just sitting there and saying nothing!" She replied: "It's your job – what do I know about wigs?" I'm sure she had strong views about her characters, but generally she'd put herself in the hands of the professionals around her, and just let them do whatever they wanted.'

For Renwick and the wig, unfortunately time hasn't been the great healer it's made out to be. 'The hair looked awful. It was on a par with the robin in the first series, and makes me squirm every time I see it – even now. We tried making it look less hideous when filming the airport scene by putting a band round to take the edge off it, but it still looked terrible.'

Filming the night scene for Episode One, 'In Luton Airport, No-one Can Hear You Scream', saw Renwick involved in discussions with Richard Wilson about two aspects of his performance which although to some people might appear trivial, revealed the depth to which the writer would go to extract every ounce of brilliance from a given performance.

In his journal on Wednesday, 4 July, he recorded: 'Another example tonight of the way in which Richard's belief in the honesty of his performance can threaten the poetry of a scene: as he is discovered standing by the fence, gazing wistfully at the remains of his old home – surveying, in effect, the last twenty-five years of his life – Margaret quietly appears at his side and he goes into his reflective speech about the tree. I said I thought it would be more powerful if he just sensed her arrival but didn't actually turn to look as she joined him. "But you wouldn't do that," is his response. "If your wife suddenly turns up you're going to look round." An argument I cannot disprove of course, and so in the shot he turns to look at her. But for my money it's a shame because it breaks the spell. Richard would argue the alternative is too stagey, an example of actor's trickery that has no basis in real life. The trouble is, we are not shooting real life and I think you have to decide to what extent these artifices are legitimate in order to elicit tears or laughter.'

And then there was the scene involving the two irate neighbours – played by Michael Robbins and Doremy Vernon – where Wilson's inclusion of an extra word in one of his lines halted filming. Renwick recalls the incident which took place while the Meldrews were at the scene of devastation. 'Michael Robbins shouted:

Yet another 'final' touch-up from make-up supervisor Vanessa White.

"Do you know what time it is?" And the line I'd written for Victor in response was, "Time you stuck your head down a waste disposal system." But Richard said: "It's time you stuck your head down a waste disposal system." Susie and I, in a muttering way, agreed that we didn't want the "it's" in there, so asked him not to say it.' Renwick acknowledges that one might argue about using the word 'it's', but to him the word's absence is essential in order to retain the rhythm and timing of the line. 'Richard's timing was invariably impeccable, but this was a rare occasion when it wasn't. Nowadays, to avoid any friction on the set we'd probably just cut the word out in the edit.'

Susan Belbin recalls the numerous takes before Renwick and she were happy with the line, and although it reveals how particular the writer could be, she feels it was fully justified. 'Those three letters make such a difference to the rhythm.'

Even Richard Wilson agrees that although at the time he was probably fed up with having to reshoot the scene, Renwick deserves the right to pick up on any slight deviation from the script. 'The sound and rhythm within a line are very important. People have classed David as the Beckett of the sitcom. In Beckett, you can't change a line – or even a word – otherwise the rhythm has gone. David is pedantic, but I think he's right to be. The only problem is the speed with which we have to do things, as actors. Because I knew I'd be in for a hard time if I didn't, I tried as much as possible to learn every word, but it does take time to be that accurate and we didn't have it.'

Although Wilson doesn't recall the discussions with Renwick about the script, he admits: 'I used to lose my temper quite a lot, because it's very tiring. But I've always said that David could never be a director because he doesn't have the people skills – he's too intro-verted, too shy in a sense. Yet he behaves like a director at times – and he particularly did on *One Foot*. However, his most recent project, *Love Soup*, is his most minimal piece of work, which I think is great. I see in that a sort of calming down and opening out. I think it's some of his best work.'

It wasn't the first time Renwick's insistence about a gesture had met with Wilson's disapproval. 'I remember in the first series, there was a scene where Victor had been beaten up by Arsenal fans,' Renwick recalls. 'He had a plaster on his head and I wanted Richard to shake his head in a particular way, in rhythm to the radiators that were clanking upstairs in his house, which he didn't want to do. He got quite upset about it.'

Wilson admits that Renwick is 'right most of the time', but adds: 'At the end of a long day's filming, it can irritate you at times. You'd keep saying a line or keep changing a word, and you'd realise that you're doing it because ultimately it sounds better. Occasionally he'd give way, but other times he wouldn't budge.'

While the first two episodes of the series were being transmitted in early October, David Renwick and his wife, Ellie, were sunning themselves in Los Angeles, but whilst waiting to jet off from Heathrow Airport, Renwick's spirits were lifted by some positive early reviews in response to the opening episode. Jennifer Selway in the *Observer* stated: 'There's a likeable element of measured black farce in David Renwick's comedy.'[iii] Other broadsheets reporting the show's return included the *Daily Telegraph*, which informed its readers that the new series 'promises to be as full of the soured milk of human kindness as the first'[iv], while *The Times*' critic felt that although the sitcom was 'over-reliant on the splendid Richard Wilson to sustain its one, fairly obvious, joke, *One Foot in the Grave* deserves another outing.'[v] He heaped further praise on Richard Wilson, stating that, 'Played straight, *One Foot in the Grave* could be bleak and harrowing, but Wilson's Victor Meldrew softens the pain and makes it palatable.'[vi] *The Sunday Times*' critic, though, wasn't so keen on what he saw of the second series, noting: 'Not as funny as the recent *Waiting for God*, the script forces its main protagonists . . . to indulge in the kind of bravura overacting generally reserved for low farce.'[vii]

Other critics watching the return of the Meldrews included Pam Francis, writing for *Today* newspaper. Although she noted the opening instalment contained a couple of 'golden moments'[viii] and that she 'quite liked it'[ix], she was also critical of certain elements of the programme, asking why 'British writers rely so heavily on toilets, bottoms and bladders to get easy laughs'[x], referring to the scene where Victor, upon returning

Richard's timing was invariably impeccable, but this was a rare occasion when it wasn't. Nowadays, to avoid any friction on the set we'd probably just cut the word out in the edit.

DAVID RENWICK

from holiday, is forced to endure a rectal examination by customs officials. She also believed that any decent moments were often spoiled by 'feeble jokes'[xi]. While Jane Oddy in the *Sun* slated the sitcom, admitting that, 'After half an hour of this, I was so bored I had both feet out of the living room door'[xii], claiming Victor's ranting and raving was as 'funny as a bad case of piles'[xiii]. Geoffrey Phillips in the *Evening Standard* brightened up an otherwise negative response from the tabloids by remarking that the show 'returned in cracking form for the second series'[xiv].

A mixed reaction from the press continued a trend set during the first series. Audience figures didn't change much either, remaining on the same levels established during the opening season, with just under nine million viewers tuning in. There was still a sizeable chunk of the audience, encompassing members of the public and critics alike, who remained undecided about the show. John Lyttle's review in the *Independent* is a case in point. He wrote: 'It's not easy to say whether David Renwick's study of a prematurely retired ranter has been, in formal terms, good, bad or indifferent; a brittle, angry undertow has, however, ensured that the tone is unlike any other comedy's.'[xv] Lyttle's observation was spot-on: the tone of Renwick's show was dissimilar to other offerings in the world of situation comedy, hence it felt more at home carrying a

Victor's accidental demolition of two tortoises led to many complaints.

was one of the funniest sequences in the episode, and for Renwick 'one of the most satisfying areas of all in comedy . . . when you just can't trace the provenance and all the traditional mechanisms and tricks of the trade have absolutely no bearing on what you're watching. It's just funny – don't try to analyse it.'[xvi]

Later Victor accidentally threw Kylie, the tortoise, in the garden incinerator, only for a replacement, amid the confusion, to be buried alive. Some viewers, horrified by such images, complained to the then chairman of the BBC, Marmaduke Hussey. When the chairman also received a letter from Scottish Labour MP Frank Doran, then representing Aberdeen South, who was acting on behalf of a constituent, Renwick's views on the offending scenes were requested. He prepared a detailed response, explaining primarily that, in his view, the incident was certainly not wilfully malicious and that the viewers' horror was echoed by the reaction of the characters. At the same time, he informed the chairman of what he strived to achieve through his scripts. After explaining the two forms of comedy programmes on television: broken comedy, containing a collection of unrelated sketches, and situation comedy, which followed a continuous narrative, he pointed out the former appeared to cater for a wider range of tastes, attitudes and ages. He wrote: 'Sketch shows have kept pace with changing times and attitudes, evolving in a very radical way into a range that extends from conventional pieces such as *The Two Ronnies*, *Morecambe and Wise* and Russ Abbot, to the more marginalised forms epitomised by *Monty Python*, Spike Milligan and Alexei Sayle.'[xvii] Renwick didn't feel such variety existed in the form of situation comedy. 'With a few exceptions (*Reggie Perrin*, *Fawlty Towers*, arguably *The Young Ones*), situation comedies today retain very much the same wholesome, conventional flavour they did in the early sixties . . . For some reason there seems to be a resistance to change in this department – to adopt a sharper, quirkier approach, taking more risks with ideas and execution in an attempt to nudge sitcoms into the 1990s.'[xviii] Pointing out that this was precisely what he was trying to do via *One Foot*, he

comedy-drama moniker. An array of black moments and shocking storylines were scattered throughout the six series of *One Foot*, often leaping out at you when you least expected them. These carefully constructed scenes imbued the scripts with a unique richness, setting the show apart from its peers in the congested television arena. Renwick isn't a conformist and has never been one to bow to pressure or to steer his writing down the well-worn paths trodden by a myriad of writers before him.

Renwick's attitude towards his writing, which saw him regularly conjure up moments of controversy to cause a deliberate reaction from his audience, meant he always trod a fine line in his attempts to inject freshness and originality into an arguably jaded genre. This was highlighted by a storyline within Episode Two, 'We Have Put Her Living in the Tomb', whereby Victor got into all sorts of bother when he looked after his goddaughter's pet tortoise. The viewer knew Victor's day was destined to nosedive when the tortoise inadvertently wandered onto the main road and ended up with a white line down its shell when the local council's line-painting vehicle happened to pass by. It described his show as 'despite its veneer of traditional domesticity . . . an intrinsically "dangerous" programme, designed to subvert the genre by refusing to conform to existing preconceptions.'[xix] This, he felt, was implicit, given the BBC's decision to transmit *One Foot* at 9.30 p.m.

Regarding the episode itself, Renwick reminded Hussey that violence had been a fundamental in comedy since the advent of moving pictures, but regretted that his work had caused distress, when all he was trying to do was entertain his audience. He explained that, 'In reality there is nothing funny about an animal suffering. But we didn't see an animal suffering. All we see is a smoking shell. The rest is left to the imagination.'[xx]

Now, sixteen years since the episode was transmitted, Renwick finds it amusing that people complained about the scenes. 'It's not that I revelled in the cruelty of animals, it's just that I didn't feel the real horror of incinerating a live animal. Had we seen the charred remains of a smoking cat on the shovel it would, of course, have been indefensible. I just didn't think that the image of smoke gushing out of a tortoise shell was that unsettling – it's difficult to define what will seem funny and what won't; it's like the scene from an earlier episode with the frozen cat. That always struck me as a very funny image.' It wouldn't be the last time Renwick would find himself defending his sitcom.

The transmission of the third episode, 'Dramatic Fever', on 18 October marked an important juncture in the show's long-term development. Although audience figures would make a sizeable leap forward during the next series, 'Dramatic Fever' saw the show attract more than ten million people for the first time; save for two episodes in the final season, audiences wouldn't drop below this level again. The episode found Margaret returning to amateur dramatics and Victor wandering along to watch preparations for the company's forthcoming production. However, while the

It's a tricky business writing sitcoms, as Victor finds out in

rehearsal was beset with real-life disasters, including a man falling off a lighting gantry, Victor, sitting alone in the auditorium and thinking it was all part of the show, found it highly amusing. Conceptually, this was one of Renwick's favourite ideas. 'I think it was very funny. Someone had just plummeted from the overhead walkway and people were rushing to his assistance while things were crashing about their ears. Victor strolled in and assumed it's a rehearsal, and just sat there chuckling away. It was Richard at his reactionary best, but the absolute killer for me in that sequence was him taking a packet of M&Ms from his pocket, removing his cap and really settling down to enjoy the fun: that's what makes it real.' The scene was shot at the Palace Theatre, Watford, and Wilson was expected not only to chuckle but howl with laughter. It's a difficult task for any actor, including someone of Wilson's talents, because even the eyes can, to discerning observers, reveal when a laugh is false. Wilson asked director Susan Belbin to empty the auditorium of everyone bar the cameraman, the sound recordist and Belbin herself, so that he could psych himself up with the minimum distraction before executing what was a very believable piece of acting.

The fourth episode, 'Who Will Buy?', saw the appearance of veteran entertainer Jimmy Jewel, who'd made his name as a music-hall comic before later reinventing himself as an actor in successful shows like *Nearest and Dearest* and *Thicker Than Water*. Jewel's character was called Albert Warris, coincidentally the name of Jewel's former music-hall partner and cousin, Ben Warriss. For Renwick, the preparatory stages for the episode hadn't got off to a good start when he classed the read-through as the worst within the series. 'Mostly it played to bleak silence, and the presence of Jimmy at the table – grim and unsmiling throughout – gave the proceedings an all-pervading air of gloom. Once you break through the bleak exterior of course, and get chatting to him, he is a mine of fascinating anecdotes.'[xxi]

Jewel was playing a blind man in one of the most emotive episodes in the entire show. Margaret befriended

him when she delivered flowers to his home, but on a subsequent visit, noticing the front door of his basement flat ajar, became suspicious and entered his

Renwick chose the name Albert Warris before ever considering Jimmy Jewel for the part – 'a spooky coincidence'.

property to find Albert dead on the floor, having been battered to death. Renwick had, once again, turned situation comedy on its head, shocking his audience with a murder. Jewel took his acting seriously, and the way the scenes were executed in front of the studio audience impressed Renwick, particularly the interplay between Jewel and Crosbie. 'The Albert scenes played with much disciplined sensitivity I thought, and Annette's reading of the imaginary letter bringing a real tear to the eye.'[xxii]

For a time, though, Belbin and Renwick thought they had hit a crisis when Jewel refused to appear without his wig, stating that he'd wear a cap instead. Believing that to do so would 'undercut the poignancy of the character,'[xxiii] Susan Belbin, as director, had to resolve it. After the dress rehearsal that Saturday afternoon, 18 August, Belbin broached the subject in his dressing room. 'He'd never performed without his wig,' explains Belbin, 'and when the costume designer tried getting him to remove it before the dress rehearsal, he refused.' Deciding not to make an issue of it, Belbin completed the dress run, knowing that she could discuss the matter with him afterwards. 'Jimmy was a

lovely man, so when the moment was right I said: "Jimmy, you don't want to take your wig off, do you?" He told me he'd never been seen professionally without his wig – ever, so I replied: "Your performance is lovely, so heart-warming and totally believable. However, it would give that extra edge and sense of vulnerability if you didn't have it on." I told him it would be the icing on the cake, but he still didn't want to do it. Then he looked at me, took my hand and said: "I'll do it for you. The first time in my career that I've ever been seen without hair, and I'm doing it for you." And he did.'

Renwick says: 'Ultimately I think it became a question of how much he trusted our judgement. Once his insecurities had been allayed and he was persuaded that we were treating it all very sensitively the problem disappeared.'*xxiv* The episode, meanwhile, was the blackest to date and caused a stir among viewers: for many, such moments provided the programme with an extra dimension, lifting it head and shoulders above its conventional counterparts; with Renwick's product you never knew what was lurking around the corner. Yes, there would always be much humour from the situations in which Victor found himself, but then a moment of sadness or pathos would hit you right between the eyes, almost making you recoil. For other people, though, *One Foot* remained an enigma and would occasionally offend, which happened in the case of 'Who Will Buy?' Having watched the scene in which Margaret stumbles across Albert's body, some viewers wrote to the BBC's *Points of View* programme, complaining that it was 'in bad taste'*xxv* and 'offensive'.*xxvi*. Renwick wasn't unduly concerned by such complaints because he realised that the approach he took, stepping beyond the boundaries of expectancy in the world of situation comedy, wouldn't always meet with everyone's approval.

'Love and Death' found the Meldrews visiting their friends Vince and April at their seaside guest house, and 'Timeless Time' closed the second series, with Victor suffering insomnia. This last was a bravely scripted episode considering it took place in just one location, the Meldrews' bedroom, and was deliberately void of plot and a welter of comic ideas. Renwick was delighted with the results.

Georgina Hale, who played April, thought 'Love and Death' was the funniest script she'd ever read.

over I managed to convince myself that it wasn't really much cop and I finished the day generally pretty deflated.'*xxxvi*

As well as strands of pathos, the episode was full of humour, particularly in the running sequence involving 263 garden gnomes arriving on Victor's doorstep despite him only ordering one. While he considers what to do, the gnomes fill up his entire house before eventually being gunned down by Patrick, who's seeking revenge after the Meldrews accidentally drink an £850 bottle of wine intended for Pippa's father. The sequence, originally planned for inclusion in Episode Two, was an example of Renwick's frugality. When 'We Have Put Her Living in the Tomb' ended up too long the entire gnome routine was cut, but instead of losing such a fertile idea, Renwick stored it away for future use.

The logistics of arranging 263 garden gnomes in readiness for the location shoot in Bournemouth wasn't easy. Renwick bought a gnome from his local Homebase as a template but, as Susan Belbin explains, there was still plenty of work to do. 'It's easy writing "263 gnomes are delivered to his house", but you can't just ring a garden centre and order that many; then there are other considerations, like being of similar height and having a certain expression on their faces: we knew it would be funnier seeing smiling, brightly coloured gnomes gunned down than horrible, grey granite ones. All these matters had to be addressed.'

Visual effects designer Chris Lawson, who joined the production team for Series Two and remained for the rest of the show's run, was responsible for making the gnomes from thin casting plaster. He estimates around five hundred gnomes were made in total. When Renwick supplied an example, Lawson carried out some modifications before producing a mould. When they were delivered, some were fitted with a detonator inside: at the appropriate moment, they would be blown up to give the impression they were being mowed down by Patrick with the machine gun.

It needed, however, a team effort to paint them in time for filming, with make-up designer Jean Steward and her assistant pitching in. She recalls: 'A lorry-full of gnomes turned up while we were on location but many were still unpainted. Whenever Chris and his team weren't doing anything else, they'd get their paintbrushes out. Between shots, we'd give a hand. Then the

dressers got involved and other people, too; it was like a production line. Some people were doing red hats, others waistcoats, but all painting furiously.' Jokingly, people started criticising each other's handiwork. 'Bantering like: "I'm wasting my time doing perfect hats – look at the state of your waistcoats!" Others would paint the waistcoat and trousers the wrong way round – there was plenty of joking going on.'

After the episode was recorded in the studio, any remaining gnomes were destined for the scrap heap. When the cast and crew heard about the gnomes' fate, many of them, including Angus Deayton, bagged one. Jean Steward recalls: 'By that time, I'd got so attached to them that before the recording I decided to secure one for my mum's garden. I searched for a well-painted one and other people started doing the same; by the time we reached the afternoon's rehearsal, everyone in the studio was running around among the gnomes putting their initials on the bottom of the feet. It was hysterical seeing all these people leaving Television Centre that evening with a gnome tucked under each arm.'

The garden gnomes for the Christmas Special were deliberately designed to give viewers a feeling of Santa Claus.

CHAPTER 9
Series Three

A year passed before we met the Meldrews again, this time in a fifty-minute Christmas Special, 'The Man in the Long Black Coat'. The show had originally been scheduled for transmission on Christmas Day until *Keeping Up Appearances* usurped its prime-time slot; consequently, *One Foot* was shifted to the evening of 30 December, which Renwick regarded as a graveyard slot. It was a decision that infuriated him and he didn't hesitate to relay his concerns to Susan Belbin. Although the director made her protestations to the BBC hierarchy, it was to no avail.

Nevertheless, fans of *One Foot* were just happy to see an episode being transmitted over the festive period. Renwick had begun working on the script back in May, already aware that a third series had been commissioned. Following his usual gruelling method of working, ideas would randomly arrive, and he would then evaluate their potential before assembling them in an orderly fashion. By mid-May, he was confident he'd garnered enough material to make a start on the Christmas script. The words were flowing and Renwick was suitably relieved, informing his journal: 'I'm feeling unrealistically fertile at the moment – once I get going on these scenes I feel I could just coast on for ever, I just so love the characters and enjoy the writing. It's a world of difference from this time last week, lying face down on the carpet.'[i] Before the end of the month, Renwick was holding a crisp, completed script in his hand, and as he arose early on Friday, 24 May and prepared some coffee, he reread the script, regarding it as 'pretty solid and workmanlike'[ii]. Belbin's verdict was, as ever, swiftly received, and although Renwick noted that it was 'strangely, not gushingly over the top this time'[iii], it remained positive, with the director applauding the script's subtleties. As a writer, working in isolation, hearing another person's view can, at times, put a bad day into perspective, perhaps lifting the writer out of a period of melancholy, which is what happened on

Tuesday, 11 June, when Belbin called Renwick to deliver her thoughts on the script for Episode One of the next series. As he recorded: 'My mood generally improved a lot when Susie called with profuse praises for the first episode – "brilliant, you've done it again" etc . . . which lifted me more than I can say.'[iv]

In 'The Man in the Long Black Coat', Victor's neighbours complained when a mysterious man sold a pile of manure to the Meldrews and dumped it on the front path instead of his allotment. No sooner was it shifted than Dr Whale, from the borough council's

> *Normally when you book an actor, even if you only require them for one day, you have the option to use them for the whole week. But when Eric Idle said 'one day' he meant 'one day'.*
>
> SUSAN BELBIN

Health and Public Safety Department, arrived to inform Victor that his manure wasn't all that it seemed – it may be radioactive. Playing Mervyn Whale was ex-Python Eric Idle, whom Renwick held in such high regard that he classed it a great honour having him in his show.

Idle was required for a scene being filmed at Plot 147 of the North Bournemouth Allotments in Priestly Road, Bournemouth. Breakfast was available on site from 7.30 a.m. on that overcast September morning. The pressure was on because Idle's busy diary meant he was free for only one day. Everyone hoped that the capricious English weather would behave itself as they prepared to shoot the scene depicting Dr Whale's arrival at Victor's allotment to inspect the manure. 'Normally when you book an actor, even if you only require them for one day, you have the option to use them for the whole week,' says Susan Belbin. 'But when Eric Idle said "one day" he meant "one day".' As rehearsals for the first scene drew to a close, the first drops of rain from an increasingly angry-looking sky were felt. Within minutes, filming was brought to a halt and everyone retired to the unit bus, in the faint hope that perhaps the weather would eventually clear. It never did, and Susan Belbin knew that unless she sorted something out, Eric Idle wouldn't be appearing in the show. When it became inevitable that filming would be abandoned for the day she climbed onto the bus where Idle was reading. 'He was returning to America and, yes, we had the option to recast and film the scene at the end of the schedule, but didn't want to.' Belbin liked a challenge so decided to try and persuade Idle to allow them one more day. 'He knew the rain wasn't going to give up and suddenly said he'd return tomorrow. I told him there was a slight problem about money so he very generously agreed to come back the following day but didn't want another fee, which was marvellous.'

After a brief spell of rain, Wednesday, 25 September boasted lengthy spells of hot sunshine and before long the allotment scenes were in the can. Renwick was impressed with Idle's performance. 'Eric was on fine form, chirpy ad-libs flowing throughout the day, redolent of the comic invention and interplay on a *Python* set . . . I was impressed by the man's professional equanimity and accommodation for all the usual bothersome retakes and adjustments, and there's no question he has that innate "comic" gold dust that you can see almost tangibly crank into gear when we go from rehearsal to take.'[v]

The Christmas episode was recorded in front of a packed house at the BBC studios in White City on Sunday, 3 November. The recording proceeded smoothly, receiving an enthusiastic reaction from the audience. A sequence gaining more than its fair share of laughter saw Victor mistake a tea caddy for an urn containing ashes. He was then horrified when he accidentally dropped the container and its contents spewed across the carpet. Meanwhile, in true Renwick style, viewers' tears of mirth were turned into tears of woe in the closing scenes: Pippa's discovery that she was pregnant was shortlived when an accident while driving a bus results in hospitalisation. In one fell swoop she lost her baby, job and licence, for drink-driving. It's a real tear-jerking moment, beautifully played by the

cast, particularly Janine Duvitski. But achieving such brilliance wasn't easy. During rehearsals for the hospital scene, Renwick was vexed because he didn't sense the actors were taking the situation seriously. Annette Crosbie recalls: 'Corpsing didn't happen very often but for some reason Janine and I couldn't get through this one, and David [Renwick] got very cross. The men [Richard and Angus] were all right, but every time I looked at Janine, that was it.'

Considering the moment now, Renwick admits his assessment of the situation was probably incorrect, stating that perhaps his own anxiety was to blame for his reaction. 'It's very frustrating when things aren't working as you'd hoped, which is probably what I was thinking at the time. The healthy thing about rehearsals is that you're allowed the latitude of experimentation, as opposed to when you're filming on location and have little time to try things out. On location, you end up with a mass of purely practical considerations getting in the way. Of course, these have to be addressed but usually an instant solution is required with no time to perfect anything. And so the purity of the comedy tends to get swamped by technicalities. Plus there is often a kind of stultifying inertia from all the waiting around that seems to penetrate the material.'

Renwick once toyed with the idea of writing studio-based scripts only because he found the whole filming process infuriatingly slow. He shared his thoughts over lunch with Richard Wilson at the Inn on the Park's Four Seasons restaurant. Although Wilson sympathised with Renwick, he had reservations about how it might 'diminish the texture of the show and limit us visually'[vi]. 'Financial constraints have probably changed this now, but in the old days I got the impression that filming took as long as it took, that at the end of the day the BBC would cough up. Eventually it became a case of, "No, there is only so much money and, therefore, so many days of shooting." So people pulled their socks up and couldn't hang around saying, "Oh, it's drizzling again." The sense of urgency on the set was a problem at times, and wasn't helpful in terms of people's energy levels; nothing tires actors more than inactivity. It's exhausting packing a lot of work into the day, too, but at least at the end of it you feel you've achieved something. But the greatest frustrations are those moments when a script I felt so overwhelmingly confident about, which contained some bullet-proof moments or lines of dialogue and interactions, just falls flat on its face.'

The closing scenes in the hospital dripped pathos, which Renwick was aware wasn't entirely to Richard Wilson's liking. Throughout the series, Wilson often commented that the scripts were becoming too sentimental or overly serious. Although Renwick always listened carefully to his leading man, valuing his advice and opinions, this was one area on which he wouldn't compromise: his unswerving attitude towards the structure of his scripts meant emotionalism was essential. Richard Wilson acknowledges that the subjects Renwick tackled are what helped set *One Foot* apart from other sitcoms. 'It was good that Annette and I were actors rather than comedians, which a lot of sitcoms used in those days, because David was writing some serious stuff, covering pathos, death and tragedy, as well as comedy, which is why it was such a breakthrough and wonderful to do. I did, however, think it got a bit sentimental at times and remember fighting that. I have to say, David is a bit of a sentimentalist.'

Renwick's journals refer to several occasions when Wilson remarked on such moments in the scripts, including the 1990 Christmas Special, 'Who's Listening?' After rehearsing for another episode back in August 1990, Wilson gave his initial reaction to the Christmas script, classing it 'too long and not funny enough'[vii]. Renwick, recalling Wilson's appraisal, added: 'Too many serious moments, too much moralising, not tight enough and generally overwritten. What it boils down to is an ingrained aversion to anything that smacks of schmaltz.'[viii] Later, while rehearsing the Christmas episode, there was an exchange of views between Wilson and Renwick regarding how a particular scene, in which Margaret buys Victor a watch only to find he's bought one himself, should be played. Renwick noted: 'For my part, I'd never seen this as a comic moment, it was meant to be just very moving . . . Richard wanted to play it as if he's pleased with himself, so you get a mischievous delight that Margaret's been squashed. I said I thought he should be visibly discomfited – although he'd done nothing wrong he would inevitably feel guilty and awkward. Once again

it's Richard's aversion to anything that smacks of being treacly or mawkish.'[ix] Although pathos is an important ingredient in the show, it's the comedic elements that drive *One Foot*. 'It's rewarding when those moments come along, but I only feel confident when I've got some comedy because that's much harder to do.'

Regarding Wilson's aversion to sentiment, Renwick says: 'If you look at Richard's work, the kind of material he directs in the theatre, he has a much harder-edged sensibility. We all have our thresholds and his is quite high. Of course, you never want to be accused of being corny – but then what's corny anyway? *It's a Wonderful Life* I guess you'd have to define as corny, and I know it's manipulative, but it always moves me intensely. I think pathos can be a very valuable counterweight to the comedy; you just have to be careful how you use it.' But, as Renwick points out, it wasn't just Wilson that felt this way. 'I remember Annette saying she wasn't wild about the speech in "Timeless Time", where Victor and Margaret talk about their son. We put some music underneath and I know she disapproved, and felt it was hammering the point. Maybe she was right. I haven't watched it for a long time.'

'The Man in the Long Black Coat' was watched by just under eleven million, four million fewer viewers than its rival on the night, the 1988 comedy-horror movie, *Beetle Juice*. An exasperated Renwick wrote: 'Clearly there is not yet a *One Foot in the Grave* audience of any significance out there. And perhaps there never will be.'[x] Time would soon prove him wrong, but he was suitably buoyed when he heard the 1991 Christmas Special had been nominated for a BAFTA award for the second year running. Again, it was up against *Only Fools and Horses* and *Drop the Dead Donkey* as well as *Mr Bean*, and there was a double dose of cheer when it was announced that Richard Wilson was a nominee for 'Best Comedy Performance'.

The awards ceremony was held at the Grosvenor Hotel, London, on Sunday, 22 March. From the table occupied by Renwick, Belbin and Crosbie, the view of the stage was obscured, which the writer felt was a sign that perhaps it wouldn't be their year again. Even Susan Belbin admits she didn't think the show would win. 'I have a habit of twisting my legs around twice when I'm sitting down,' she says. 'We were tucked right around the corner and because I didn't think we'd win, I took my shoes off and decided to relax and enjoy the event. Suddenly, I heard the words: "And the winner is . . . *One Foot in the Grave*!" I'm there trying to unlock my legs and find my shoes, which I struggled to put back on; and if that wasn't bad enough, on the way to the podium, I tripped over a camera cable!'

Renwick was equally surprised when the result was announced. A rush of emotions raced through his body as he weaved his way between countless tables en route to the podium. Without thinking, he hurried over and kissed the flamboyantly dressed presenter – none other than Dame Edna Everage, alias Barry Humphries. To add to his embarrassment, he headed back to his seat without collecting his award. 'When I went up with Susie I just assumed there was only one trophy between the two of us. I was halfway down the steps before I realised there was one for me as well.' And regarding planting a kiss on Humphries' cheek, he says: 'Of course, I don't make a habit of kissing men in drag on live television, but Barry Humphries is so convincing as that character you just forget yourself.' To add to the triumph, there was a tumultuous round of applause when Richard Wilson was invited to collect the award for 'Best Comedy Performance'. It was the first in a string of awards bestowed upon the series and those involved in its success, including Wilson being declared 'Best Comedy Actor' and *One Foot* 'Best Comedy Series' at the 1991 Comedy Awards held at the studios of London Weekend Television.

More good news for everyone associated with *One Foot* arrived when the opening episode of Series Three, 'Monday Morning Will Be Fine', was transmitted on 2 February 1992. It attracted nearly fifteen million viewers, beating the previous best by almost four million. Excepting a handful of episodes scattered throughout the remaining three series, figures wouldn't drop below fourteen million. The decision to repeat the first two seasons during the summer months of 1991 helped improve *One Foot*'s standing within the pantheon of television treasures. Susan Belbin had predicted correctly

that the show would take off around this time in its life. 'It's the age-old story of a show starting slowly and becoming a classic BBC third series success. The good thing was in those days that was acceptable. No one expected a show to be a hit until the third series – you were allowed time and money to help it grow.'

This was the stage in the sitcom's life when Renwick brushed aside his seemingly ever-present feelings of self-

> *Of course, I don't make a habit of kissing men in drag on live television, but Barry Humphries is so convincing as that character you just forget yourself.*
>
> DAVID RENWICK

doubt to allow himself, for a moment, to enjoy the success story he'd created. A journal entry for late February 1992 reads: 'Emerging from the BBC I reflected how encouraging it was to note the way the show's profile has now increased there . . . There's no question it seems finally to have achieved the status we all hoped for. And it's a very strange feeling. The top show on BBC1 after the two soaps. It's actually impossible to get your head round it.'[xi]

The opening episode saw the Meldrews' house being burgled and a case of mistaken identity at the local pub leading to a host of problems for Victor, including spending ages in the pouring rain, courtesy of a rain machine hired by visual effects designer Chris Lawson. The night shoot was a traumatic experience for everyone concerned, starting when the team fell behind in the filming schedule after smelling gas. Murray Peterson, the production manager on the series, remembers the episode well. 'The requirements for the house where we filmed were extremely specific and, therefore, hard to find because the bushes and the back door had to be exactly in the right place for shooting purposes. Eventually we found a property and began filming. We were catching up on the schedule when someone smelt gas, so all the equipment had to be switched off.' The Gas Board was summoned but no leak could be detected; after just over an hour and a half, with everyone standing around in darkness, the crew switched on their equipment and just managed to complete the filming before daylight.

In a later incident, proceedings were interrupted again, this time by an unfortunate accident involving Richard Wilson. 'Someone slammed the car door on his fingers. Luckily they weren't broken, but we had to rush Richard to hospital,' recalls Susan Belbin. 'He was wonderful about it, such a sweetheart. The hospital was

More cruelty inflicted on a helpless performer as she is thrust between Richard Wilson's legs.

locked up when we arrived and we had to knock on the door. You can imagine their expressions when they opened up and Victor Meldrew was standing there!' Belbin kept in contact with the rest of her team back at the house via walkie-talkie, but communications went awry, as she explains. 'Someone asked what I wanted them to do, to which I replied something to the effect of, "We will be back, stay there – we'll be back to carry on." And the person at the other end thought I said, "Go home," so after

Richard and I had sat there for hours while he got his fingers sorted out, we returned to the location to find everyone had gone!'

After the first episode we were presented with 'Dreamland', which concentrated on reflection and contemplation of the past. This time comedy took a back seat as drama came to the fore. Here was a script containing more straight narrative than any that had gone before. It focused on Margaret's aberrant behaviour, which manifested itself in an unannounced departure from Victor in order to find space and time to review her life, only to realise that she was better off in her current situation. But before she casually strolled back into Victor's life, he nearly suffered a coronary through sheer worry, heightened by the fact the police find a coat, similar to Margaret's, on the canal towpath. He began anticipating life on his own, until she returned, having taken a day's holiday from the florist's to visit Margate.

No episode, of course, is devoid of comedic moments and one particular scene had the studio audience doubled over in paroxysms of laughter when it was recorded, back in November 1991. The Meldrews had been invited to Nick Swainey's house for the evening, and after a game of Scrabble, in which Victor inevitably came out the loser with fortune against him again when he picked seven letter Es, we heard from upstairs a series of bangs of a walking-stick, rings of a bell, hoots on a horn and whistles; it was a code devised by Mr Swainey for his unseen mother, who supposedly lived with him. He scuttled off to get his little notebook to decipher the code, only to find all his aged mother wanted was a digestive biscuit. 'I love those mad moments,' enthuses Renwick.

Owen Brenman enjoyed references to Swainey's mother, too. 'There are shots of Nick telling the Meldrews that his mother is up at the window, so why don't they give her a wave? But there isn't anyone there – all you see is the net curtain shaking in the wind. I never really knew if she existed or not, although in a later episode Nick heard banging on the ceiling and went upstairs to see her, so there must have been someone there.' Another scene showed Swainey practising archery, shooting arrows through the back door towards a target standing in the front garden. To execute the scene, Brenman spent a week taking archery lessons.

Although unsure, Renwick believes the introduction of Nick Swainey's mother was probably a one-off idea that materialised when he began constructing the script for the first episode of Series Two, when Mr Swainey and the Meldrews first became neighbours. It was a device to worry Victor, who happened to be in the garden at the time. The mother's anonymity is reflective of Renwick's style of giving little away to retain a sense of mystery. 'I love understatement and I love giving the audience just enough information and then leaving the rest to their imagination,' he says. 'Like all those incidents in which bizarre misfortunes befell Victor, instigated by person or persons unknown. You never knew who was making malicious calls to the fire brigade in one episode, or who exactly had broken into his bedroom and daubed the walls with graffiti. Victor may refer to "those bastards" or whatever, but you never actually see them. I find that anonymity very funny – it gives you a sense of Victor against the world, as opposed to just one or two specific individuals.'

In 'The Broken Reflection', Renwick enjoyed being reunited with veteran actor Richard Pearson, who'd played defence secretary Michael Sumpter in the 1986 big-screen version of *Whoops Apocalypse*. This time he was cast as Victor's long-lost brother, Alfred, who paid an unexpected visit to the Meldrews from his home in New Zealand. Victor and Alfred hadn't clapped eyes on

each other for twenty years and instead of feeling a sense of excitement regarding his impending visitor, Victor felt nothing but despair because he believed they no longer had anything in common. What's more, Alfred, being hard of hearing and having some peculiar foibles, did little to increase his popularity. Margaret's attitude towards Alfred ameliorated her husband's initial frostiness somewhat, but gradually Victor's antipathy towards his brother broke down and he began finding an emotional bond that he didn't know existed. Such shifts of emotions were helped along by reminiscing about days in Dibley Street, a terraced house on top of a hill, where the five members of the family lived, and memories of a father whose homemade beetroot wine was so potent, the smell was rumoured to have knocked budgies off their perches three streets away.

Sharing memories drew them closer, and another affecting scene unfolded, thanks partly to a fine, delicate portrayal by Pearson. 'Victor had such a chip on his shoulder about Alfred, as people often do in their families,' says Renwick. 'He's the brother we know Victor can't

Brothers Grim . . . Richard Pearson was the ideal choice to play Alfred.

stand, so before he appears we're imagining some kind of loud, uncouth yob to turn up, and then in comes this wonderfully benign, congenial, slightly dreamy old character, perfectly rendered by Richard Pearson.' Having eventually warmed to his brother, next morning Victor took him a cup of tea in bed, only to find he'd gone. Victor was abashed to discover that Alfred had returned to New Zealand after accidentally switching on a dictaphone and hearing a remark from Victor making it clear that he wasn't welcome. 'There are two ways in which you derive fulfilment on this kind of show: one is getting huge belly laughs, and the other is when you become genuinely emotionally involved with the characters. It's all you can ever ask for in a drama: that you care about the people you're watching enough to worry about what happens to them and feel their anguish and pain. And even though I wrote it, I find those scenes between Victor and Alfred very moving and very touching.' Watching the episode in the living room of his Hertfordshire home, Renwick was

Filming is always physically uncomfortable: you're often not wearing the right clothes for the season you're supposed to be in. So you're either boiling or freezing to death, while the whole unit is standing around you dressed properly, looking happy.

ANNETTE CROSBIE

pleased with the final product, regarding it as a strong, compact piece of television. 'Susie had done a splendidly pacy job on the editing.'*xii*

For eagle-eyed viewers, the sudden appearance of a small bandage on one of Pearson's fingers in the scene where he was opening a parcel on the Meldrews' kitchen table was the result of an earlier accident.

During the recording, Pearson used a knife to open the package. 'It was too sharp, which was a little naughty because all knives are supposed to be blunt on set,' admits Susan Belbin. Pearson sliced his finger and the extent of the bleeding left the director no alternative but to stop the recording. 'I had to get him to hospital, so we left the rest of his scenes that night because he needed stitches.' He returned the following week and completed his scenes, hence the bandage. 'He was so good about it and I felt sorry for him. It was a bad cut.'

15.6 million people tuned in for the following instalment, 'The Beast in the Cage'. They saw a sterling episode, with the Meldrews and Mrs Warboys stuck for hours in bank-holiday traffic with tempers beginning to fray. It wasn't just viewers who enjoyed the instalment, either. Writing in the *Sun*, Garry Bushell classed Victor's grumblings in the motorway snarl-up as 'the funniest moment all week'*xiii*. He viewed it as 'simple but hilarious – like all great comedy it was based on real human reactions in believable situations.'*xiv* In the *Daily Express*, Margaret Forwood regarded a scene where a driver alongside Victor passed him a mobile phone, which the furious driver behind had called in order to ask Victor to move forward a few yards as the 'cleverest bit of writing of the week'*xv*. And equally complimentary in the *News of the World*, Charlie Catchpole compared *One Foot* to *Hancock's Half Hour*, where nothing much was happening but 'the writing and acting were sublime'*xvi*. Fans of the show, who were lapping up Victor's continual diatribes and his wife's constant frustrations, were writing to the papers, one saying that 'hilarious is the only word for this show'*xvii*, another recommending Crosbie and Wilson for an Oscar because 'they really cheer me up'*xviii*.

The episode, which was conceived by Renwick while dining out at an Indian restaurant the previous summer, was filmed at Vauxhall's test track at Millbrook,

Filming for the half-hour traffic jam episode took over two weeks to complete.

Bedfordshire. Miserable weather, including drizzle and mist, disrupted the filming schedule and meant over four days were spent at the track, and with the car's windscreen having been removed to aid filming, Wilson, Crosbie and Mantle were exposed to the chill wind that swept down into the valley. Even the blue sky that greeted everyone on the first day once the mist had cleared caused its own problems with lighting continuity, and if that wasn't enough to worry Renwick, an incident in the catering bus at lunchtime left him speechless – literally. While he was eating his meal, a piece of pork lodged itself in his throat and he began gasping for breath and spluttering; terrified, he started jumping up and down in panic until Richard Wilson saved the day. 'David suddenly started choking and I told him to have some water but it didn't help. It became worse and worse and I got up and hit him on his back. He began panicking and rushed off the bus, trying desperately to get rid of this piece of meat. I followed him and gave him an enormous whack on the back – I hit him so hard I hurt my hand. Luckily, the piece of meat came out. I was in a terrible panic, too, because if it hadn't worked I don't know what I would have done. I still shake when I remember it.'

Annette Crosbie rates the episode among her favourites, even if it wasn't one of the most comfortable to film. 'Filming is always physically uncomfortable: you're often not wearing the right clothes for the season you're supposed to be in. So you're either boiling or freezing to death, while the whole unit is standing around you dressed properly, looking happy.' Crosbie explains that when you work for David Renwick, you've got to be prepared for all eventualities. 'Just take some of the situations we found ourselves in, like Richard and Doreen with their feet stuck in a bag of cement and Richard buried up to his neck in the garden. Because it's filming you're doing it over and over until all the technicians get it right at the same time.'

Richard Wilson agrees with Crosbie's views, before pointing out that Renwick's requirements haven't changed. 'He made me suffer incredibly in *Whoops Apocalypse*,' he says, with a wry smile on his face. 'I was crucified in that along with Richard Pearson. We'd done the shot, but for some reason it hadn't worked and I remember hearing David say: "We could leave them up there and see what the light does." I said: "Excuse me, did you say 'leave them up there'?" Richard [Pearson] then said he was fine, so perhaps I'm very Victorish and a bit of a complainer!'

In 'The Beast in the Cage', pretending they were travelling during a May bank holiday meant summer gear was worn. 'It was freezing cold and the three of us were trying to hide hot water bottles on our laps,' says Crosbie. 'We were stuck there while certain scenes were being reshot over and over – it was wearying. It never seemed to occur to David that we might just be getting a bit tight-lipped about the whole thing. We were cold and uncomfortable, and if we wanted to go to the lavatory you had to get out of the car. It was almost a case of saying: "Please, miss, may I leave the room?" You'd be driven to the lavatory. And David was always frowning – there was never a smile. At the read-through

'The Beast in the Cage' originally related to the fact that the Meldrews were on their way to Whipsnade Zoo, but the dialogue was cut.

he'd laugh like the rest of us because he loves hearing his work come to life. But after that, deep frowns. You'd look at him to see if the bit you'd just done was OK and all you'd see was deep gloom.'

Filming on the episode wasn't a happy experience for Renwick, either. Inclement weather and failing light meant he was tense. He classed the second day of filming as 'a thoroughly, dismal, unconstructive day in which the grim, grey light prevented us from shooting any more than cut-in shots inside the car'[xix], leaving him to wonder 'how the hell we would ever complete the show by this time tomorrow, and fearing that we wouldn't.'[xx] Fortunately, the following day was more productive, despite conditions remaining poor, largely due to Belbin moving the production along. Forgetting the dreary British climate, it was an episode Belbin enjoyed filming. As soon as she read the script, she decided that apart from opening and closing shots, she wasn't going to take the camera out of the car, in order to establish a sense of claustrophobia.

All the effort invested in the filming, and the discomforts endured by Wilson, Crosbie and Mantle, paid off because 'The Beast in the Cage' was a ripping

episode. Renwick, however, wasn't enamoured of it: after viewing an earlier rough cut he regarded it as flat and unstimulating. But for many, it contained several excellent scenes and lines of dialogue, including a beautifully written piece where a contemplative Victor viewed a car journey as a mirror image of one's life.

VICTOR: First fifty-odd miles on the go all the way, a sense of direction, bowling along. Get past sixty, everything slows down to a sudden crawl and you realise that you're not going anywhere anymore. All the things you said you were going to do that never came to anything. And you can't turn the clock back. One-way traffic gradually grinding to a complete halt.
MARGARET: Same for everyone, I suppose.
VICTOR: I suppose.
MRS WARBOYS: And you just have to try and make the best you can of it.

If 'The Beast in the Cage' was proof that you can make a successful comedy show without movement, 'Beware the Trickster on the Roof', the penultimate episode in Series Three, provided evidence that one ignores the old adage 'don't work with animals' at one's peril. Of course, Renwick didn't heed the advice, with several storylines necessitating the use of animals, but is first to admit that introducing a cow into the Meldrews' confined back garden wasn't such a good idea. When Uncle Rodney died, the Meldrews were asked if they'd like to acquire any of his possessions; they opted for Lot 362, a cot with a slightly damaged back leg, only to discover it was a misprint and should have read 'cow with a slightly damaged back leg'! What a shock for Victor and Margaret, then, when they walk out into their back garden and find a cow chewing the grass. 'As a writer you're constantly having to evaluate material,' says Renwick. 'A hundred thoughts may pop into my head, and most of them I throw out immediately because they're not even worth considering. Now and again you chuckle out loud because you've thought of a real cast-iron comic premise you know will work. And then there are all those middle-order ideas that might possibly be useful or might end up looking completely naff. And at the writing stage you have no way of telling which way they'll go. As far as the cow business was concerned, the only thing that persuaded me I might get away with it was the extra touch of the slightly damaged leg. When you see the cow in the garden there's a bandage round one of its back legs. That one tiny detail was what sold it to me, although it probably passed most viewers by completely.'

Renwick enjoyed employing extraordinary sight gags, like the cow in the garden, but the problem is that animals are inevitably unpredictable, and it was a restless cow that was transported to Tresillian Way to make her screen debut. Production designer Linda Conoboy, who worked with John Bristow on the episode, remembers clearly the day she spent with the cow, called Dawn, in Bournemouth, mainly because it was quite an effort getting the animal up the alley leading into the Meldrews' garden. Murray Peterson, production manager on the series, adds: 'There was one bit where the cow was getting restless, and then it heard its calf, which was back in the lorry. There was a sudden panic and it charged through the gate, but right in the way was the prop master, who ended up being pinned against the fence with the cow's horns either side of her! The cow eventually went hoofing off down the alley to find its calf.'

It was also a challenge trying to get the cow composed in the studio. In the scene, Patrick and Pippa are inside their house looking out towards the conservatory when the cow suddenly appears. 'We had to make sure she didn't run riot, especially with all the electric cables around the floor,' says Conoboy. 'Things

like that can't be planned for because you never know what animals will do. Fortunately it worked out.'

Another idea in the episode caused a few headaches for visual effects designer Chris Lawson. One day, while standing in his back garden in Luton, Renwick noticed a nearby television aerial that resembled a face. The idea of using such an aerial symbolically to represent a mischievous figure of fate, which Victor believes is conspiring to make his life a misery, amused Renwick, so he decided to incorporate it into his script. The writer passed a photo of the aerial to Lawson to help him construct a replica. 'I made a rough design on the floor. The wire leading to the aerial was scooped, to make the mouth, and there were other bits that made the eyes and nose. Then I had to put it up on this roof, which wasn't the best of working platforms. It took me a while to get right. When you're working up close to something, you can't see clearly what you're

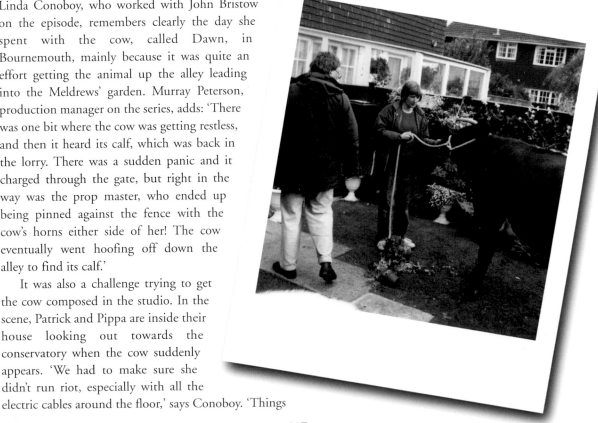

Working with animals, like the cow in 'Beware the Trickster on the Roof', is always fraught with problems.

Special effects wizard Chris Lawson created an artificial bottom to receive the hypodermic needle that Victor throws from his car in the final episode.

doing, so I had to keep coming down to look, then go back up to alter it.'

Chris Lawson had worked for Susan Belbin on a couple of occasions, including Michael Aitkens' motorcycle courier sitcom, *Roy's Raiders*. Although it only lasted six episodes, it was enough time for her to gain his respect. 'She was terrific,' he says. 'One of her favourite sayings was "page one". If you'd made a mess of something, she'd say: "Let's go to page one." That meant, "You've made a mistake here." But if something went wrong and it wasn't your fault, she always understood. She built a team who worked well together.'

He admits, though, that *One Foot* could be frustrating to work on at times. 'David wrote fantastic scripts but could be very demanding at the last minute. For the betterment of the programme, he would come in and say if he thought you'd headed off in a different direction from what he'd envisaged, but often there wasn't a lot of time to put it right.' It could be 'infuriating' when he'd invested much time and effort trying to interpret what was required, only for Renwick

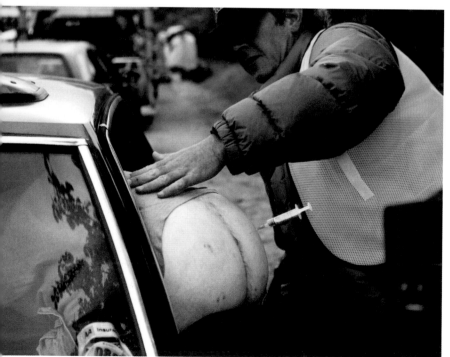

to arrive on the scene and ask him to change his plans. 'I suppose you saw it as your own input suddenly being eradicated,' suggests Lawson. 'You might talk to Susie, and she'd say: "Yes, that looks all right, but we'll check with David." Then you thought: "Here we go!"'

Susan Belbin tried addressing areas that might be incorrectly interpreted by any member of her team by scouring each script with a fine tooth comb and, if necessary, double-checking Renwick's requirements before issuing it to her team. Although this strategy helped reduce the volume of incidents where differences of opinion arose, it was impossible to eliminate every occasion, and from Renwick's point of view, many aspects of the production, including visual effects, couldn't be assessed until they were in situ. Belbin was aware that for many of her team the experience of having the writer heavily involved was new. 'I eventually told everyone to take instruction from David. But, of course, from time to time you got new faces arriving who perhaps weren't privy to that, so there could be some huffing and puffing or heavy sighs occasionally.'

Chris Lawson thinks *One Foot* broke new grounds for a situation comedy, not just in terms of the themes it explored, but also in setting the fashion for writers' increasing involvement in a show's direction. 'With David's scripts, you had to really study them to ensure you'd done absolutely everything required in any given episode. In the old days, the writer delivered their scripts to the producer-director and while the team went off to make the programme, the writer would start on more scripts. Then, you listened to the director and the producer was who you answered to. The new style of working means writers are around more, and, of course, David, having written the script, had the right to express his views.'

The third series closed with 'The Worst Horror of All', which was transmitted on Sunday, 8 March at 9.05 p.m. The show's popularity was continuing to grow with just over sixteen million viewers settling down to watch another eventful week in the life of Victor Meldrew. The episode was a positive cornucopia of humorous sequences, serious moments and sight gags, like the scene where Victor found a Citroën 2CV dumped in the skip he'd hired. It was just one of countless incidentals seen in Renwick's programmes. 'You can't build a whole episode around them, but it's good when you come up with some. All you hope is that people can relate to them.'

For Susan Belbin, the episode revealed everything she liked about Victor Meldrew's principles and morals. It had been over twenty years since he was last offered a full-time job, which explained the ray of sunshine lighting up his life the morning the postman brought good news. He began his job as doorman at the Norfolk Royale Hotel, but before the day was out was picking up his cards after revealing his contempt for a

Another five-minute wonder: Victor's job as a hotel doorman ended with a toupee being tossed down a drain.

supercilious couple who'd just arrived at the hotel. While they were demanding that Victor grab a fur coat they'd left on the back seat of a taxi, Victor noticed a legless man on the opposite side of the street alighting from his vehicle. The poignant image led to Victor losing his temper with the snooty couple, and in the process he pulled off the man's toupee and dropped it down the drain. 'I watched this episode again recently and wasn't sure how comfortable I felt about the heavy-handed cut to the man with no legs getting into a wheelchair,' explains Renwick. 'Victor was having a hard time with this very objectionable couple who wouldn't even get out of a cab until the doors were opened for them, then over the road you see this man struggling to climb out of his vehicle. It was rather ponderous satire, but I suppose it made the point.'

CHAPTER 10
Series Four

The fourth series, transmitted in early 1993, marked the acme of David Renwick's sublime sitcom. Audience figures reached their peak during this season with each episode attracting at least sixteen million viewers: among the high-flying instalments was 'The Trial', the only script not to feature Annette Crosbie, which was seen by nearly 18.5 million; and if that didn't send everyone associated with the show jumping for joy, seeing that year's Christmas Special, 'One Foot in the Algarve', top the ratings chart with a staggering twenty million audience, becoming the most watched episode in the show's history, certainly did.

The show's indubitable rise to the top of its tree was fully deserved, yet the self-effacing David Renwick, who has never taken his hard-earned success lightly, was only too aware that the ephemeral nature of the television world meant sustaining the show's popularity couldn't be taken for granted. The public's fondness for the show and the actors was exhibited in many ways; being stopped in the street and receiving a burgeoning pile of fan mail are concomitant with fame, and for Wilson and Crosbie, both seasoned professionals, being recognised while out shopping wasn't new. But nothing could have prepared them for the reaction from the show's legions of fans. Crosbie didn't mind members of the public stopping her to talk about *One Foot*. 'We did the show to give pleasure and if people take the trouble to tell you how much they enjoy it, that's great.' She recalls an occasion when she was crossing a busy intersection in Edinburgh. 'I was against the lights so had to rush; I'd reached the middle of the road when a woman grabbed my arm. I couldn't move. Sometimes, people recognised you but didn't know why, and she was trying to tell me I'd been in something else! We were in danger of being run over – it was crazy.' People stopped her frequently to share stories. 'I remember at an airport a man said he worked in an old people's home and watching *One Foot in the Grave* was the highlight of the residents' week.'

Although the exposure from appearing in *Only When I Laugh* and *Tutti Frutti* meant Richard Wilson's face was occasionally recognised by the public, playing Victor meant he became a national figure. He recalls innumerable occasions when he came face to face with fans of the show. 'I have two very good Glaswegian examples,' he says. 'For a time, I was Rector of Glasgow University and was walking down a city-centre street when this Mini drove onto the pavement beside me. A man jumped out, shouting: "I must have your autograph for my son. He thinks you're wonderful." I was taken aback – it was my first car-jacking autograph! I couldn't believe it when he told me that his son was only four – and already a fan of the show.' Another time, Wilson was in a stationery shop when he happened to glance out the window and noticed a bus driver waving furiously from inside his cab. Wilson obligingly waved back and essayed a smile but soon realised the driver wanted to speak to him. 'I thought he'd pulled in at a bus stop but when I came out of the shop I realised he'd stopped his bus, full of passengers, to say how much he enjoyed the programme.'

At times, it was difficult coping with all the mail the show generated,

Richard Wilson always made time for his fans, young and old.

This couple were immortalised with a fleeting shot in 'Love and Death'.

and Crosbie and Wilson received all manner of requests. 'The strangest letter I've ever had was while appearing in the West End [during the run of *One Foot*] and someone wrote: "There's a photograph of you in the West End and I notice you have some nasal hairs. These can be removed – would you like me to come and do it for you?" Then there was a request from someone wanting a photo of me in the nude, and if not, then stripped to the waist, and if that wasn't possible, just a photograph!' But nothing beats the package that arrived at Wilson's London home the week after an episode showing Victor regularly visiting the lavatory. 'This beautiful box arrived, well wrapped. It was a two-month supply of prostate pills. A note said: "Dear Mr Wilson, this is our latest product, just in case this is a real problem you have. Please find enclosed a two-month supply of prostate pills. If they're not required, maybe you can pass them on to somebody who needs them." I couldn't believe it.'

But it wasn't all congratulatory letters the leading players received: Wilson and Crosbie were recipients of some vicious hate mail in response to the scene showing Victor removing a frozen cat from his freezer. 'One, which was sent to both of us, was very threatening,' says Crosbie. 'It was written in red and said: "You in *One Foot* will wind up dead." Of course, you don't respond to letters like that – you just hope for the best. But I did ask David [Renwick] in despair once to stop writing about animals because he didn't have to put up with the letters. But it wasn't just the letters I objected to; I didn't think it was fair on the animals.' Crosbie refers to the final episode in Series Four, 'Secret of the Seven Sorcerers', where doves are seen flying around the Meldrews' lounge, as a prime example. 'We worked with netting all over the set and had to keep catching the birds – I hated it: you don't use animals like that. Then there was the episode with the little dog who had to be put in a box for Patrick's birthday. That also upset me because, of course, he didn't want to go in the box. I used to get cross with David. I can see it's funny, but the whole business of animals interned in a studio isn't good.'

The wheels were put in motion for the fourth series in March 1993, when Renwick began gathering thoughts and ideas for the six scripts. A random sample of entries from his journals during April 1993 revealed, once again, the highs and lows of scriptwriting, from dreaming up storylines that on closer examination lacked mileage to the delights of discovering everything fits into place and a script is complete. During a weekend in April, he'd endured 'a solid day of thinking and thinking and thinking but making no progress. I began by imagining I'd got enough for a two-parter, but quickly realised I hadn't enough even for one. Agonising back and forth over this thought about a 100-year-old woman erroneously getting into Victor's bed, how on earth could this be contrived, was it truly funny anyway . . . '[i] Although he worried about the strength of the idea, he eventually went with his instincts and the scene turned out to be one of the funniest moments in the fourth episode, 'Warm

Champagne'. By the start of the following week, the running order for the episode he was focusing on was consigned to the bin, leaving him to contemplate whether he'd 'ever come up with another solid script again'[ii]. But by the end of the week, he'd finalised the third script, 'Hearts of Darkness'. His upbeat entry confirms that 'after all the aggro I'm extremely pleased with it – more so than the other two, and on reading it back I didn't want to change a word. A nice mix of character, predicament, farce and relationships, with very few actual spoken jokes.'[iii]

Only when the final word had been typed and Renwick was entirely satisfied with a script would he involve director Susan Belbin, who delighted in receiving his work. At no point would the writer discuss storylines or potential plots with Belbin, which left her eagerly anticipating what the next buff-coloured envelope from Luton would bring. 'He wouldn't tell me anything,' says Belbin. 'When he'd sent in the first four scripts, intermittently, and we'd meet to begin casting those episodes, he'd often arrive relieved and jolly because he'd finished Script Five and had a plot for Six. But even then he wouldn't tell me anything, not even a hint of what was going on; he didn't want to clutter my mind with snippets of information.' Needing peace and quiet, Belbin usually read the scripts at home before ringing David Renwick to convey her thoughts.

As well as casting and discussing the scripts, one of Susan Belbin's early tasks for the new series involved an unexpected trip to Bournemouth. Location filming had been scheduled to begin mid-September, but soon after the usual negotiations to secure the houses in Tresillian Way began in earnest, rumblings of discontent among the residents were detected. Belbin recalls: 'Word came back to me that they didn't want us back, they'd had enough, which could have been very serious. It wasn't anyone from the houses we used that was unhappy, because we were

paying them to compensate for any disruption – it was a neighbour further down the road.' A meeting was convened with residents in the local church hall, and over tea and biscuits Belbin intended to appease any disgruntled residents. 'I was truthful and told them what we'd be doing and approximate dates. There were a few moans but generally everything went well and agreement to film there again was reached. When the meeting closed, I even received a round of applause!' As the hall began to empty, several people approached Belbin. 'They told me there was never really a problem; it was just one person who'd complained, and that was because we weren't filming at his place and he wasn't getting any of the action.'

A note said: 'Dear Mr Wilson, this is our latest product, just in case this is a real problem you have. Please find enclosed a two-month supply of prostate pills. If they're not required, maybe you can pass them on to somebody who needs them.' I couldn't believe it.

RICHARD WILSON

Local resident Mike Lewis, who lived in Nick Swainey's house, understands that the inconveniences associated with filming a television series in a suburban street are, largely, unavoidable, but realises that not everyone welcomes the intrusion. 'Whereas we were being paid, many of the other owners were inconvenienced without getting the benefits.' Kelly Southgate, whose house was used for the Meldrews, agrees with Mike Lewis. 'When you consider there were nearly forty people plus the equipment, it's bound to be disruptive. Some of the complaints were probably to do with jealousy because obviously the BBC couldn't pay everyone on the estate, and you can't please everyone

Director of photography John Rhodes (standing) brought a very filmic look to Series Four, and the Christmas Special 'One Foot in the Algarve'.

either. At times, though, I think the BBC did start taking things for granted a little. People who weren't being paid had their share of disruption. Having said that, there was one time when I came down at 7 a.m. and they'd taken my front door off!'

With filming arrangements finalised, the series kicked off with 'The Pit and the Pendulum', with Richard Wilson engaged in arguably his most uncomfortable piece of filming. When Patrick's cherry tree invaded Victor's rockery and began strangling his junipers, he hired the excessively hairy Mr Kazanzi to repair the damage. But a series of incidents and misunderstandings resulted in Victor confronting Mr Kazanzi, who took umbrage at Victor's accusations and retaliated by planting him up to his neck inside the chasm he'd dug in the garden. In reality, Wilson was crouched inside a wooden box buried in the earth with a supply of hot water bottles to keep him warm. He remembers it as a problematic day, mainly because it took three attempts to shoot the sequence. 'We shot it once and there was a camera fault; we shot it again and it didn't look right, which annoyed me because they should have realised that beforehand. So we had to shoot it a third

time. It wasn't very comfortable inside that box, mainly because I couldn't do anything, even scratch my nose! It was miserable because I was in the hole for long spells – two or three hours – and to top it all, there was a wind blowing right down the garden.'

Director Susan Belbin confesses that she was to blame for stopping the filming on one occasion, and even now, whenever she sees the scene, it still doesn't convince her. 'In one scene, when Victor is in the hole, he has a flowerpot on his head and Angus comes in and takes it off. Because of the camera angle being very low, it looked as if Angus just slid it off, rather than lifting it. It made me think that viewers would believe there was a hole at the back of the flowerpot and that he wasn't really under it. I don't know where my brain was at the time because it wasn't until I saw the rushes that I realised, but by then Richard was out of the hole and we were doing other things. So we had to do it again.' Belbin felt awful putting Wilson through such discomfort once more. 'Richard was lovely. He moaned, but you love him for it, because I'd moan too. I have no objection to him moaning about being put in a hole on three occasions.'

Annette Crosbie sympathised with Wilson's predicament. 'Down at that level, there was a terrible wind blowing,' she says. 'You'd be amazed at the number of people – all members of the crew – who wanted to take a photograph of Richard in the hole, all people who should have known better. They thought it was so funny and were shrieking with laughter, but Richard couldn't get out and I think people should have been a little more tactful.'

Allowing a film crew into your back garden isn't conducive to maintaining an attractive plot, as visual effects designer Chris Lawson explains. 'Every time we went to the house, either the rain poured and the lawn became a quagmire or we dug it up, like the massive hole for the box to go in. I remember having to go back to do some reshooting of Victor in the ground; it had rained recently and the water table had risen so much, we couldn't push the box in the hole. Then we tried refilling the hole and it turned into a mud bath. But every time we'd finished on the site, a landscape gardener repaired the garden.'

Keeping the residents sweet was a crucial job, but occasionally an oversight caused some headaches everyone could have done without, like the time fake snow was being used in an episode. Nick Wood, who worked on the fourth series as production manager, recalls: 'We omitted to tell everyone to shut their windows. Of course, it being summer, nearly the whole street had their windows open and the fake snow blew into their houses. We had to do a big PR job at half a dozen properties, but everyone was all right in the end.'

Cast as Mr Kazanzi, alias the Hairy Man, was Daniel Peacock, although at one point Renwick had envisaged either Rik Mayall or Robbie Coltrane playing the part. The script dictated that the character wouldn't just possess a little bodily hair, he'd be covered in it. Director Susan Belbin arranged a meeting with make-up designer Jean Steward to convey her requirements. 'I assumed Susie would cast someone who fitted the bill perfectly in terms of their hairiness,' says Steward, 'but that wasn't the case.' Steward thought a T-shaped piece of chest hair might suffice but was wrong. 'Susie said she wanted him covered in hair. My partner, Peter Robinson, worked as the gaffer on the series and he's

covered in hair, so when Susie said she wanted the character as hairy as Peter, I knew I had a job on.' After taking some Polaroids of her partner's body, she asked a wig-maker in London to make the hair. 'They did a fantastic job. You couldn't have one big strip, so had to piece dozens of bits together, like a jigsaw puzzle, some on his forearms, tops of his hands, fingers and so on.'

On the day of filming, Steward and her assistant, Vanessa White, who took over the mantle of make-up designer for Series Five and Six when Steward became make-up department manager, rose at the crack of dawn to prepare Daniel Peacock for the day's filming. 'The poor actor had to kneel down for nearly two hours while we stuck, with spirit gum, every little piece of hair on his body.' What made the job even more laborious was the tendency of spirit gum to dry out, causing pieces of hair to lift or peel every time Peacock bent his arm. 'It was a cold day and Daniel had to stand around much of the day stripped to the waist. He couldn't wear a coat to keep warm because that would flatten and disturb the hair, but we didn't want him freezing so Richard Winter, the costume designer, gave him one of the foil sheets emergency services give people to prevent hypothermia.'

My partner, Peter Robinson, worked as the gaffer on the series and he's covered in hair, so when Susie said she wanted the character as hairy as Peter, I knew I had a job on.

JEAN STEWARD

The filming schedule wasn't kind to Peacock, with all the close-up shots left to the end of the day. 'By then, pieces of hair had fallen off and been stuck back on about a dozen times,' says Steward. Eventually, though, they reached the end of a gruelling day and Steward and White shepherded Daniel Peacock to their make-up van to begin the tedious job of removing the pieces of hair, with the help of spirit gum remover. It took about an hour, by which time they all had blinding headaches thanks to the fumes emitted by the gum remover. The following day, just as the make-up team thought they'd

> *Danny Peacock was made to look impressively hairy . . . Vital that having heard Victor describe him as the Wild Man of Borneo you then understand what he was talking about, and I think on this occasion the make-up department did us proud.*

DAVID RENWICK

seen the last of the Hairy Man, they received some bad news. Steward recalls, 'We were told there had been a technical problem with the camera. They'd known all day yesterday that it wasn't behaving properly, but nobody bothered to suggest sending for another; all the previous day's scenes had to be reshot – I couldn't believe it.' If Steward and White thought their previous day's headache was bad, what they were about to experience was much worse. All the pieces of hair had been cut to make them fit, so there we were with this big box of misfit pieces, which required all the spirit gum being cleaned off, as well as making sure the hair was dressed to go back in the right direction. As expected, results were nowhere as good as first time around.'

Nonetheless, David Renwick was pleased with the efforts of the make-up department, noting in his journal that 'Danny Peacock was made to look impressively hairy . . . Vital that having heard Victor describe him as the Wild Man of Borneo you then understand what he was talking about, and I think on this occasion the make-up department did us proud.'[iv]

A juxtaposition of emotions in the closing stages of

the episode underline the adroitness of Renwick's writing: after the hilarity of seeing Victor buried in the garden, the viewers' are suddenly sharing Margaret's sadness upon hearing that her mother has died. Cutting to show Victor's sorrowful reaction when he's in such an incredibly bizarre predicament, is a powerful piece of television, aided by an emotive performance by Annette Crosbie. Renwick, realising her investment in the poignant scene had taken its toll, noted: 'Annette gave a terribly moving performance on the speech about her mother dying, and after the camera had cut she disappeared into the house and I could see that the subject matter had affected her very personally. So I followed her outside the front door and gave her a consoling cuddle as she erupted in a flood of tears.'[v]

The return of the show was welcomed by all quarters of the national press. In the *Today* newspaper, Pam Francis wrote 'every moment was a gem . . . welcome back to TV's best sitcom'[vi]. Equally complimentary was Sally Brockway in the *Sun*, who enthused, 'This ace comedy . . . is the funniest show on the box since *Fawlty Towers*. There were dozens of dotty situations crammed into the show and the Meldrews milked them for a barrel load of belly laughs.'[vii] Maureen Paton, in the *Daily Express*, singled out Richard Wilson and Angus Deayton for praise, stating, 'Theirs is a superbly sarcastic double act.'[viii] But she also hailed others for their performance, including the Hairy Man himself. 'The show has such high production values that even the guest parts are strongly cast. Enter Daniel Peacock, who does a lovely line in cunning gormlessness for various *Comic Strip* films – and did not disappoint here.'[ix] As the month wore on, other positive reviews in the press, including the *Sunday Times* and the *Stage and Television Today*, which felt the show was 'justly celebrated for its hilarious black humour, its sharp writing and its spot-on characterisation',[x] helped relieve Renwick's usual anxieties regarding whether *One Foot*'s popularity was waning. The *Sun*, in particular, was in Victor Meldrew mood and during February 1993 even ran a 'Draw Victor Meldrew' competition for its readers.

The second episode, 'Descent into the Maelstrom', found Margaret bed-bound with Victor acting as nursemaid and having to attend his cousin's sixtieth birthday bash on his own, although a mix-up at the dry cleaner's, means a limited choice in terms of attire – it's either a mix-and-match outfit or a gorilla costume. The gorilla outfit was picked up inadvertently by Mrs Warboys, and the scene is one of David Renwick's favourites because he feels it completely embodies what he regards as Doreen Mantle's strengths as a performer. 'She can place that gorilla costume down on the back of a sofa without any sense of self-consciousness whatever. She really makes you believe she sees nothing odd about it; the way she does that is priceless. It's something you can't teach.'

Mantle was the oldest member of the regular cast and brought with her a wealth of experience, particularly on the stage. Impressed with the actress from the day he first met her at the audition, Renwick believes her contribution to the show was immense. 'In theatre, which she loves, she says it's never worth anyone coming to see the production until about three weeks into the run, when the actors have had a chance to hone their performances. So the schedule we had on *One Foot* was sadistic as far as she was concerned. I know she found learning lines taxing, which I can understand, especially when you get out there in front of a studio audience. She would be the first to admit how hair-raising she found the whole thing, but the bottom line is that she was always incredibly good value. I don't think you'd find anyone who worked on the show who'd disagree with that.'

Mantle is able to qualify and expand on Renwick's reference to learning lines being taxing. She says: 'David's skill and success as a writer is largely due to his innate sense of what works, and the precision with which he seeks to perfect it. I never had a problem learning the actual lines, it was about being absolutely strictly accurate in their delivery. This was due to not having a lot of time for rehearsing, but also David's idiosyncratic style of writing which made it challenging, at times, to get it accurate.'

Intending to name each episode after an Edgar Allan Poe story, Renwick ran out of apposite titles after the first two shows and plumped for 'Hearts of Darkness' for the third instalment, arguably the most controversial Renwick scripted. What was meant to be a pleasant day trip in the Norfolk countryside for the Meldrews, Mrs Warboys and Nick Swainey turns into a nightmare, and Victor ends up trudging off alone to summon help. He stumbles across a retirement home, but soon discovers that it's more like a rest home from hell. With the staff exhibiting reprehensible behaviour towards the residents, he launches a one-man crusade to help restore some order and dignity to the inmates.

He announces his intentions to Miss Lander, who runs the home, in a frank exchange:

VICTOR: Oh, sorry, I very nearly forgot.
LANDER: Nearly forgot what?
VICTOR: I nearly forgot to call you an evil, loathsome bastard. I wouldn't treat a sewer rat the way you treat these people, and I shall be calling the Social Services department first thing in the morning to tell them about the sickening brutality that goes on around here in the name of geriatric care.
LANDER: I have to look after the welfare of all my residents, not just one or two. You haven't the first understanding of the way their minds work, or the destructive behaviour they are capable of.
VICTOR: I'm sorry – what language are you talking in now? It appears to be bollocks!

Richard Wilson thought the dramatic shift in the episode's mood from one of laughter during the lion's share of the script to one of seriousness when Victor enters the retirement home was too much of a leap. He questioned whether a little preparatory work preceding the scenes depicting ill-treatment of the old people would have cushioned the shock for viewers. But it's exactly that reaction which Renwick enjoyed engendering in his work. The sense of Renwick's satisfaction upon eliciting the desired response from the studio audience watching the recording is almost palpable. He noted that 'you could sense the sudden chill in the audience as the tone grew darker and it all got a bit disturbing.'[xi]

The episode cast light on the delicate and shocking issue of mistreatment of the elderly. Scenes of the

'Hearts of Darkness' was thematically inspired by the film *Apocalypse Now*, itself based on the novel by Joseph Conrad.

outraged by the treatment dished out to the residents in their care. He adds: 'The scenes in which the old people were being mistreated would only have been offensive if we were asking people to laugh at them – and quite obviously this was not the case. As a society we tend to treat the elderly quite shamefully, and I like to think that by showing Victor tackling injustice on their behalf we were offering a small message of hope.'*xii*

Director Susan Belbin knew as soon as she read the script that the episode would generate viewers' complaints – and she was right. Within minutes of the episode airing on that Sunday evening, forty people had phoned the BBC to register their disgust. Days after, letters were still arriving. 'When you show someone hitting an old person, you know you'll get a reaction from viewers,' admits Belbin. 'David and I were interviewed on *Biteback* [a BBC programme airing viewers' comments] and had to defend ourselves. Actually, you don't defend yourself, you say: "Go out into the big wide world and see what it's like." People then come back at you, saying: "But this is comedy." And the reply to that is if you want to get a message home to people, use comedy.' Belbin received numerous letters from viewers, some terrified because their own mothers had just entered a home. 'I wrote telling them that the majority of homes are perfectly all right, but that you have to look carefully at these places because some may not be. We're all aware that mistreating residents in homes does happen. You have to be responsible in what programme you make, and with "Hearts of Darkness" I think we were in the way we showed it.'

residents being hectored and ill-treated, with one old man being slapped and kicked, wasn't what the traditional sitcom viewer had come to expect, but then this wasn't conventional comedy. *One Foot*'s history to date had entitled it to be considered the cradle of the dramcom, to coin a phrase, the comedy-drama which on the surface possessed many of the qualities and facets of a traditional situation comedy but which, upon digging beneath the surface, revealed a darker, menacing structure. 'There is a problem when you insert scenes like that in the middle of what's regarded as a nice safe comedy show,' admits Renwick. 'It upsets people's equilibrium: they're not prepared for it, so they react in a far more horrified fashion than if it was a drama. But then the whole curve of the episode was that it began with a conventional shape, and then suddenly you're plunged into this dark Conrad world, where all this nastiness is taking place, and our hero eventually rides to the rescue.' As Renwick points out, in order to enjoy that moment of triumph when the staff of the nursing home get their comeuppance, viewers had to be suitably

The episode also contained the sitcom's first nude scene. A bedraggled Victor Meldrew, whose trek to summon help meant traversing rough ground, arrived at the nursing home filthy and was invited to take a shower, only to be interrupted by Miss Lander just as he was stepping from the cubicle. 'I had several nude scenes,' recalls Richard Wilson. 'There was a joke about my bottom because I kept saying: "David Renwick just wants to see my bottom." In the film of *Whoops Apocalypse* [which Renwick co-wrote] I had to show my bottom with writing on it. But David wasn't happy with the writing and did it himself. So after that, I was always saying: "I've got to show my bottom again!" It didn't worry me, though.'

However, attempts had been made to save Wilson having to appear nude in front of actress Janet Henfrey, who was cast as the stern Miss Lander. Several devices, including flesh-coloured underpants, were considered before Belbin decided to take the bull by the horns and suggest to Wilson that he complete the scene in the buff. 'I said to him: "Look, we're going to be messing about for ages; you're going to get fed up and be cross with me, so are you up for doing it naked? We're all this side of the camera." He said he would, so we had a laugh about it, then shot it. It was filmed on location in a real house, which meant we couldn't get many people in the room anyway, but I didn't tell everyone it was a closed set because that would have only attracted more interest – there was no big deal made at all.'

While 'Hearts of Darkness' was shot largely on location, the fourth and fifth episodes in the series, 'Warm Champagne' and 'The Trial' were largely studio-based. The fourth instalment saw Margaret, suffering post-holiday blues, surreptitiously arrange a rendezvous with a man she met while away: her tryst was short-lived, however, when she quickly realised it was Victor she loved. While that episode focused heavily on Margaret Meldrew, 'The Trial' spotlighted her husband, the only character to appear. Reminiscent of the memorable Tony Hancock episode 'The Bedsitter', this well-honed soliloquy saw Victor on jury service, but after five days of waiting for the phone to ring, he was yet to set foot inside the courtroom. Endless hours of waiting allowed him time to, among other things, flick through the medical dictionary and assume he'd got every illness under the sun and question whether his decision to kill a woodlouse but not a crane fly was symptomatic of a prejudiced society.

VICTOR: I suppose if I was religious I wouldn't have killed that woodlouse. It wasn't doing anyone any harm, just walking across the floor minding his own business, going for a quiet stroll along the gripper rod. Then, for no apparent reason, I just callously murdered it in cold blood. Discrimination. Didn't do that with the daddy long-legs, did I? No, he was picked up in a nice fluffy duster and shaken out of the window – talk about a classless society.

Richard Wilson, who feels the script was 'beautifully written', was given two weeks to learn the dialogue, which he classes as 'a great luxury'. Although being on his own for the entire half-hour meant having to cram more lines into his head, it did, curiously, ease the pressures involved in recording. He explains: 'Because I was the only thing the cameras could point at, I didn't have to be too exact with my marks. I also got all the rehearsal time and it was an enjoyable episode. It's the only occasion I can remember where we had to stop recording because the audience wouldn't stop laughing.' The scene referred to was one of many highlights in the episode, showing

I said to him: 'Look, we're going to be messing about for ages; you're going to get fed up and be cross with me, so are you up for doing it naked?'

SUSAN BELBIN

Victor sitting in an armchair while contemplating answers to his crossword, accidentally daubing ink all over his face thanks to a leaking pen. 'It's a wonderful image,' enthuses Wilson, 'and was great to act.'

Susan Belbin says she would never have dreamt of suggesting storylines to Renwick, but admits 'pleading' with him to write a one-man show for Wilson. 'I wouldn't go as far as saying it was my suggestion, because it may have been on David's list of things to do anyway. But I certainly nagged him about doing it. The way David writes, the way he thinks, it was an inevitable episode, whether Hancock had done it or not. It was a great episode to work on – just Richard and myself at rehearsals most of the time. It took ten days to rehearse because thirty minutes is a long time with just one man learning the lines. It was wonderful watching Richard develop his performance.' Referring to the pen-leaking scene, she recalls: 'We couldn't shut the audience up but eventually finished the episode.' While editing the programme, Belbin, who classes 'The Trial' as her favourite episode, knew the amount of laughter couldn't be retained, leaving no alternative but to rerecord the scene the following week. 'Even then, the audience roared with laughter, but not on the scale of the other lot!'

Like Belbin, David Renwick enjoyed watching Richard Wilson's performance evolve. The read-through was virtually void of laughter, such was the actor's style of absorbing the lines and gradually transforming it into the performance millions of people, including Renwick and Belbin, had come to expect. Renwick acknowledged that this was 'par for the course now with Richard'*xiii*. He had every confidence in Wilson, noting that 'as soon as we began to put it on its feet it showed signs of life, and I know that once he's assimilated all the material and starts to interpret it internally it will all take off.'*xiv* By the following Monday, 23 November 1992, when Renwick spent the day at the BBC's rehearsal room helping block the episode, he was enchanted by Wilson's performance. Renwick noted: 'Richard has now come into his own and is enriching the whole thing with some masterful timing, reactions, looks and various subtle touches. It's a joy to just sit back and watch it.'

It was a joy for viewers at home, too, who delighted in Wilson's monologue, and when the episode was transmitted on 28 February, it was also enjoyed by critics. In the *Evening Standard*, Victor Lewis-Smith felt *One Foot* had the gift to 'transcend time altogether, flowing so effortlessly that afterwards you cannot imagine how so much construction was squeezed into a meagre half-hour slot.'*xv* He added that, 'Script, acting and direction combined to produce a genuine *tour de force*.'*xvi* He spotted

influences of Czech novelist Franz Kafka, whose work included portraits of lonely individuals trapped in an indifferent world, Hitchcock for the 'sinister establishing shot of a lone raven perched against a thundery sky, with the camera tracking into and passing through the rain-swept front window'*xvii*, and, of course, Hancock. As far as Lewis-Smith was concerned, *One Foot* was an 'impassioned plea for the traditional virtues of immaculately crafted scripting, performance and directing'*xviii*. Meanwhile, Martyn Harris, writing in the *Spectator*, classed *One Foot* as an 'accurate picture of idleness in retirement . . . which grows more ambitious with every episode.'*xix*

For Renwick the Hancock episode, 'The Bedsitter', was a key influence in his decision to tackle the idea of a one-man show. 'I sat down and watched it again before I embarked upon 'The Trial' to give me confidence. I remember Susie nudging me, trying to persuade me to write it, but I didn't need much encouragement because it's the sort of thing I love.' At one point he even considered writing an episode without either of the Meldrews. Set next door in the Trenches' house, Victor and Margaret's voices would only have been heard through the wall, with the entire story seen from Patrick and Pippa's perspective. The concept, however, was jettisoned once Renwick failed to dream up enough ideas to fill the episode.

For once, having to cut material from a script proved useful for David Renwick when he was asked to supply a sketch for 1993's Comic Relief, as he was able to offer excess material from 'The Trial' – a sequence showing Victor Meldrew musing to himself in the bath.

The fourth series was brought to an end with the screening of 'Secret of the Seven Sorcerers', a sad moment in the life of Jean Warboys who suspected her husband, Chris, of having an affair, only to bring about her own personal disaster by hiring a private detective to investigate. Although her initial suspicions were proved wrong, she was devastated when her husband eventually moved in with none other than the female detective Jean had hired. Mrs Warboys cut a forlorn figure as she informed Victor and Margaret of her shocking news, but she'd perked up sufficiently by the time the Christmas Special, 'One Foot in the Algarve', was transmitted on Boxing Day 1993, jetting off to Portugal to meet Afonso, a pen pal she'd been writing to for thirteen years.

CHAPTER 11
Heading for the Algarve

accept his own interpretation of the character. 'He was a big name, hugely respected in comedy. We didn't know what to expect from the part, but we knew we'd get his version, which probably meant it being wacky and off the wall.' Belbin was looking forward to working with Cook. 'He was a legend as far as David and I were concerned. I knew it was going to be a challenge because it's no secret that Peter had led a very colourful life. But as it transpired, he was one of the nicest, easiest people I've ever worked with.' She recalls him phoning before leaving Heathrow Airport. 'It was a Sunday, a day off, and I was lying on my bed in the hotel. Peter was flying out to join us and decided to call. He said: "Susie, I'm at the airport. What Sunday newspapers do you want brought out?" He knew I'd have to wait twenty-four hours before the papers arrived in Portugal otherwise, so decided to bring some over for me – it was such a sweet thought.'

When David Renwick first met Cook in Belbin's office at the BBC to discuss the part, he classed him as 'large and infectiously affable'[iii]. He added: 'He's not the sort of person to offer an in-depth analysis of the characterisation – mostly he just preferred to talk about moustaches. The main thing is he is undeniably a funny man, and I was pleased that we never got round to asking him to read. I don't think it would have proved very much and indeed might well have put us off him. The character doesn't have a huge amount to say in the show anyway – his function is principally visual: the recipient of an ever-escalating series of slapstick violence. After he'd gone we decided to take a risk and offer him the part.'[iv]

The venue for the first day's filming on Sunday, 2 May was Victoria Station, and again two of Renwick's biggest bugbears in relation to filming were evident. He thought the scenes were being framed too tightly, which could, in his view, kill the effect of his visual comedy. Renwick discussed the matter with Belbin, pointing out that they needed to adopt the style used in the studio, whereby pulling back and showing the entirety of a shot afforded viewers the chance to feel part of the action.

He also detected a lack of urgency during the early part of the day, resulting in some scenes having to be shifted to the following day's schedule due to fading light. As far as he was concerned, it was another example of why he'd once contemplated writing studio-based scripts only. But Renwick's focus was primarily on Cook. Initially he found himself encouraging Cook to speed up his performance; the following day, he offered advice on a particular scene, noting later: 'A jokey performance that works well in the context of a sketch show can seriously damage the credibility of a narrative piece like this. The stuff where he is searching through his pockets, for instance, required a structured approach, as does all comedy business. And it's something even skilled actors fail to recognise: that because the success of the action is all based on rhythm you need to "block" it all out by numbers to begin with, and then apply the fluency afterwards. As a result I had to slow down his actions to make them more coherent, and prevent it from being just a slurred mess.'[v]

Once all the UK-based scenes were in the can, the team jetted off to the Algarve. Susan Belbin hoped her visit would turn out better than her first trip. Earlier, she'd travelled to Portugal on a recce and it soon turned into a nightmare. After spending an entire day scouring the countryside for suitable locations, Belbin and members of her design and camera team headed for a beach bar. It was out of season and tourists were scarce. Stepping off the deserted beach into a little shack, the team decided to put thoughts of work to the back of their minds and unwind. But relaxation soon turned to panic when their car's alarm went off. 'We'd parked it no more than fifty yards from the bar,' says Belbin, 'but by the time we reached it, someone had already broken in and swiped, among other things, my passport.' Equally devastating was the loss of the director's pile of notes. 'All the work I'd done for "One Foot in the Algarve" had gone, as well as other people's possessions. We didn't know how we were going to get home – it was terrible.'

That night, back at the hotel, Belbin was more despondent than she'd ever been in her life. She'd had enough and for a while wondered whether she wanted to continue with the production. 'It was a huge blow, and what was particularly frustrating was that the people who grabbed my bag didn't want the paperwork – they probably dumped it. It's very difficult working up that level of enthusiasm again: it clouded my enjoyment of a project which suddenly became a chore.'

Finally boarding the plane at Faro Airport, she couldn't wait to get home, but she hadn't seen the last of her troubles. 'I didn't think we were going to make it back to London!' she exclaims. 'The plane hit turbulence, worse than I'd ever experienced. When your drink ends up on the roof of the plane, you fear the worst. If we hadn't been strapped in, we'd have ended up on the ceiling, too. People were screaming, it was awful, but we suddenly got a fit of the giggles because it seemed the only way we could get through it.'

Fortunately, the journey to Portugal for filming was less troublesome, but as Belbin greeted everyone at the first-night cocktail party at their base, the Prainha Club Hotel in Portimao, Renwick was already concerned about a 'feeling of everyone succumbing to a frivolous holiday mood, instead of worrying about the gargantuan task that lies ahead of us'.[vi]

Progress was slow during the early days before being hampered further when the elements began ganging up on the team. 'It started raining on the first day of filming,' recalls Richard Wilson. 'The "Algarve" episode was a bit of a disaster. I remember getting dressed for a night shoot and putting on thermal underwear and also wearing gloves. I thought to myself: "This is not what I hoped the Algarve would be like." It was so cold.'

No one would have predicted inclement weather in Portugal during May, but Belbin was kicking herself that she hadn't arranged weather insurance, which she'd originally considered. 'It would have only cost around £600. I went to my then departmental manager and told him I was concerned because we only had a finite time over there [seven weeks to make the ninety-minute show] so we'd have to motor.' For peace of mind, Belbin regarded it a worthwhile investment. 'He said we could have it if our budget allowed. I thought the department should take it out on our behalf, but he

didn't agree. Stupidly, I didn't override him or go behind his back, which I should have done.' For a time, it looked like the BBC's parsimonious attitude would have a lasting effect on the production.

Wilson and Cook had already worked together on Renwick's 1986 film *Whoops Apocalypse*.

When the heavens opened, temperatures dropped and thunder and lightning set in, affecting several days' filming in an already packed schedule, Belbin was duly worried. 'We did what we could, but it was a nightmare. You're working in a foreign country where logistically it's difficult. You have actors flying in and out, and it's not like phoning somebody in Richmond and getting them to travel to Television Centre quickly; it was difficult altering plans. Having to cancel facilities and rebook them because we couldn't use them as planned due to the weather became expensive.'

But, slowly and painfully, they completed the scenes, and Belbin was grateful she'd had the chance to work with Cook. 'He was wonderful,' she says, before recalling a particularly awkward piece of filming which saw him with his leg and arm in plaster. 'As we reached remark about Peter." I then returned to my seat and sat down.' Lin Cook was soon confronted by the man's irate wife. 'She had a go at me, but I retorted: "Just ask him to repeat what he said and I'll whack him again!" Then the sound engineer intervened and led her away. I felt elated and pleased with myself, but didn't say a word to Peter: I couldn't bear to tell him that someone had insulted him.' It was a year later, when Peter Cook was filming *Black Beauty*, in which he played Lord Wexmire, that Lin finally confided in her husband. 'It just came out very naturally one day while we were having a discussion. I wanted to let Peter know that I stood up for him and always would.'

For the first time in the show's history, David Renwick wasn't around for the entire filming schedule. While in the UK he'd accompany the production team throughout the filming period, but he didn't want to stay in Portugal for the whole seven weeks. 'I thought I'd see

get the words more or less right and hit their marks it's felt that the take is a success and we can move on. Thank goodness I'm going home tomorrow, leaving them to their own devices.'[vii] Thirteen years later, Renwick admits the anxieties involved in filming the feature-length instalment were largely to blame for his melancholia. 'Generally, it was very successful,' he says, although he admits the film needed substantial editing before being fit for transmission.

In hindsight, Susan Belbin believes she let Renwick see the film too early, and should have conducted a complete edit before showing him. 'It hadn't had its final cut by any stretch of the imagination,' she says. 'He was anxious to see what had come out of Portugal, so I let him watch what I can only term as a joined-up series of scenes; it was a disaster because there were shots he didn't like and wanted removed which would have looked better a little further down the line, once we'd completed some editing.'

Belbin admits she can't remember why the episode's length became such a problem, but does point out there are always opportunities to tighten a film, therefore slicing seconds and minutes from the overall length. 'You can lose up to two minutes on a thirty-minute programme purely by tightening up. By that I mean if we had a car driving along the road, if it's not actually moving the story along, you can take it out. If someone pauses for too long before answering, you can cut. It may only be seconds, but it all mounts up.'

The first assembly of 'One Foot in the Algarve' ran to two hours eight minutes, a staggering thirty-eight minutes over length. When Renwick arrived at the editing suite on Friday, 16 July to see the results of the filming, his initial feeling was one of 'total desolation'[viii]. He regarded it as 'paceless, sprawling, lacking in fluidity, barely funny most of the time, with some really off-key performances and inexplicably badly

> *He was anxious to see what had come out of Portugal, so I let him watch what I can only term as a joined-up series of scenes; it was a disaster because there were shots he didn't like and wanted removed which would have looked better a little further down the line, once we'd completed some editing.*
>
> SUSAN BELBIN

things kick off, then leave them to it.' It was probably for the best because his diary entries during this period reveal he was frustrated with the progress being made and relieved to return home. He wrote: 'What astonishes me is the lack of urgency on set while we're actually shooting, which is when it really matters . . . Basically, if the actors staged moments throughout.'[ix] Renwick tried his utmost to sound constructive, while Belbin listened and tried to be accommodating, but tweaking scenes wouldn't solve the problem, so an entire strand had to be removed.

Renwick knew he was guilty of overwriting. A surfeit of ideas meant episodes were regularly being trimmed to fit the time slot in the schedules, which ultimately meant losing some golden lines of dialogue. Renwick claims this was largely due to feelings of insecurity concerning the 'comic voltage of the material. If I'm not a hundred per cent confident about one thing I try to bolster it up with another.'[x] He adds: 'I didn't have the courage to thin things out and allow it to breathe. But I never made an apology for trying to provide as rich an experience as possible in every episode. When someone sits down to watch the show, you want to give them value for money. Yes, a certain amount of it is down to lack of confidence – "Is that funny enough? Maybe it's not, so I'll have to see if I can think of something else that's as good or better." But by and large, I don't regret that.' Writing to the required length has always been Renwick's problem, he admits. 'When I compile my running order, I allot a number of pages per scene, then make adjustments so they add up to what should be the required script length. As I'm writing a scene, I have a pretty good idea how long it should be. Occasionally things spread and then I'll try shortening another scene further down the line to compensate. But it's a real juggling act and, of course, the number of pages is only a rule of thumb – mostly it's all down to intuition and experience.'

Extracting a complete storyline from 'Algarve', though, was no easy feat. To draw an analogy, Renwick's writing is like a spider's web: his scripts are full of intricately woven storylines and sub-plots which make them complex to edit. An off-the-cuff remark in the early stages of a script may resurface later and develop into a comedy strand. Chris Wadsworth, who edited the first four series and three Christmas Specials, including 'Algarve', was fully aware that removing an entire strand would be a challenge, particularly as the product had already been edited by the time it reached his cutting room. He says: 'Not having access to the original film material meant I wasn't able to recut with, say, extra close-ups and made the whole process

clumsier, but the main problem with *One Foot* was that the scripts were so intensive and plot dominated – there were plot points in every scene. You had to keep your wits about you. If you were removing a line, you had to look out for back references because some might have been critical to the plot. You had to edit with great care.' Although Wadsworth regarded Renwick's scripts as among the funniest he's ever edited, he knew the plot was so decreed that it meant his choices for editing were limited. 'Very often you had no option but to remove excellent material, just to get a plot point through.'

Usually, if an episode overran, Wadsworth reached the required duration by a series of shavings, deleting a few seconds here and there throughout the episode. He acknowledges, however, that editing 'Algarve' was a major challenge. 'We virtually had to unpick it. We [David Renwick, Susan Belbin and Wadsworth] all came up with ideas regarding what bits we could lose; it was a little heartbreaking but I think what materialised was a much better product.' He affirms that one of the golden rules of situation comedy is never to take your actors away from their home base because it rarely works; however, he classes 'Algarve' as one of the rare exceptions.

An inordinate time was spent reviewing the film before a decision was finally taken on which storyline should be dropped. In the transmitted version of 'Algarve', Victor was seen rushing to the aid of a Portuguese shopkeeper and performed the Heimlich manoeuvre when she began choking on a sandwich. It was a brief moment but originally spiralled off into a major storyline before becoming a casualty of the edit. 'The script seemed top heavy at the end of the day,' explains Renwick. 'There was the strand with Peter Cook, the one with Mrs Warboys and her pen friend who may or may not have murdered his wife, the one involving the boxer, and then a whole strand with Margaret suspecting Victor of having an affair with Isabella – it just seemed there was one thread too many.'

A line remaining in the film, where Isabella, the shopkeeper (played by Anna Nicholas) whom Victor saved from choking, warned him to look out for jellyfish on the beach, was a remnant of this original storyline. It was there to set up a later sequence when Victor found he had trodden on one of the jellyfish and Isabella ended up sucking his toe to extract the poison. Inevitably, Margaret stumbled upon this provocative scene and incited Hugo to exact the revenge he was already seeking for the incident with the donkey in the bathroom. And so at her behest he hauled Victor away and socked him in the jaw, thus proving to his father, finally, that he did indeed have the 'killer instinct'. In the next scene, which remained in the film, Margaret was seen feeding a badly beaten Victor. 'It was a problem to edit because we had to keep that scene in while removing the event that led up to it,' recalls Renwick. 'What happened in the end was that we went directly from the scene with the donkey urinating in Hugo's bath to the bit where Margaret's spooning food into Victor's mouth, and I added a couple of lines that referred back to Hugo breaking Victor's jaw in the bathroom – which, of course, was never shot.' The lines were dubbed on afterwards, and close inspection reveals that Margaret's lips don't even move. 'It's not perfect,' says Renwick, 'but on balance it was worth doing because it meant we could tighten the whole thing up and basically use the donkey scene as the film's big comic crescendo. I wouldn't say it was my own favourite moment in the show but, of course, it got howls from the audience when we screened it in the studio.'

Renwick's remedy for reducing the show's running time may have been efficacious, but when the film was finally transmitted on Boxing Day, he noted: 'All my basic reservations remained, although the added thrust of the audience laughter seemed to suggest it was all very amusing.'[xi]

The Christmas Special was welcomed by much of the national press. Tom Sutcliffe, in the *Independent*, wrote: '"One Foot in the Algarve" won out by a neck, if only because it kept faith with its dark glee at other people's catastrophes to the very last frame.'[xii] Other journalists examined the question of whether situation comedies can be extended beyond their thirty-minute boundaries and still entertain: Hugh Herbert and Garry Bushell

clearly felt *One Foot* achieved that. Herbert, in the *Guardian*, stated that sitcoms can be stretched to feature-length 'if you give it one big new element'[xiii] with Peter Cook being singled out as that new element. Bushell, meanwhile, regarded Victor Meldrew as 'an inspired comic creation'[xiv], adding: 'Stretching a sitcom works if the plot is strong enough. And David Renwick's sensational script delivered a comedy of terrors . . . strong currents of black humour flowed below the surface.'[xv]

> 'One Foot in the Algarve' won out by a neck, if only because it kept faith with its dark glee at other people's catastrophes to the very last frame.
>
> TOM SUTCLIFFE, *INDEPENDENT*

But not everyone was enamoured of the feature-length episode. Journalist Pam Francis had known David Renwick for some years. When she was a cub reporter on the *Barking and Dagenham Post* she attended the same journalism course at Harlow Technical College as Renwick, who was then employed by the *Luton News*. It took time for Francis to become a fan of the sitcom, hence her often negative reaction when reviewing the show in the various publications for which she wrote. Writing in the *Today* newspaper, she didn't agree with her contemporaries who felt the extended episode had worked. She stated: 'One of the problems with removing Victor from his own backyard and plonking him in Portugal . . . is that you lose the domestic trivia which act as a fodder for much of his madness. Plus all those extra characters and sub-plots to fill ninety-five minutes somewhat dilutes the magic of Meldrew.'[xvi]

Inevitably critics' views differed, but with twenty million viewers tuning in to watch on Boxing Day, BBC executives enjoyed their Christmas just a little bit more thanks to Victor Meldrew et al.

CHAPTER 12
Series Five

Watch *One Foot in the Grave* and you can't fail to be impressed by its sense of movement and fluidity. The stylistic approach adopted by director Susan Belbin became one of its trademarks. It broke away from the traditional look of the domestic, sofa-based sitcom, where characters remained static and events unfolded within the confines of the living room.

Belbin determined not to take *One Foot* down the cosy sitcom route, à la *Terry and June*; she knew, however, she couldn't avoid the obligatory sofa, although she would have loved making the series without the usual baggage associated with the genre. 'David had written a

Susan Belbin waits (more or less) patiently while Jimmy Grimes and John Record set up a crane shot.

show that was a million miles from *Terry and June* but people have to live in a house, and nine times out of ten they have a settee. If there hadn't been one in the Meldrews' house it would have been noticeable.' To avoid rooting her characters in the sitting room, Belbin tried to keep the characters on the move, replicating real life. 'If you had a long-standing marriage like Victor and Margaret's, you wouldn't spend all your time sitting next to each other on the sofa, talking face to face, you shout from one room to another, chat to people while washing up and things like that, which is what I tried to create.'

A prerequisite in achieving her aim was an apposite set for the Meldrews' house. She arranged with her production designers (Nick Somerville for the house in Series One and John Asbridge for the design used from Series Two) to design a composite set, to allow non-stop movement from one room to the next. Belbin wanted the show to look natural, and to create a system whereby the comedy was given every assistance – continual interruptions would hinder this from happening. She says: 'You can't be funny if you're interrupting the flow all the time. You'd get on a roll and then have to say: "Right, hold it there. Cameras take position. Over to the next set, thank you. OK, ladies and gentlemen, do you remember where we were? So and so has just washed his hands and now he's going to come in through that door . . ." It's bad for the audience, dreadful for the actors and awful for the comedy.'

What Belbin perfected was a method where the episode was recorded in the studio almost continuously from one scene to the next. One of her biggest frustrations as a director had been the frittering away of valuable time while recording a programme in front of a live audience, and she wanted to avoid the same happening with *One Foot*. 'So much time was wasted in the studio. You would have all the sets across the front of the studio, and perhaps a couple at the back, which the live audience wouldn't see. We'd stop and start a lot as we moved between sets. I wanted it to look and feel like a proper house so that the actors could walk freely between the rooms.' Belbin strategically positioned cameras in various points within the set, enabling her to pick up the characters as they walked from one room to the next. For most episodes, this meant using seven cameras – sometimes more – when the norm was four. 'It saved time,' states Belbin. 'Obviously using so many was expensive, but it was balanced by saving time in the studio.' She acknowledges that her working method posed additional challenges for members of her production team. 'I think the technical lads hated me at first, but they rose to the occasion. It's all right putting lots of cameras in the set, but where do you put the lamps and microphones? Eventually, though, everyone enjoyed working this way.'

The most cameras Belbin used was nine for 'Love and Death', the episode from Series Two which saw the

Normally programmes are rehearsed for five days and recorded on the sixth, and so that the cameramen and the rest of the crew involved are able to do their jobs a camera script has to be available for them the day before the recording. A camera script breaks down the writer's script into a sequence of pictures, and at the same time confirms which camera will take which picture. It normally runs to about three or four hundred different shots. This meant that, as the script needed to be typed and copied, it had to be produced at the end of the day I saw the programme for the first time. At first the script felt extremely thick (after a while one can usually guess the length of a script by its feel) but not knowing the speed of the actors' delivery I put that out of my mind. I'd worked with Richard Wilson before, but he was the only contact I had had with the programme – if you're a comedy director you normally watch other directors' programmes a couple of times, but only to see what the programmes are about or if they're doing something different. Not having

(Top) Renwick on set with the cast during the final series. (Bottom) The production designers did a sterling job on *One Foot*.

Meldrews staying at their friends' coastal guest house. The set required an upstairs, allowing the Meldrews to climb the stairs to their attic bedroom, so scaffolding was assembled. Being a complex set, it wouldn't be the easiest episode to record, particularly with nine cameras to coordinate. Rehearsals at the Acton rehearsal rooms were brought to a halt when Belbin received disturbing news: her mother had suffered a heart attack and the director was needed in Scotland. 'The doctor said: "No going home and packing bags; you get on a plane now."'

Just days before the studio recording, an experienced hand was required to cover for Belbin's absence, so distinguished director Sydney Lotterby was asked to step into the breach. The then head of comedy, Robin Nash, phoned him on the Wednesday, asking if he'd take over the programme. Lotterby recalls: 'I would start the next day as the rehearsals were in the middle of a six-day period.

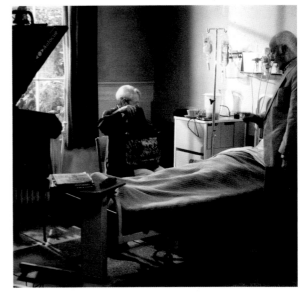

143

anything to do with the casting or the script, and at the time only being on nodding acquaintance with David Renwick, this would be a completely new programme for me.

'When I arrived at the rehearsal room I'm not sure who was taken aback the most: the actors hadn't been told I was taking over and I was terrified to see that there were,

it seemed, hundreds of scenes, which meant the studio would be crammed with scenery and dozens of actors, none of whom I knew. Apart from this, Susie had ordered and planned for nine cameras. I felt this rather excessive but it was the way Susie worked and as a visiting fireman I wasn't going to change anything just for change's sake.

'The next two days I spent trying to catch up. I didn't know the script – an absolute essential for any director – and hoped the actors wouldn't notice; if they did they were all too polite to say. My greatest difficulty was that not having studied the programme to any degree, I was not aware of how the principal actors reacted to various things. The attitudes of the visiting guest characters were usually quite obvious, but the leading actors were a different matter. However, I needn't have worried for both Richard and Annette were kindness itself and put me straight if I erred. Strangely, I don't remember David being around at rehearsals, which in retrospect is amazing, for he's one of those authors who's extremely possessive about his scripts. I can only put this down to the fact that if he was there, there couldn't have been any major differences between us. But I had enough troubles of my own – remembering everyone's

Rehearsals for the final series took place in a church hall just behind the Hammersmith fly-over.

names, and having to keep refreshing myself of the intricacies of the plot.

'The recording day is split into two parts: rehearsing with cameras, costume and lighting, and then the actual recording in front of the audience. The day went remarkably smoothly, thanks to the extreme professionalism of the cast and ability of the helpful crew. I think I managed to sort out the script in my mind, but I'm not sure how David took to my visual interpretation of it. It was never mentioned – he, I believe, is of a different school from myself – but here I had the advantage because he was unable to see how I'd shot the programme until it was too late. I'm sure the cast would have gained more direction if they'd had their usual producer, but when it had finished and I'd edited the programme (the script was too long), I'd enjoyed the programme as well as the challenge it had given me. And I came away feeling full of gratitude that so many professional people had helped me. Secretly I envied Susie being able to produce the series.'

By the time the episode was being recorded in front of the studio audience, Belbin had returned to London and was ready to begin work again. Taking over someone else's show is never an easy task, partly because each director has their own style of working, and the difference in styles is evident when comparing 'Love and Death' to the Belbin-directed episodes. Nonetheless, Lotterby had stepped in at the eleventh hour to resolve a problem and his experience prevented the episode's potential cancellation.

An aspect of the studio set that afforded the show a three-dimensional quality was the use of a fourth wall. Traditionally, sets were constructed with just three sides, leaving an opening through which the audience watched the action and the technical crew, including the cameramen, would operate. This format, however, restricted the angles at which the cameras could record the action. To overcome this obstacle, Belbin employed a fourth wall, a false structure erected in front of the set. Although it occasionally blocked the audience's view, it afforded the cameramen the opportunity to shoot back towards the audience, therefore providing a new angle. 'You're making a television programme, not a piece of theatre,' says Renwick. 'That's the difference: the fact the show is being made for people who subliminally, at least, feel they're inside a real house. Those rules were all broken, much to Susie's credit. Her leadership and confident approach were a huge factor in the show's success.'

Members of Belbin's technical team relished the idea of being associated with this innovative pro-

Rehearsal props were sometimes past their best by the day of recording.

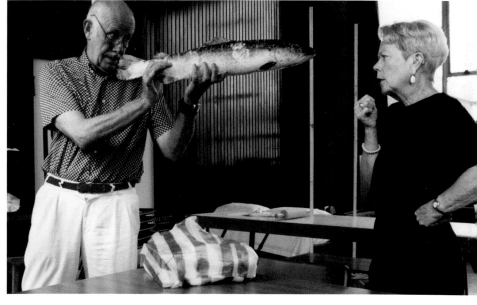

gramme. Laurie Taylor, sound supervisor on three series and two Christmas Specials, had the additional headache of knowing that Belbin disliked radio mikes. One of the most difficult areas of the set for fixing microphones was the staircase and hallway, and the view down the staircase towards the toilet and front door became one of its most recognisable shots. 'It was a confined space and we had to use fishing rods and booms stuck in all sorts of corners,' recalls Taylor, who admits that the more cameras used, the more complicated shooting became. 'As well as sound, lighting becomes more difficult because every light on the set casts a shadow somewhere; it's being aware of where the shadows fall. Everything requires discipline and a degree of forethought, which is very hard work. I had to provide sufficient public address for the audience, for them to hear and laugh. But if the whole thing became too open and echoey, it would no longer sound like someone's living room. To prevent this, I needed the microphones as close as possible to the people speaking. We were always treading a fine line.'

Taylor acknowledges that with Belbin shooting the episode as continuous action, rather than the more traditional stop-start method, extra pressure was placed on the cast and crew, testing their expertise to the full. 'There was incredible pressure, but that's the nature of the business,' he says philosophically. He points out that teamwork was crucial. 'It was a vast collaborative effort, and there had to be a clear set of ground rules regarding what had to be done.' Discipline was key in the show's success. 'If, for example, a cameraman was to panic and offer wider shots than in rehearsal, it might reveal other cameras and almost certainly the booms which were working to the edge of the shot. It affected the actors, too. If they weren't in the exact position they were expected to be, the whole thing could fall apart. Initially everything was set by the choreography and ability of the actors to get it right.'

The style was, in many respects, reminiscent of drama: the use of wider camera shots in the studio and on location, where other directors would have chosen to cut tight, helped make it a superior piece of comedy. John Record, film cameraman on Series Two and Three, and four Christmas Specials, didn't work in the studio, but whenever he watched an episode he enjoyed seeing Belbin's style of directing. He particularly liked how she'd linger on a scene, aiding the humour in the process. 'An example is that she'd allow Victor to walk through the front door, walk past and out of shot. Then you'd hear, "I don't believe it!" without Victor being in vision. She was brave enough to let the shot carry on, when a lot of directors would have cut to a close-up of Victor saying the line. The way Susie did it made the scene funnier.'

Leading lighting director Christopher Kempton worked on virtually every episode of the show. To help create the correct ambience inside the set, softer and more realistic sources of light were used. Kempton says:

'There was much more lighting through the windows of the house, and certainly fewer lights overhead than you'd normally have on a situation comedy. This was partly because Susie wanted, at times, to shoot up into the ceiling; normally, of course, you wouldn't have a ceiling on the set because the lights are there.' As with the microphones, finding convenient positions to place lights wasn't always easy, so when the set was changed between Series One and Two to accommodate the Meldrews' relocation, Kempton spoke to production designer John Asbridge, who was designing the new set. Although he realised continuity with the exterior of the house used in Bournemouth took precedence, he hoped Asbridge could incorporate some of his wishes. 'Big windows at each end, and glazed front and back doors so that light could come through even when it was shut, and a window in the downstairs toilet meant there were places where I could use light in a realistic way.'

The painstaking details, which helped shape the sitcom, were evident in Kempton's lighting, too, such as trying to reflect the passage of time via the colour and angle at which light entered a room. 'In most situation comedies it's either day or night and no one's interested in anything in between. But those details were important on *One Foot in the Grave*.' The passing of the day was particularly relevant in 'The Trial' from Series Four, where Victor found himself housebound while waiting to be called for jury service – a call that never came. To accentuate the wastage of time, Kempton used different colour light, such as blue to project a colder feel as the day wore on.

He feels the style of lighting was brave for its time, perhaps even pioneering. 'If you look at most of the sitcoms now, they're lit more in that style. Sometimes when I was afraid that perhaps I was doing too much in terms of lighting, David was always very encouraging. The more filmic and drama-like, the more he liked it.' Kempton, though, admits Renwick was, at times, exacting. 'Our schedule was very demanding: on recording day I'd start at seven in the morning, getting everything ready for rehearsals at ten. That went on until six in the evening, then we'd record in front of the audience at around half seven. David would sometimes turn up later in the day and want something altered, and although you could see his point, you wished he'd said it earlier because it would have made it easier to change. Fortunately, David generally liked what I did. Yes, you could see him getting frustrated at times, but he's a very charming man and was always quick to tell you when he liked something.'

When Kempton, who classes the show among the best he's worked on, joined the series, he'd only recently been promoted to lighting director, and believes he learnt much about his trade from his days on *One Foot*. 'When I look back at the first series, some of it looks pretty awful from a lighting point of view because I was trying, desperately, to do things that I hadn't done before. The lighting was much better in the next series.'

A whole year had passed since viewers had last seen the Meldrews on their screen. But the success of the previous year's Christmas Special, 'One Foot in the Algarve', meant Renwick was being pressurised to write another festive instalment. Not having a script in mind, he devised a plan in conjunction with director Susan Belbin, which would alleviate the need to pen a further script for the Christmas period. Transmission of the fifth series had been scheduled for Autumn 1994, but Renwick and Belbin decided to make the first episode, 'The Man Who Blew Away', forty minutes in length. By emphasising that the episodes must be shown in the intended order, it would force the BBC schedulers to begin the series at Christmas.

The opening episode was transmitted on Christmas Day. Although the inclusion of some snowy scenes added a seasonal touch, Renwick admits it wasn't a show he'd have designed for that time of year. 'It's listed as a Christmas Special, which in a sense it was because it went out on Christmas Day and got fifteen million viewers. But it was really a slightly bloated first episode.' The main thrust of the script was rather sombre, finishing on a downbeat note with news that an acquaintance of the Meldrews' has committed suicide. Victor and Margaret's lie-in was interrupted by a phone call from the loquacious Mr Foskett, whom the Meldrews met whilst holidaying at Weston-super-Mare seventeen years ago. Victor and Margaret were now rueing the day they suggested he pop in if ever in the neighbourhood. It was a troubled Mr Foskett, though, who arrived on their doorstep. With Victor and Margaret unable to get a word in edgeways, Foskett –

played by Brian Murphy of *George and Mildred* and *Last of the Summer Wine* fame – delighted in telling his audience that when his wife left him, he tried committing suicide thirteen times in the space of three years. Renwick, who's forever keeping viewers on their toes, used the cry-wolf scenario to good effect when upon hearing the shocking news that his second wife, Loretta, had deserted him, too, he later took his own life by jumping from a seventh-floor window at the police station, where he'd been taken after attempting suicide by climbing on to the Meldrews' roof. One's emotions endured a rollercoaster ride, though, because the closing scene showed the Meldrews becoming the recipients of an unexpected package, containing Mr Foskett's treasured collection of antique dentures, which he'd bequeathed to his friends for the kindness they exhibited when he needed it most. A touching finale, but as Renwick admits: 'It was never my intention to be that bleak on Christmas Day. The nation will probably not have thanked me, but that's the way it came about.'

Actor Brian Murphy, who was also cast in Renwick's *Jonathan Creek* before his character was killed off, was the result of the writer's principle of looking for

And as if that's not bad enough, he's taken Victor's chair.

'funny people'. Renwick explains: 'When we were throwing casting ideas around we often found ourselves looking back at classic sitcoms. That's how we ended up with Diana Coupland, who was in *Bless This House*, and Stephen Lewis and Michael Robbins, from *On the Buses*. These were actors who brought a great sense of character, and a natural gift for comedy. And Brian Murphy was always top of my list for Mr Foskett.'

> *I told Susie [Belbin] that at my age I'd done so many things, but being naked on screen was something I hadn't, so let's make it a first. Susie told me not to worry because she'd have the studio cleared, apart from the technicians, but I looked at her seriously and said: 'Don't worry about that, because when I take my clothes off, that will clear the studio.'*

BRIAN MURPHY

Murphy was delighted when asked to play the character; he'd become an avid fan of the show and admired Renwick's writing, particularly his predilection for treading into uncharted territories. Murphy had another reason for watching the show: he'd worked with Richard Wilson during the 1970s at the Oxford Playhouse, where Wilson co-produced a production of Gogol's *The Government Inspector*.

One of the scenes saw a naked Mr Foskett, who had clambered out of the Meldrews' bathroom window on to the roof, hanging precariously from the guttering. Clinging on, he steadily inched his way along, passing the Trenches' office window in the process, just as Patrick is meeting potential clients. 'We were in the studio and I was given a flesh-coloured codpiece to cover the naughty bits,' recalls Murphy. 'We started the recording but it soon became apparent that they were having problems. The codpiece was noticeable, so I agreed to remove it. I told Susie [Belbin] that at my age I'd done so many things, but being naked on screen was something I hadn't, so let's make it a first. Susie told me not to worry because she'd have the studio cleared, apart from the technicians, but I looked at her seriously and said: "Don't worry about that, because when I take my clothes off, that will clear the studio."'

When she took the material to the editing room, Belbin was left with a little touching up to do. 'We got Brian to stop so that his genitals were behind the upright of the window, but there was a tiny bit showing, so I had to paint it out electronically.'

Taking over the editor's chair from Chris Wadsworth was Mark Lawrence, who remained with the show until its conclusion. He'd previously worked with Belbin and on Renwick's *Alexei Sayle* series, although he'd never met the writer. Lawrence feels he learnt much from Renwick about the craft of editing. 'The first time I met David I was working on the Brian Murphy scene where he was swinging outside the window. David and Susie came up one lunchtime to have a look at it. I said: "I've edited this together, but didn't want to milk it too much." All David said was: "Why not?" I didn't have an answer to that! I've held that memory ever since, and as David pointed out, "If the audience are laughing and enjoying it, let them laugh and enjoy it." He was absolutely right, of course. David was one of the first people to really teach me anything about pacing: he's brilliant at just slowing everything down, to encourage the real humour. He's one of the few writers who could almost be an editor and director as well. He's so aware of the shots in progress.'

The opening instalment in the series met with a mixed reaction from the press. While Stephen Pile in the *Daily Telegraph* classed it as the 'best sitcom script of the season'[i], others weren't so impressed, with A. N. Wilson in its sister paper, the *Sunday Telegraph*, referring to an 'achingly unfunny Christmas *One Foot in the Grave*'[ii]. Meanwhile David Thomas in the *Sunday Express* was reflecting that 'life chez Meldrew seemed less outrageously entertaining than in days gone by.'[iii] And even the show's staunch supporter in the tabloids, Garry Bushell, writing in the *Sun*, felt *One Foot* was 'a let-down . . . the story was bitty, the dialogue fell well short of the visual gags and it all seemed to peter out like a duff indoor firework.'[iv]

The series continued on Sunday evenings, which under normal circumstances would be regarded as the prime slot in the schedules for any show. It was a slot Renwick fought over, although in hindsight he wishes he hadn't been so vigorous in his argument when he heard, during the summer of 1994, that Alan Yentob (controller of BBC1) was considering moving the show back to its earlier Thursday evening slot. When he arrived at Belbin's office at Television Centre on Tuesday, 12 July to be greeted by such news, he was irate. He later wrote: 'I threw a tantrum and said I might as well take my next project to Yorkshire then, and Susie was very supportive and immediately communicated my dismay to Martin Fisher, who sent a memo to Alan Yentob.'[v] Yentob responded quickly, advising Belbin that it wasn't definite and if Renwick wanted the show transmitted on Sunday evenings, then it would be. 'We had started out on Thursday evenings,' says Renwick, 'but Series Three and Four were shown on Sunday, which was where we got our biggest audience. And, of course,

with irresponsible vanity I regarded any kind of switch as a demotion.' A breakfast meeting between Yentob and Renwick was convened at the Halcyon Hotel in London's Holland Park on Friday, 18 November. Yentob's concern was to protect the show; he was worried that *A Touch of Frost*, which was transmitted by ITV on Sunday nights, was becoming increasingly popular and might affect *One Foot's* ratings. 'Rather foolishly, he did as I asked and put us out on Sunday nights anyway,' says Renwick, who acknowledges the decision led to a significant drop in his show's figures for the fifth season. Whereas Series Four had averaged 17.5 million, Series Five only pulled in just 12.5 million. It was still more than respectable, but losing five million viewers per episode was a major disappointment for Renwick, Belbin and the BBC.

With just over fifteen million watching 'The Man Who Blew Away', the series peaked at just under 16.5 million with the screening of Episode Two, 'Only a Story', which Renwick had originally planned in a completely different form. 'I thought it would be nice to write an episode based entirely upon Victor and Margaret discussing a detective show they had just watched on TV. I wanted to have a go at all those labyrinthine crime dramas my wife and I had sat through where you switch

From old Vic to Queen Vic: Barbara Windsor's next part would be in Eastenders.

off after two hours without the faintest clue how it was meant to fit together. We can't be the only couple who have sat there desperately trying to figure out who killed who and why, and whose head was it they found in the freezer, and – my favourite line in almost any episode — who was that dwarf in the bowler hat who kept running through the woods in slow motion? I think if I ever had to nominate a line of my dialogue that absolutely epitomised what I find funny that would be it. Anyway, after all the usual mental torture I realised I wasn't going to come up with enough material to sustain thirty minutes, so it ended up as just that one scene between Victor and Mrs Warboys.

Somewhere between the lamps and the turnips: Windsor and Wilson.

'The Affair of the Hollow Lady', which starred Barbara Windsor as redheaded green-grocer Millicent Miles, saw Victor being pursued by the flirty Miles, who got her comeuppance for daring to unsettle the Meldrews' relationship when Margaret clobbered her. Garry Bushell in the *Sun*, who'd classed the opening instalment of the series as 'below par'[vi], enjoyed this episode. As well as praising Windsor's performance, he felt Renwick had 'found his form'[vii].

A memorable feature in the episode was the lifelike waxwork model of Mrs Warboys. Jean, who was hospitalised after her car careered into a ditch while returning from her sister's in Blackpool, won the model as a prize. 'Mrs Warboys couldn't stand it, and nor could Doreen Mantle,' smiles Renwick. 'The irony was, it never looked as convincing on screen as it did in the flesh. The first time we saw it on location in Bournemouth it was just scary – absolutely, unspeakably funny because it was Doreen to a tee. But for reasons I've never been able to fathom, it never looked as accurate when it was photographed.'

Visual effects designer Chris Lawson coordinated the work, which entailed an alginate cast being taken of Mantle's hands and face. 'Taking an alginate of the face, for example, involved a cold water paste being mixed very thickly and slapped onto Doreen's face,' explains Lawson. 'That goes off in just over a minute, and then you put a plaster bandage on to hold it in shape. It's then carefully lifted off the face, leaving a perfect replica from which you can take an impression.'

Victor and Margaret were in reflective mood for the next episode, 'Rearranging the Dust', a script that impressed Richard Wilson so much that he tried persuading Renwick to use it for the Christmas Special instead of 'The Man Who Blew Away'. While waiting for what feels like an eternity to see a solicitor regarding making a will, Victor remarked that his buttocks were turning into 'fossilised fuel'. There was a series of incidents, including getting chewing gum stuck on his fingers, knocking a barometer off the wall and nearly demolishing the waiting room's glass-topped table, and a riled Margaret claimed it was worse than taking a child out for the day.

As their wait continued, the tone of the episode turned towards sentimentality: Margaret recalled the moment they first made love, before confessing a case of mistaken identity brought them together thirty-seven years ago, because there was a power cut and when the lights came back on she realised she'd grabbed the wrong man. Victor, who was usually quick to enunciate his views about life, especially those aspects that irritated him profusely, struggled to express his more intimate emotions. In a touching scene, he confided in his wife that she was his first choice. Spotlighting the difficulties people experience in revealing their true feelings, it was a surprised Margaret who, after considering her husband's confession, said: 'I suppose there are lots of things you never say but you think about saying, and something always crops up – life goes on. Somehow you never quite get round to putting it into words.'

Just as she turns to Victor, smiling, perhaps feeling the urge to reciprocate, someone walks into the waiting room, stopping her in her tracks. It was another lost moment in the lives of the Meldrews. Journalist Pam Francis, who'd changed her opinions of the programme over the years, reported: 'It was on the tip of Margaret's tongue to tell him how much she loved him. Not so much as we do.'[viii] At the *Sun*, Stafford Hildred felt Wilson was on 'hilarious form'[ix] but applauded Crosbie for stealing the show with her account of their first intimate moment together; he quoted Margaret's wonderfully funny lines: 'You took a long time to get going. You had your hand in my blouse for half an hour, twiddling with a wasp.'

Richard Wilson regarded it as 'particularly tender' when the characters showed their love. 'They were a contrasting pair but clearly joined to each other. It's a very Scottish thing in a way, that they weren't luvvy duvvies all the time. I'm not saying that is a good thing particularly, but it's that their love and trust for each other was just there – they didn't have to go around showing it all the time. I suppose I understand that in my own sphere: when my mother died my father was lost – he didn't know what to do. He'd depended on her, and their partnership. He didn't live a long time after my mother died.'

Among the audience on the night of recording was the BBC's new Head of Entertainment, David Liddiment, who'd joined from Granada, where as Director of Programmes he'd commissioned, among others, successful dramas *Cracker* and *Band of Gold*. Soon

> *David [Renwick] and I had set up this way of working, so we were doing our own thing and just forgot what the rest of the world were up to. We were quite innovative – not just in the writing, but in the way we produced it.*
>
> SUSAN BELBIN

after arriving at the corporation, Susan Belbin invited him to watch an episode of *One Foot* being recorded. She recalls: 'A few drinks were arranged to welcome him and I introduced myself. We got chatting and I said: "If you'd like to come and see a recording you're more than welcome. I know it's your job to do so, but I'd be pleased if you came along."' Liddiment chose to watch 'Rearranging the Dust', and was suitably impressed. 'I ran through thirty minutes in real time, with only a couple of little retakes at the end,' says Belbin. 'David [Liddiment] said he'd never seen anything like it done before in sitcom. I was surprised to hear him say that, because by then it was the norm for us. But then, David [Renwick] and I had set up this way of working, so we were doing our own thing and just forgot what the rest of the world were up to. We were quite innovative – not just in the writing, but in the way we produced it.'

Liddiment remembers watching the recording of this single-location episode, and being 'thrilled' with Belbin's approach. He says: 'She ran it like a live half-hour, which impressed me. Having been involved in several sitcoms before, I knew it was a strange hybrid form: it's the nearest thing to theatre on television, but with all the equipment and the stops and starts. The two things contradict each other because the audience come in to watch a performance and all they get is a fractured sequence of scenes or half-scenes. But the truth is, the public enjoy seeing the entrails of television studios and what goes on,

An irritating morning rehearsing this fifth episode – a prevailing attitude of 'everything we're doing is perfectly OK' which needled me because it certainly wasn't.

DAVID RENWICK

so that becomes part of the pleasure of being in a studio audience. Nevertheless, there is real added value if you do what Susie did, but that's only possible with a writer up to creating a half-hour that can be filmed that way. Overall, it was exciting to observe because it was like watching live TV.' Liddiment acknowledges it was a new approach to recording a sitcom, but says: 'In a way, it was a return to the way early sitcoms were made. Few programmes had the luxury of expensive editing in the early days of television, so were either transmitted live or telerecorded live and screened later that night or a few days later. It really was harking back to those days when essentially it was a live medium.'

Originally, David Renwick had a 'half-baked aspiration' to make 'Rearranging the Dust' a purely visual episode, which explains the abundance of visual business. Sadly, his attempt to write an episode in which no one actually speaks never came off because once again he couldn't dream up enough material. He didn't, however, experience that problem with Episode Five in the series, 'Hole in the Sky'. Although it remains one of his favourites, the production process was far from straightforward, as his diary entry for Thursday, 3 November reveals: 'An irritating morning rehearsing this fifth episode – a prevailing attitude of "everything we're doing is perfectly OK" which needled me because it

certainly wasn't. After a bite of lunch I waded in with Richard and Annette first of all, delivering a long list of performance notes, together with another meaty cut because we were still overrunning. The witch stuff has now all been removed, which is a shame conceptually, and it means I'll have to think of a new title for the episode. Still, it avoided my having to persuade Richard to say "*barley* sugars" instead of "barley *sugars*" which was killing the joke.'[x] Despite the constant challenges involved in preparing the episode for the day of recording, everything came together in the end, drawing a healthy response from the studio audience. Renwick was pleased with the outcome. Everyone had survived a stressful period, which was par for the course whilst working on *One Foot*. Renwick noted a conversation he'd had with Annette Crosbie in the BBC's Green Room, after the recording had finished, where she professed that 'in the thirty-eight years of her career this was the hardest thing she had ever had to do, because of the incredible precision required, and that sometimes she felt like a puppet and just did as she was told.'[xi]

David Renwick is aware that he's partly to blame if performers and crew regarded *One Foot* as one of their toughest jobs, but feels that quality is rarely achieved without effort. 'It's a wafer-thin line between confidence and arrogance,' he says, 'but I have to look back at all the shows and series I've done over the last thirty years and say that the more closely I've been involved or consulted in the production process the more successful they've been. For years I would meekly defer to the judgement of others when in my heart of hearts I knew that this piece of casting was a disaster, or that shot was far too tight for you to enjoy the humour of the situation, or that person's choice of stress in a sentence was completely killing the joke. And I've got all the tapes at home, where there's stuff I can hardly bear to watch because it offends me so much, because I just think – that could have worked, the potential was there on the page; it didn't have to be that embarrassing. But with *One Foot in the Grave*, because we all worked so much harder to get every particle of it right I'm actually very proud of the results. I think the heartache was worth it, and presumably there's some correlation between this and the popularity it has enjoyed.'

As recorded in his journal, the 'Hole in the Sky' script overrunning necessitated the cutting of a sequence and, consequently, eliminated the need for Renwick to approach Richard Wilson regarding the emphasis he required on the words 'barley sugars'. Renwick says: 'Thank God I didn't have to say anything to Richard about that one because he hated being given line readings. Some actors, like Janine, actually welcome it, but Richard never did. And that's fine, it just meant I had to learn what to say and what not to say.' An example of where Renwick felt Wilson was using an inflection incorrectly occurred in the 1996 Christmas Special, 'Starbound', when Mrs Warboys brought a stuffed cocker spaniel to the Meldrews' house. Victor, believing the dog was still alive, had built a kennel especially for the animal. 'He's standing there with this bowl of dog biscuits, open-mouthed with disbelief, and Mrs Warboys says: "I thought everyone knew about Nippy." And Victor's line is, "Well, I didn't!" All through rehearsals he was saying: "Well, *I* didn't" in a kind of plaintive, defensive sort of way, which for some reason wasn't funny. And it was just one of those instances where I couldn't find a logical route to my objection – it was totally intuitive. I could only say how I thought it should sound, which was not an option. And so I just trusted to luck, that on the night, when the audience reaction was driving him along, the sheer momentum of the exchange would somehow culminate in the correct delivery – which is exactly what happened. Once the scene had really taken off, with an energy of its own, Doreen says: "I thought everyone knew about Nippy," and Richard rasps back, "Well *I didn't!*" Both "I" and "didn't" equally stressed, with almost palpable venom, and for the first and only time it made me laugh.'

There were plenty of funny moments in 'Hole in the Sky', and Renwick is particularly fond of a sequence involving one of the McKendrick twins, played by Christopher Ryan, continually feigning injury at the Meldrews' house while working on their loft conversion. 'It's the cry wolf principle turned on its head. You present the viewers with a situation in which this guy is pretending to be horribly wounded, to wind Margaret up, then you repeat it, and now you assume it's for real, but Margaret isn't buying it any more. Then eventually she realises and goes into a complete panic – at which point you reveal that he was actually still faking it. That to me is what comedy is all about: confounding the expectations. Setting up a surprise element, then not delivering the surprise at all, which is actually a much better surprise.'

An equally busy offering in terms of its content was the closing episode in the fifth series, 'The Exterminating Angel', although surprisingly it recorded the series' worst audience figures at just under 10.5 million. In the episode Victor was employed, briefly, as a chauffeur, ferrying Lewis Atterbury around in his Merc, BMW and Jag, but a series of disasters soon found him receiving his cards. The fifth series contained its fair share of robust episodes, maintaining high standards in terms of scripts, production and acting. Although the BBC hierarchy reassured Renwick that the dip in audience figures wasn't a reflection on the quality of material, he realised his insistence on screening the episodes in the show's previous slot on Sunday evenings, against the advice of Alan Yentob, had seriously backfired.

Another of Renwick's comedy heroes from the sixties: John Bird in *The Exterminating Angel*.

CHAPTER 13
Crossing the Big Pond

The history of British television is littered with homegrown shows which seem to suffer travel sickness. Although the programmes achieve success here, they fail to shine when shown abroad. Such are the vagaries of television, it's never easy predicting which will succeed and which will disappear swiftly without trace.

Of those which attract interest from foreign television shores, the station's executives have to decide whether simply to screen the existing product using subtitles or consider making their own version of the programme. All too often, sadly, when a successful British television series is adapted for a foreign market, it loses much of its richness and vitality in translation. Styles of humour differ between cultures and, frequently, companies that set out to remodel the show's fabric to suit their viewers' tastes and attitudes end up with a product that is a wan shadow of its original.

Considering the success of *One Foot in the Grave*, it was inevitable that eager television executives would come calling to discuss acquiring rights. The show was featured at the 1993 Montreux Festival in Switzerland and topped many stations' wish-lists. Wolfgang Maier, of Germany's pay-per-view station VOX TV, was just one of those interested, declaring: 'This is the funniest show I have ever seen. Victor is fantastic. He is very British but we also understand him.'[i]

Many companies decided to employ subtitles and subsequently transmitted the programme in its original format, but a Swedish television channel was first to knock on Renwick's agent's door to discuss making their own version of *One Foot in the Grave*. The project never materialised and it was a German network that eventually became the first to adapt the show. A five-strong party from ARD Television flew to London and attended rehearsals at the BBC on Thursday, 13 October 1994. Suitably impressed, they reported back to their bosses and thirteen instalments were commissioned. Made by one of ARD's regional stations, Cologne-based WDR (Westdeutscher Rundfunk), two series of *Mit einem Bein im Grab* were transmitted between 1996–97, with a third season proposed but later cancelled. Donning typical Victor Meldrew attire, including cap and mac, was seventy-one-year-old German actor Heinz Schubert as Viktor Bölkoff, alongside Brigitte Böttrich as his screen wife,

Margret. Both performers' careers had been confined largely to their homeland, save for Schubert's appearance as Aaron Levine in the 1966 Michael Caine movie *Funeral in Berlin*. The sitcom, directed by Thomas Nennstiel and Frank Strecker, was shortlived.

The most successful adaptation, in terms of longevity and audience reaction, also received its first airing in 1996. In May 1995, Caryn Mandabach from the Carsey-Werner Company in America contacted Renwick's agent, Brian Codd, to discuss securing the American rights.

The broadcaster's major successes included *The Cosby Show*, starring the legendary comedian Bill Cosby, and they saw an adaptation of Renwick's sitcom as the perfect vehicle to entice Cosby back to the small screen. By the beginning of July, agreement had been reached and Renwick jetted off to New York to meet Mandabach and her then colleagues, Tom Werner and Marcy Carsey. The following day, over breakfast at the Carlyle Hotel, they talked about the project: it was during the meeting that Renwick discovered that Cosby's name was in the frame to play the lead role. When asked for his views about the comedian's suitability, Renwick said he regarded him as ideal for the part. That evening, everyone dined at Cosby's New York home, and as every hour passed, Renwick became increasingly convinced that Cosby – whom he recalled seeing in the 1978 Neil Simon film, *California Suite*, playing the irascible Dr Willis Panama – was right. 'I had no doubts at this stage about his suitability for the project, based on his personal charm and his insight into what sorts of things were funny.'[ii] Renwick believes Cosby had reached that point in his life when the premise of the sitcom was particularly relevant. 'The concerns, frustrations and irritations of life generally must have appealed. His comedy has always been based upon observation, as well as the broader aspects of social interaction and relationships.' Everyone was trying to entice Cosby back to television because of his audience appeal and the fact that his original sitcom, *The Cosby Show*, had been arguably the most successful sitcom in America. Renwick believes Cosby knew this was a good vehicle to mark his return.

The programme was appropriately titled *Cosby* and saw the comedian playing Hilton Lucas and Phylicia

Rashad his wife, Ruth, practically reprising their roles as Dr and Mrs Huxtable from *The Cosby Show*. As the project developed, it became clear that Carsey-Werner wanted Renwick to play an active role in the programme. In his journal, he wrote: 'Caryn and Tom say they are still very keen on my work and want me to be fully involved as a "partner" in all this. They say I should now think more as an executive producer rather than a writer, as we try to decide the best way forward. They've read my script and their reaction seems to be a rather guarded one, saying cryptically that some things could work and some couldn't . . . They asked me yet again if I couldn't see myself relocating to NY for six months in order to devote myself more fully to the series. And I had to explain that my method of writing is too slow and insular for me to be of any use to them . . . Meanwhile they would keep me in the picture about how it was all progressing and would be grateful for any input I could offer. I put the phone down feeling quite relieved.'[iii] Renwick didn't entertain thoughts of uprooting to New York to play a key role in writing the scripts. 'I couldn't have done that,' he says. 'I was happy for them to send the scripts for me to comment on, which is how it worked for the first season. Scripts were faxed, I'd read them and fax notes back to the writers.' Renwick worked through each script with a fine-tooth comb, commenting in detail, but he says: 'I don't think many of my suggestions were ever implemented.'

The similarities between *One Foot* and its US spin-off *Cosby* were sometimes less than obvious.

As the first season reached its climax, Renwick and his wife, Ellie, spent a week in America, observing the team at work. 'They were a great bunch of people, and it was fascinating to watch. Everyone said they were thrilled to meet us and enjoyed receiving my notes each week. David Landsberg, the head writer, laid the essential problem on the line to me: Cosby does what he wants, basically. Most of the changes are entirely random; he will reject parts of the script halfway through the week simply because he's grown bored with them, and apparently forty per cent of the show is improvised. "It's like jazz," he said. "Giving him a script is like saying this week it's in the key of C." If you ever heard him do one of the jokes they'd written it was a real event. The general consensus was – we love your faxes, you're very often right and it's nice to hear from someone who knows, but there's not a cat in hell's chance any of it will ever be put into practice. They seem, though, to be full of admiration for his comic genius, his ability to pull any show out of a hole, and his general niceness.'

Tom Werner, however, confirms Cosby, the writers and producers always collaborated. He says: 'I've never enjoyed a healthier, more creative relationship in all my years producing American series.'

Landsberg, reflecting on Werner's comments, says: 'I can see how Tom would say that, because he was in Los Angeles getting more shows on the air while my staff and I were in New York facing the everyday problems created by "shoot from your hip" rewriting and improvising. Tom rarely made an appearance in New York, and when he did his comments, although sincere and sometimes constructive, usually careened like a driverless race car into the writer's pit crew who now faced at best a complete rewrite, if not a totally new story and script. Much like war, there are those in Washington DC who give their thoughts and opinions, and those who face the actual battles that those thoughts and opinions create. All in all it was a wonderfully difficult and rewarding two years. I got to work with some incredibly talented writers, actors and crew. I made a terrific salary. I got to know and have a warm relationship with David and Ellie Renwick, and of course spend day after day in both admiration, affection and occasionally fear of one of the most influential comedians of my generation.'

The pilot episode was transmitted by CBS on 9 April 1996, the beginning of a four-season run. The premise followed a similar track to *One Foot in the Grave*, with Cosby playing a man who loses his job in the aviation industry unexpectedly and suddenly finds he has plenty of time on his hands. Many of the episodes in Season One were loosely based on Renwick's original scripts. 'In the first half-dozen or so there was quite a lot of my material. But there were

fifteen writers employed on the show and gradually I noticed all the dialogue I had suggested was being stripped away. In the end, the only thing left that was recognisable from *One Foot in the Grave* was the cap.

They asked me yet again if I couldn't see myself relocating to NY for six months in order to devote myself more fully to the series.

DAVID RENWICK

Still, I continued receiving a weekly credit and a royalty, which proved very lucrative.'

Despite early shows containing some of Renwick's input, many critics writing for papers this side of the Atlantic failed to spot similarities with *One Foot*. Quentin Letts, writing in *The Times* days after the American public were introduced to 'a sanitised, scrubbed version of Victor Meldrew'[iv], felt that having secured the rights, 'American television chiefs set about ruining the product.'[v] He believed that the 'cutting edge of the comedy was left on the cutting-room floor'[vi] and while based on *One Foot*, it was 'impossible to tell that they came from the same source'[vii].

Tom Werner, however, believes that any successful series is a 'meld between the actor and the character and the writing, and a carbon copy of Victor Meldrew didn't fit either Mr Cosby or American television.' He adds: 'What inspired us was the tone David Renwick brought to the project, and the fact that many people are given so little respect as they age.'

For four years, *Cosby* entertained the American public, and for CBS having a luminary like Bill Cosby appearing regularly was a major boost for their schedules. 'I believe *Cosby* – while never reaching the amazing ratings levels of *The Cosby Show* – was quite a successful series. We made ninety-six episodes, which is remarkable for any project – most never even get picked up for a second year. As for what *Cosby* meant to CBS, it did quite well on their network for four years and the show that followed it, which inherited our great lead-in, was none other than *Everybody Loves Raymond.*'

The show evolved during its four-year run and by 1998 a reporter in *TV Guide*, previewing the forthcoming season, wrote: 'New executive producer Tom Straw is aiming for a more familiar Cosby-sitcom tone, reducing the farcical elements and stressing stories about Hilton's surrogate family.'*viii* Straw added: 'When you have Bill and Phylicia, you don't need plot after plot.'*ix* As the reporter noted, 'We feel such a comfort level with Cosby – and for that matter, Rashad – that the show's lack of focus hardly matters.'*x*

It's rare for a homegrown programme to be Americanised and remain, in British people's eyes, a satisfactory product. But for the Americans, seeing the programme for the first time, the sitcom was welcomed. Its arrival met with almost universal approval from American critics. A reporter in *Variety* enthused: 'There's something immensely reassuring about the combination of Bill Cosby and television'*xi*, while a contemporary at the *New York Times* reported that 'Cosby's new comedy may not take off instantly, but it holds plenty of promise. It's Cosby, so it's funny, that's probably sufficient.'*xii*

When the show premiered in September 1996 (by which time the chief writer and original co-star, Telma Hopkins, had already been replaced) nearly seventeen million viewers tuned in. Of the wife's early recasting Tom Werner says: 'We felt America loved the relationship between Bill Cosby and Phylicia Rashad, and that any other pairing would inevitably be compared to the wonderful chemistry these two share. There were some risks in the reteaming, but we saw it as comparable to reuniting Fred Astaire and Ginger Rogers in movie after movie.'

It was the highest-rated comedy series screened in the 8 p.m. slot since, ironically, *The Cosby Show* earned a

thirty-nine per cent share of the audience for NBC in 1994. But the figures didn't remain so buoyant and although it enjoyed a four-year life, Renwick wasn't surprised when the curtain finally came down. 'The ratings nose-dived, deservedly so in my opinion. The show became so flabbily indulgent you couldn't even tell what Cosby was trying to achieve any more. He was clearly trying to educate his audience through the series – one episode involved a fairly tedious dialogue between Bill and William Shakespeare – which is all very worthwhile, but not at the expense of the entertainment.'

While acknowledging it's laudable to try and raise an audience's attitudes and beliefs through television, Renwick points out that it's crucial a balance is struck. 'Cosby's son, Ennis, was tragically murdered during the first season, which was incredibly traumatic. You could understand why he would want to wage this personal crusade to elevate the aspirations of the black population of America, to show them that, yes, blacks can be successful professional people. Nothing wrong with the message, but you have to make it palatable – good comedy with a good story.'

'Like jazz': Renwick once watched Cosby improvise for fifteen minutes during a live recording.

CHAPTER 14
The Specials

1998 TRIC AWARDS
ONE FOOT IN THE GRAVE
CHRISTMAS SPECIAL

By the time the episode 'The Exterminating Angel' closed Series Five, viewers had been house guests of the Meldrews on thirty-three occasions. David Renwick had provided over seventeen hours of scripts and writing an entire series each year was becoming increasingly difficult. 'It was starting to feel like I was on this treadmill, and the only way off was to reroute my energies into something else.' The BBC, though, was anxious to retain not only a programme which was one of its most treasured assets in the winter schedules, but also a highly respected writer who had become a fine exponent of his art. A compromise was struck and Renwick agreed to write a Christmas Special. As it transpired, he ended up writing festive shows for the next three years. 'I really think they're among the best shows we ever did,' says Renwick. 'Writing at greater length enables you to develop the stories in more interesting ways, with basically more twists and turns in the plots. It's a completely different form, and although the discipline of keeping it tight and funny is the same you find that the overall scale of the thing demands more thought and skill. To be honest, it always ended up feeling as if I'd written a whole series, because the work involved was enormous.'

The first of the Specials, 'The Wisdom of the Witch', was transmitted on Christmas Day 1995. On the eve of the Meldrews' thirty-seventh wedding anniversary, a nightmare was seemingly unfolding before their eyes. While dining at a Chinese restaurant, Margaret explained to Victor that an unexpected meeting with a witch hadn't augured well for his future: not only would he be visited by a plague of devils, his life could meet a sudden end, so he was advised to avoid long journeys. Unfortunately, though, he's unable to postpone the hundred-mile trip to sort out the rambling country house left by his recently-departed cousin Ursula.

Nearly a year had elapsed since the actors last played their characters. Switching roles and adopting a plethora of personalities is par for the course in the acting profession, but it's easy to underestimate the effort and concentration involved. Even though a character is familiar, revisiting that person, particularly after a lengthy period, is challenging – even for an actor of Richard Wilson's calibre. When filming began at the end of September 1995, it took a moment for Wilson to rediscover Victor. While filming the Chinese restaurant scene, when a fellow diner's booming voice irritated Victor, Susan Belbin realised something was wrong. 'It just wasn't happening. David and I looked at each other and I said: "Richard has lost it; he's left Victor in London." Actors, especially those like Richard, are hugely professional and work very hard. You don't want to upset them, so I took it upon myself to tell him privately. We broke for lunch early so I ushered him behind the make-up caravan and said he hadn't brought Victor with him. Richard hadn't realised, but when we reshot the scene, everything was fine – Victor was back.'

'It was Richard speaking rather than Victor. There was no real edge; he was just saying the lines,' adds Renwick, who observed in his journal that day: 'An uncharacteristically flat performance from Richard . . . by lunchtime we still hadn't got a version that worked, and I said Susie would have to have a quiet chat with him and then we could remount

Patrick's 'Ronald Coleman' moustache needed constant attention in 'The Wisdom of the Witch'.

Patrick's lunch with his secretary (Joanne Engelsman) lands him in a spot of bother.

Even a show as slick as *One Foot in the Grave* isn't exempt from occasional technical hitches or accidents. A scene at cousin Ursula's house, where Patrick and Victor have fetched up for the weekend, sees Victor tangling with the thuggish boyfriend of Patrick's new secretary. In the ensuing struggle, they fell from a bedroom window on to the roof of the conservatory below. The stuntman hired to portray Victor was the experienced Gabriel Cronnelly, who frequently doubles for, among others, Sean Connery. Among those watching was make-up designer Vanessa White. 'I remember he didn't want his hair cut too short because he was attending his daughter's wedding the next day, so as he was playing Victor, I put a bald cap on him.' While preparing the conservatory roof with artificial snow, it collapsed and was rebuilt swiftly, ready for the stunt. 'The stuntmen were going to fall through the roof and land on cardboard boxes. The new glass, though, hadn't collapsed as planned. It repelled them a bit and Gabriel cut his face. Blood was everywhere. The cuts were mostly superficial but the ambulance was called, just in case. Thankfully he was all right and able to attend the wedding.'

the scene in the afternoon. I don't know what she said during the lunch break, but when we did it again he seemed to lock back into the character with more energy, and actually made me laugh again. It confirms my general philosophy that the only way you can remain successful is to remember how close you always are to failure.'[i]

Renwick says he enjoyed the restaurant scene because it highlighted one of his favourite dynamics between the two characters: Margaret's indifference to Victor's terror. 'During the meal she talks about this male witch she's met in the sweet shop, who's predicting all these dire misfortunes that will befall Victor, completely oblivious to the effect it's all having on him. The way she just breezily lobs in expressions like "the wrath of Lucifer" – as if it's an everyday event that needn't concern him, and you can feel his blood's running cold while she's more preoccupied by her chopsticks. Another situation like that, which I always enjoyed, was when he's just got up one day and she walks in through the back door and says the whole street was evacuated during the night because of an unexploded bomb. And all the alarming details are just thrown away as she bustles about, getting the milk in, while Victor's reduced to a gibbering wreck.'

White was another member of the production team given her first designing job by Susan Belbin. Two series of Paul Mayhew-Archer's newspaper-based sitcom, *Nelson's Column*, were transmitted between 1994–95, and Belbin, who produced both series as well as directing the first, gave White her big break. 'Susie was always ready to give a helping hand. In those days, it was hard moving up the BBC career ladder, and many of us have Susie to thank for giving us a start.' On *One Foot*, when the previous incumbent, Jean Steward, was promoted to a managerial post, White, who'd worked on the show as Steward's assistant, stepped up to become make-up designer. The first episode she was responsible for was 'The Man Who Blew Away', which she'll never forget. 'On the first morning I picked up my gas hair tongs the wrong way and promptly burnt my hand. So there I was, the new make-up designer standing around with my hand in a small bucket of cold water!' She enjoyed working on the programme, though. 'I loved it. Having been the assistant, taking over wasn't too difficult because I'd made up the majority of the cast before.' She classes sitcoms as a 'nice, gentle entrance into the world of design', although acknowledges there was an intensity associated with *One Foot*, thanks mainly to the exacting

Artificial snow and a wind machine were used to create a seasonal atmosphere for 'The Wisdom of the Witch'.

standards set by David Renwick. 'The visual side of the show definitely came from David, rather than Susie [Belbin] or Chris [Gernon], when she took over. He thought about his characters so intensely that he knew exactly what he wanted. I realised that if we were shooting when David wasn't around, it was likely we'd end up reshooting something, so I'd always take lots of continuity photos!'

'The Wisdom of the Witch' was watched by just under seventeen million, the highest audience for the three Specials shown between 1995–97. Sam Brady on Teletext classed the episode as the only special that year which lived up to expectations. Even before its screening, Alan Yentob had contacted Susan Belbin about further instalments. Ideally, he wanted another

series, but at the very least another Special for 1996. Although he wasn't prepared to write an entire run, Renwick agreed another Special. He began working on 'Starbound' in May 1996, and it was the usual struggle. In his journal, he wrote: 'Desperately trying to conjure up Victor thoughts and once again drawing a total blank. Feeling at an absolute low ebb, that panic-provoking void wherein you just drift about aimlessly without any feel of "funny" inside you, so all you end up doing is mechanically flitting from subject to subject, in the certain knowledge that that lateral comic curve will prove completely elusive.'[ii] The next few days were more productive, but by the following week he was still wrestling with the episode's central premise. A month later, and he continued battling with the script's structure. 'Hideously difficult trying to arrange all these disparate thoughts into some sort of a whole. I found myself typing up running order after running order, amending and adjusting each time to create some kind of overall story texture, but by the end of the day I can't really say that it had come. I convinced myself there was one element too many, took out the guy in the shed, then put him back in again, then in a panic about the possible objections to the cocaine strand I removed the stuff with Victor behaving strangely after his first day's exposure. Generally I just ended up not knowing where I was on it.'[iii]

But, as always, the script finally gelled and after Susan Belbin gave it the thumbs-up on 20 July, thoughts turned to casting and filming the exterior scenes in Dorset, which were completed during the last week of September and the first week of October. As always, it wasn't plain sailing, and while filming the opening scenes on the Isle of Purbeck, a livid David Renwick stormed off and returned to the hotel. The sequence that prompted this saw Mrs Warboys driving along a country road after picking up the Meldrews from the airport. They had returned from a disastrous weekend in Hamburg, and to top it all Victor's hernia was playing up and he was feeling travel sick. The car was fixed on a low-loader, enabling the cameraman to film through the front of the vehicle, but things weren't running smoothly. Renwick noted: 'Doreen, after being word perfect on an earlier line-run, was suddenly very erratic, prompting a host of notes when we came to a halt. Richard and Annette were also corrected on a couple of speeches, and through my headphones I heard Annette comment dryly: "Yes, I'm sure people will be switching off in their thousands because I got those two words the wrong way around." I relayed this to Susie, who misguidedly told them she could hear every word they were saying – provoking a rebellious chorus from the actors of, "We don't care!" And that was enough for me. I just jumped off the trailer and got in my car and left them to get on with it. Later on, Doreen rang back at the hotel saying she was sorry I'd been upset, which was gracious of her. But it's fair to say it was a day when tempers got more than a little frayed.'[iv]

Doreen Mantle remembers the day well. 'The morning was taken up in attaching the car to the low-loader. It was ready near lunchtime, and we drove out into Poole. The roads, however, were too noisy and busy to be able to film, so after lunch the unit moved by ferry to the Isle. It was mid-afternoon before work started. The roads were narrow, and we had to drive from the base for about ten minutes to a roundabout to turn us around and be able to film. I had three pages of monologue punctuated by a single interjection from Margaret [Annette Crosbie], and had to chew a green Opal Fruit before removing it at a certain point to demonstrate the colour of a fellow passenger's face from air-sickness when I'd been travelling in the U.S. We had no rehearsal, and on the first take I'd finished the sweet before reaching the line. Susie suggested I mime the chewing on the next take and pop the sweet into my mouth just before the line. The miming slowed up the dialogue, so I went back to chewing and used two sweets. There was almost half an hour between each take as the car had to journey up to the roundabout, et cetera. Time was moving on, the light was changeable, it was hot and stuffy in the car and we seemed to spend a lot of time at base inside the car while technical adjustments took place. It was then that poor Annette had her outburst over the missing words in her line. On a perfect take for me, Susie said I had lost my sparkle, so I had to go again – it wasn't a good afternoon. And when the scene was shown the sweet bit was cut. I haven't touched an Opal Fruit since!'

> *On a perfect take for me, Susie said I had lost my sparkle, so I had to go again – it wasn't a good afternoon.*
>
> DOREEN MANTLE

Annette Crosbie's comments were triggered by a note passed to her when instead of uttering the line, 'Best not to remind him of it, I think, Jean,' she said, 'Best not to remind him, I think, Jean.' She appreciates, however, that Renwick wrote the scripts so knew precisely how it should look and work. 'To my mind, everybody should be grateful and always try their best. I think it's sad if people can't accommodate that. It's just that that day the car was on a low-loader which meant we couldn't open the doors; it was hot and we were sitting behind the glass, boiling. The scene had taken some time owing to interruptions, which meant we kept getting notes. I got more and more tight-lipped, and nobody ever said: "Sorry, we're going to have to do that again." You couldn't even have a five-minute break because it was impossible to get out of the car. That's the one time on the show I lost my temper.'

Renwick wasn't immune to criticism but had slaved over his scripts for so long, concentrating on, among other features, rhythm, and didn't allow deviation, unless it improved the original. The accidental omission of two words from Crosbie's line brought the day's frustrations to a head. Doreen Mantle found such attention to detail made filming nerve-racking, although she recently played Mavis Bledsoe in an episode of Renwick's latest project, *Love Soup*, and missed having the writer around. 'On the day I went in to play my part, David couldn't be there and I missed him very much. I think I'd come to realise how secure he can make you feel, partly because he knows exactly how a joke should work.'

It wasn't the first time Renwick had walked off the set, having already left proceedings when the bee sequence in Series One wasn't going to plan. Susan Belbin, meanwhile, had no alternative but to continue filming and catch up with Renwick later. 'Had he not been the writer he is, and I respected him so much for that, it could have been a very different scenario. If he'd been an awful writer, I would have told him to forget it, but I put up with it because of his ability, his inventiveness and his eye for detail.'

As far as Renwick is concerned, actors are given a script and it's their job to learn it, not to paraphrase. 'I think there's a very clear distinction,' he says, 'between the wilful rewording of a speech by an actor who has given the material a lot of thought, and believes he's improving something, and the kind of approximation that occurs when they basically can't get the words to go

If he'd been an awful writer, I would have told him to forget it, but I put up with it because of his ability, his inventiveness and his eye for detail.

SUSAN BELBIN

into their head. Learning lines is a hideously difficult process – I would never pretend otherwise. But I've found over the years that the most gifted performers, certainly those with a flair for comedy, just know intuitively when they've said the wrong word, or inverted something or missed something out, because the rhythm's all wrong, and they can sense that it didn't

work. Ronnie Corbett always used to say to me that he had no problem learning a last-minute topical joke I'd written for him and going onstage that night to deliver it, because there was a certain syntax to the way it was phrased which made it funny, and that was the only way it *was* funny.

'The curious thing is that one of the imperatives for me in writing dialogue is to make every speech as comfortable as possible for the actor to say. So I'm incredibly conscious of the way one word ends and whether it will segue easily into the next, or whether there's one syllable too many in a particular phrase. And you do all that, and then a lot of actors will just paraphrase the line so it becomes incredibly cumbersome. For me, dialogue generally falls into two categories: there are speeches where all you need is to get an effect or some kind of emotion across. In those cases it's not a big deal to me whether the performer says exactly what I've written or something close. It may be a moment of great passion or excitement and whatever they come out with, so long as they're in character, you're happy to go with the flow. The rest of the time, my rule is simple. If you come up with a stronger alternative to what's written, fine. Given that I find it next to impossible to string any sequence of words together I am amazed at how hard it is for anyone else to do better.

But they so rarely do. And I suppose the only difference is that I've sat there for hours and hours to come up with my version, whereas they're usually just busking it, off the top of their head. I'm aware it sounds arrogant, but the analogy to me is a concert violinist just arbitrarily changing some of the notes around. I suppose you can make a case for the free-form jazz approach of people like Mike Leigh, but that's not a form that appeals to me. I just think, why bother to be a writer at all in that case.'

One of the principal storylines involved Patrick, whose job was on the line, trying to impress his new man-eating boss, Fenella Fortune, including letting himself be molested on a bed of tomatoes. But he couldn't believe his eyes while attending a meeting at Fortune's sumptuous home and spotting Victor, employed as a gardener. Unusually full of the joys of spring, Victor's happiness was a result of him unknowingly inhaling drugs. He merrily tore around the garden on the ride-on mower, as high as a kite, inadvertently taking a wrong turn into the house. The mower chewed up the shag pile carpet. And if that wasn't bad enough for Ms Fortune, she watched in dismay as a car, driven by drug dealer Millichope, crashed into her grand summerhouse. It was a dramatic climax to the episode and a gargantuan exercise for everyone, particularly the special effects and production design teams. Renwick classed it as a 'great team effort'[v].

After a lengthy search for a suitable location, production designer Linda Conoboy recalls coordinating the collapsing of the forty-foot summerhouse. 'We struggled to find somewhere, so got on with all the other scenes. On the last day of the first block filming we had a meeting and I said: "Look, I've seen some photographs of a place you've rejected without even seeing it. I think we should take a look." When we did, we knew it could work.'

It was a pressurised sequence to film because everyone had only one chance to get it right. 'It was amazing how it turned out,' says Conoboy. 'The car looks like it crashes into the summerhouse but it didn't hit the structure at all. We got the summerhouse to collapse by explosives and wires, pulled by an out-of-shot Land Rover. We cut out the flash of the explosion, which was only a couple of frames, so you couldn't tell when the sequence was run. Remarkably, there wasn't a scratch on the vehicle and we were able to sell it on.'

Along with Nick Somerville, Conoboy was the longest-serving production designer on the series. She enjoyed her time on the show, particularly working with Belbin and Renwick, whom she respects for speaking their minds. 'You knew where you stood, and they were always there if you wanted advice. Some people were in awe of Susie, probably because she was, arguably, the only female comedy producer at the time. When I first worked with her, I expected a dragon bearing down on me, but she was a nice, funny, friendly person who's easy to be with. We hit it off from the beginning. I respected her professionally because she knew what she wanted. We had a laugh, of course we did, but work came first – and quite rightly.

'That's how I found the whole team. With David, you could always talk straight to him. Yes, he could get upset if people weren't pulling their weight or listening to the details he gave. He was always upfront from the start, making it clear what he wanted. I'd always try my best, but if it seemed impossible it was important you told him. In one episode, Victor was given a glass paperweight with a scorpion in it. David's description of what it should look like was very detailed, but we struggled getting it to look effective. In the end, I just said: "David, this is proving impossible to make – where did you get the idea?" It turned out he had one at home and agreed to lend it to us. Sometimes it was as simple as that, but if ever you had difficulties, it was best to be frank, not surprise him on the day of filming. He didn't want us saying: "Okay, you said blue car but we could only get a grey one." The fact it was blue would always be relevant. If you paid attention to the detail in the script, it saved a lot of bother in the end. We benefited from having the scripts well in advance. With *One Foot in the Grave* we were making a very particular, detailed product, and it had to be just so.'

Cast as the vampish Fenella Fortune, a role that Renwick originally thought suitable for Joanna Lumley, was Rula Lenska. She says: 'It's rare that you receive a script which makes you laugh while reading it, but that's what happened – especially the scene where Victor enters the room on a lawnmower.' For Lenska, it was an honour being offered a part in the Christmas Special, particularly as *One Foot* has always been one of her favourite comedy shows. 'Starbound' afforded her the chance to work with Richard Wilson again. 'I've

Patrick and his man-eating
boss, Fenella (Rula Lenska).

Owen Brenman, who played
Nick Swainey, feels actors should
have been warned. 'I don't know if
they were, but it's possible someone
could be thrown by the attention to
detail in *One Foot*. I went to an
audition recently and asked the
writers if they minded me adding
the occasional "hmmm" or "ah".
They were okay with that, but with
David, you'd need a bloody good
reason to start putting them in his
lines!'

Janine Duvitski says that
everyone admired Renwick's
writing, and that he was always
right. 'I was full of admiration for
him and accepted what he said. At
times, I might think: "Oh God,
there's David. I'm going to get this
line wrong and he'll pick up on it."

known him a long time, so
when asked to do this with
Richard, it was a delight. It
wasn't a huge role, but was a solid part in a very funny
episode.'

She recalls the scene with Victor riding the mower
into the meeting room. 'We were sitting with the French
doors open and I had my back to what was already
telegraphed to the audience. I sat opposite Angus'
character, whom I was flirting with under the table,
running my foot up and down his leg. Seeing his reaction
to what was going to happen, it was difficult stopping
myself having a fit of the giggles. Although I couldn't see,
I knew what would happen. It was great fun,' says Lenska,
who admits she was pre-warned about having to be word-
perfect. 'I can't remember who told me – it could have
been Richard. But someone told me that every line had to
be spoken word for word. It's unusual in television, or in
non-classic writing, for a writer to be that adamant. Even
conjunctions had to be perfect. It made one much more
diligent about learning one's lines. It wasn't hardship for
me because it was a one-off, but I imagine that in a whole
series, having to be absolutely true to every single word
the author had written could become a bit of a problem.'

But he's right to pick up on it, even if it's just one word.
At the time you think: "Goodness, it's only a word!"
But I'm terrible at getting odd words wrong, so I welcomed his comments. Sometimes, though, he would
say he was pleased, and then you were thrilled. He
wasn't a gushy kind of man, so if he did say something,
you felt extremely happy.'

Being a writer himself, Angus Deayton agreed with
Renwick's drive to see his lines uttered as written. He
says: 'David and I came from the same stable. We'd
both initially been writers on radio and had similar
styles and senses of humour. I always have great
sympathy for writers because I know what it's like:
you've written something and then see actors
completely wreck it. It's difficult asking them politely to
do it in a different way. David was meticulous about the
stage directions in the text, so you'd often get things
underlined. I remember a line, "Good morning, Mr
Meldrew." The word "morning" was underlined. I
thought: "How else would you say: 'Good morning,
Mr Meldrew' without emphasising 'morning'?" That
was one of the more pointless underlinings, but
generally the stage notes were truthful to the way David
heard it in his head. I was in sympathy with that, but

some actors find it slightly offensive. It's a very precise art: if you get just one inflection or word wrong, the whole line is messed up. He was very careful about things and that's part of his unbelievable success.'

Deayton admits, though, that occasionally Renwick's timing for passing notes could have been better. 'He'd usually be there at the read-through, then the Tuesday but wouldn't necessarily be around for rehearsals on Wednesday, Thursday or Friday. He'd turn up next on Saturday for the recording, and you could be passed a note some half an hour before going on. We had done the tech run that afternoon, by which time you'd got all the words and movements bedded in your head, then suddenly you'd get this list of points. It was much worse for Richard because he was in more scenes. He'd suddenly find he had a dozen notes just before recording the show.' However, Deayton adds that you always respect someone who's

Richard Wilson gets to grips with a lawnmower, watched by costume designer Richard Winter.

enjoyed the level of success Renwick has. 'You respect their opinions, but in addition to that, everyone is working to make the programme as good as possible, so the reason he gives notes is to make the performances better, not for any other reason.'

Renwick's insistence on aiming for perfection ruffled a few feathers occasionally, but as Gareth Gwenlan points out, 'Most people who are professional wouldn't object.' He regards Renwick as an 'amazing writer'. 'He's incredibly hands-on. Not only is he clever, particularly with comedy, but he always has a firm vision of how it should look and sound. A lot of writers don't – some haven't even got any ideas about casting.' Reviewing the success of the show, one of its assets, says Gwenlan, was the strength of Belbin and Renwick's working relationship. 'They had to trust each other – and did. Susie was very good at handling David. Sometimes he can be slightly obsessive about his work, but for the right reasons: he cares deeply about what he writes.'

As he settled down with his wife, Ellie, on Boxing Day to watch 'Starbound', one of his favourite episodes, Renwick was impressed by the opening shot showing what appeared to be a glowing planet set against a backdrop of twinkling stars turn into Victor's inclined head resting on a speckled blanket in the back seat of Mrs Warboys' car. 'It looked sensational and the music [videotape editor, Mark Lawrence] had fished out from a library disc couldn't have been more appropriate. Arguably the most impressive opening of any episode, ever.'[vi] As for the rest of the episode, he thought it stood up well: 'I was still just about objective enough to feel it worked and was funny and mysterious and poignant in equal measure.'[vii]

Renwick was disappointed, though, with the lack of press coverage, reflecting on a 'rather hollow feeling this year; you expend all that time and energy making something and in one swift hit it's disseminated to the nation and you have absolutely no feedback whatever as to its reception.'[viii] The reviews, however, began to trickle in, although some critics had been fortunate enough to watch a preview of the Special prior to its screening. Of those, Peter Waymark in *The*

Times wrote: 'Last year's Christmas offering . . . was one of the feebler seasonal efforts but the show is in better shape this time.'[ix] Fellow journalists in the *Independent* and the *Daily Mail* stated it was 'still one of the funniest Christmas Specials around'[x] and 'an unmissable Christmas one-off'[xi].

The final Christmas Special, 'Endgame', transmitted on Christmas night 1997, saw Tim Brooke-Taylor and Marian McLoughlin playing the Meldrews' new neighbours, Derek and Betty McVitie.

David Renwick is a genius, and to see him construct the script and the plot in rehearsals, working with the actors, is something I'll never forget. I would like to have experienced it again.

PAUL LEATHER

When Victor bought a second-hand caravan he made headlines in the *Psychic News*. To his dismay, it seemed he'd lumbered himself with the most haunted caravan in Britain, containing the spirit of a Satan worshipper. When Margaret refused to step foot inside the tin box, let alone endure a two-week caravanning holiday in Dorset, Victor holidayed alone. It looked like their marriage might be on the rocks, but their car certainly was when it ended up running over the cliff. Fortunately for Victor, the caravan clung to the edge, enabling him to escape.

Fans of *One Foot in the Grave* were fortunate to be watching a third consecutive Christmas Special because, at times, Renwick was close to scrapping the idea, particularly as he faced the prospect of writing a third series of *Jonathan Creek*. 'I had enormous trouble writing the script and frequently considered ringing Geoffrey Perkins [head of comedy] to say he wouldn't be getting a show that year. The breakthrough in the end was the idea of refreshing the situation with the neighbours by having a different set of characters move in next door. I'd started out, as usual, by thinking of Patrick and Pippa, and various ways in which their paths would again clash with Victor's, but couldn't get past that sense of déjà vu, that it was retreading the same ground. Then it occurred to me, why not introduce a new couple who got on with the Meldrews like a house on fire, who can't see what all the fuss is about, and then you've got somewhere to go, because you know that before the show's over their sunny optimism is all going to come to grief.'

Renwick had worked with Tim Brooke-Taylor before, and was pleased to have him playing Derek, although others who had been auditioned for the role included Robin Nedwell, Peter Denyer and Mike Grady. 'Having Tim in the show gave it a completely new dimension. The big plus was that he brings that whole positive aura of comedy with him, based on everything you've ever seen him do, so you know it's going to be fun as soon as he appears on screen. And, of course, he was one of my heroes from way, way back, as one of the *I'm Sorry I'll Read That Again* team that first inspired me to start writing.'

But the script remained a struggle, with Renwick finding it difficult to cultivate new storylines. 'I've been trying to concentrate on more Victor ideas with the grim conviction that I'll never come up with another funny idea as long as I live. I've thought of them all already; every little germ of something in my head is instantly dismissed because it harks back to something much better from a previous series.'[xii] Although the next few days revealed the script starting to take shape, albeit slowly, he admitted a week later, 'I could easily go to pieces at this point, the thought that this really is going to be the first time I simply can't come up with it. But for the moment I soldier on.'[xiii]

Despite the worries, Renwick maintained his track record and delivered the script in plenty of time. The read-through took place on Friday, 17 October, just before the cast headed to Dorset for filming. On the thirteenth floor at Television Centre, Renwick was happy with the session, regarding it as 'triumphantly funny and entertaining'[xiv], and noted that while Brooke-Taylor was settling in to his role, Wilson was 'worryingly accurate to begin with, but deteri-orated comfortably into his usual misfiring deliveries while Annette beside him was as ever pin-sharp perfect.'[xv]

Photographs of Owen Brenman to correct certain misunderstandings about him ...

The hour-long script is a seamless example of quality writing. The episode contains, as usual, humour, drama and pathos. Much of the drama took place on a mild October day at Kimmeridge Bay, Dorset, where scenes showing Victor's car rolling off the cliff edge were filmed. Proud to have been part of this successful day's filming was

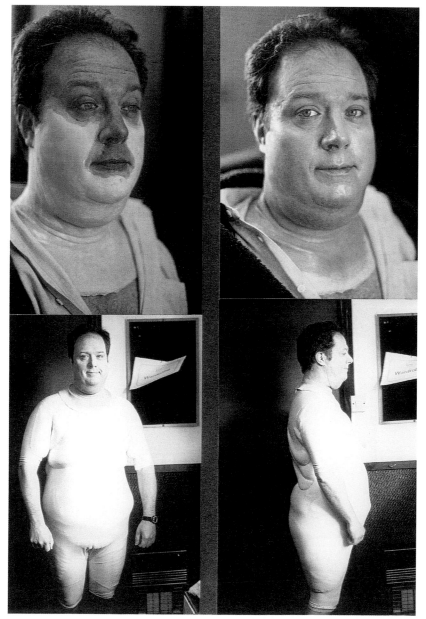

assistant director Paul Leather. It was the only time he worked on *One Foot*, but it's a job he'll never forget. 'The car needed some momentum if it was going to roll over the edge. Therefore, it was fired from a hydraulic ram, which pumps up air to a phenomenal number of pounds to the square inch, and releases it like a human cannonball. I remember the special effects supervisor saying that there was a slight chance that the rig could explode. To me, that was like saying: "Don't want to alarm you, but there is a small chance that a bomb could go off!" I remember the blood rushing to my face and getting on the walkie-talkie to the director, asking how near she wanted Richard to be to the car. There is never any certainty with effects, and you always build in as much safety as possible.'

While the car fell onto the beach below, the caravan ended up teetering on the edge, thanks to a series of heavy-duty bolts. Leather, who now directs children's and educational programmes, says: 'When the film was put together it looked stunning. But my abiding memory of the whole period was of it being a very happy affair and good fun. David Renwick is a genius, and to see him construct

...and the image that left casting directors wondering.

Nick Swainey, who reported the death of his mother during the episode, although whether she existed in the first place or was a figment of a lonely man's imagination was left to the viewer to ponder. A throwaway line in the script resulted in Owen Brenman being fitted for a fat suit with prosthetic jowls to match. Victor mentioned to Margaret that he'd noticed 'him next door' had put on weight since the death of his mother, and how it was odd that people let themselves go when touched by bereavement. 'Making Nick incredibly fat was the worst thing David did to my character, and I've never really forgiven him!' says Brenman, smiling. 'The trouble was, the suit wasn't quite fat enough so was very realistic: so much so that when we were recording in the studio, I went to the warm-up comedian and said: "When we've finished this scene, can you tell the audience that the fat isn't real?" And he just laughed at me. I had to get him to physically touch it to realise that it was latex. It was very well done but looked like Owen Brenman, the actor, had suddenly put on a lot of weight, and afterwards I started getting auditions for very fat people! It didn't do me any favours – even friends of mine said they'd seen me and thought I was ill. As I'm always struggling with my weight anyway, I looked at myself in the suit and thought: "This is the future staring me in the face." I didn't like it.'

the script and the plot in rehearsals, working with the actors, is something I'll never forget. I would like to have experienced it again.'

The highlights for me, once again, were the moments of sadness, including Margaret suffering a heart attack. The first we knew about the problem was when Victor returned from his solo caravanning break and discovered his wife in hospital. At her bedside, memories of many blissful moments together came flooding back, and he realised how lucky he was to have Margaret, whom he nearly lost before she was revived by paramedics. It was a moving scene.

Someone not so fortunate was next-door neighbour

As I'm always struggling with my weight anyway, I looked at myself in the suit and thought: 'This is the future staring me in the face.' I didn't like it.

OWEN BRENNAN

The prosthetics were supplied by Neill Gorton, who runs Millennium FX Limited, specialising in such effects. Gorton, like Brenman, wonders why the suit wasn't even bigger to maximise the reaction from the audience. 'Anyone watching might think that the line was inserted to excuse the fact that Owen had been stuffing his face over Christmas! I always wondered why David didn't make a big gag of it. I'm sure a lot of people either didn't realise, or just thought Owen had put on weight.' Gorton explains the painstaking process of applying the prosthetics. 'You start with a kind of leotard, on which we apply Lycra fabric and use pockets filled with either wadding or stuffing. If you want sections to move, like under Owen's biceps, you use a loose bag of fabric filled with lentils, because they have the right kind of weight. Once it's under a costume, if he waves his arm about, it appears to be skin bouncing around. You add weight in certain areas and padding in others so that it moves the way a fat body would move.' The transformation of Nick Swainey was the first idea Renwick dreamt up when he began planning the script earlier in 1997. The idea of seeing the character fattened up amused him, so he legitimised it by the death of Swainey's mother seeing him turn to comfort eating as he tried to cope with his loss.

Another scene involving Swainey which amused Renwick saw him giving Victor a boomerang, which he'd come across while sorting out his mother's possessions. 'Of all the absurd things you'd have in a house, it's never explained why Nick Swainey's mother owned a boomerang,' says Renwick, who admits he had to get the boomerang specially made. 'I was in the hotel the day before shooting that scene and the floor manager showed me the boomerang. The trouble was, it didn't look like a boomerang – it was more like a coat-hanger without the hook. But it was actually an Aborigine boomerang – what more can you say? It was what I'd asked for, but the problem was it didn't look effective enough. So Linda Conoboy [production designer] said she'd get one of the chippies to cut out a more exaggerated shape from plywood, and would paint some markings on it, which is what we did. That was an example of

having to cod reality up, to enhance it in order to achieve clarity for the audience.'

Renwick was once quoted as saying: 'I'll watch an episode being made and feel suicidal. Even if everyone has laughed at it I can still feel suicidal. But the worst time of all is when I watch the first rough edit. That's when I feel like slashing my wrists.'[xvi] It's not surprising, therefore, that upon watching the first assembly of 'Endgame' he felt depressed. Fortunately, though, by the show's transmission on Christmas Day, by which time *One Foot* had won the BBC's 'Best Sitcom' award for the sixth time, he was in a more positive frame of mind, stating: 'Sat down to enjoy Victor, which as far as I could tell came over as a strong, classy piece of work.'[xvii]

The Special attracted just under sixteen million people, but everyone would have a long wait until they saw the Meldrews again. Nearly two years would pass before the sixth and final series aired.

Brenman feels that Nick's fat suit wasn't quite fat enough.

171

CHAPTER 15
Bringing the Curtain Down

After the agony of writing the fifth series, David Renwick believed he'd squeezed every ounce of life out of Victor Meldrew and it was time to quit. Comforted by the knowledge that 'Endgame' had pulled in a sizeable audience during the festive period, the writer was convinced he'd taken the Meldrews as far as he could along the creative road. Just a few weeks into 1998, he was quoted extensively in the national press. The *Evening Standard* reported him saying: 'I have no new ideas for Victor Meldrew. It's as simple as that . . . I know that if I tried to write another series it would be even harder than the Christmas one. I don't want the standard to drop. There would be no point doing something I didn't believe in.'[i]

Renwick had discussed the situation with Richard Wilson over lunch at the RAC Club in London's Pall Mall, just a few days before Christmas 1997. As well as becoming increasingly busy writing his new series, *Jonathan Creek*, he told Wilson that he lacked sufficient confidence to contemplate further episodes. Although Wilson didn't want Victor killed off, believing such drastic action would conflict with the character's general ethos, he would, however, respect Renwick's decision.

Despite the press reporting Victor's demise, it's evident from Renwick's journals that he secretly hadn't ruled out revisiting the Meldrews; he was simply taking a well-earned sabbatical while pursuing other projects. The BBC was reluctant to relinquish its grip on such a classic show, particularly as its attempts to inject new life into the genre of situation comedy had floundered. Having waved goodbye to such draws as *Keeping Up Appearances*, *Only Fools and Horses* and, seemingly, *One Foot in the Grave*, the chasm in the corporation's comedy output would take some filling. Worryingly for those advocating a new era in sitcom, there was a dearth of projects that made a serious impression, while old favourites like *Dad's Army* and, now, *One Foot*, continued attracting healthy audiences whenever repeated.

BBC1's new controller, Peter Salmon, wanted Renwick to write more *One Foot*s and with the new

Behind the camera for once . . . and Victor was about to disappear altogether.

millennium on the horizon, he met the writer at the Halcyon Hotel, in London's Holland Park, on Monday, 23 February 1998. Among the items discussed was welcoming the year 2000 with a new instalment. '*One Foot in the Grave* was the number one sitcom on British television when I arrived at BBC1,' explains Salmon. 'You're grateful to be in possession of a jewel, which was beautifully acted and beautifully written. The mention of another series was enough to get ten million viewers clustered around the television, which was rare in those days and something comedy was finding more and more difficult to achieve. *One Foot* was one of the exceptions to the rule – it was a wonderful legacy from previous channel controllers.

'I wouldn't say I had an editorial plan for David: that was something owned by him and his imagination – and to some extent the production team. I hadn't worked out a plan of how *One Foot* might centre around the millennium, although it gave me a wry smile to think of Victor standing on the threshold of a new millennium, looking back and forward, in his own particular way, and probably not relishing what the future held.'

Not one to dissemble, Renwick listened to Salmon's idea but made it clear that he wouldn't be rushed into a decision. And it was a year before he finally committed to writing more scripts. Again, he was meeting Peter Salmon, but this time in his office at Television Centre. A millennium Special was mentioned once more, a 'mordant alternative to all the rest of the celebrations'[ii], but Renwick wanted to avoid another one-off episode. 'As perverse as I always am, I ended up doing exactly what no one expected: I suggested writing another series. Having a break is always helpful in this profession, and it was over four years since I'd written the last. I'd begun asking myself whether I could still do it, and suddenly it became a challenge I wanted to face. Simultaneously, though, I knew that if I went ahead, I wouldn't repeat it – it would be time to move on, so the logical thing was for Victor to die. I didn't want a repeat of *Only Fools and Horses*, where the fantastic closing scenes of the Trilogy saw the Trotters walking up the Yellow Brick Road, only for them to return a couple of years later. I didn't want people constantly enquiring when Victor was coming back, or anyone trying to persuade me. Also, killing off the lead character in a major sitcom would be a first.'

Hearing Renwick offer six more episodes was music to Peter Salmon's ears. 'That's like Christmas for a channel controller,' he says. 'Sitcoms like *One Foot* are

> *I would have liked it to run for ever because it was good and I enjoyed it so much.*
>
> ANNETTE CROSBIE

a national treasure: you get your hands on them very rarely.' Regarding Renwick's decision to send Victor to an early grave, Salmon was sympathetic. 'I assumed David was tiring of the character or frustrated about where else he could take him. After all, Victor had been

everywhere, and just about everything that could have happened had. All things come to an end, and I was grateful to have been a recipient of such a fine show. These days, most sitcoms don't get beyond a couple of series, so David having delivered several, and they were certainly barnstormers, was good enough for me.'

On Friday, 4 June, Renwick, who collected another award (the prestigious 'Dennis Potter Writers' Award') in May 1999, informed Richard Wilson of his intention to kill off Victor. Wilson was appearing at the Royal Exchange, Manchester in *Waiting for Godot*, and after the evening's performance, he dined with Renwick and his wife at the Lincoln restaurant, just a stone's throw from the theatre. 'We had already agreed this would be his final outing, so I said that death was the ultimate truth. As it had never been done before with a major sitcom character, intuitively I felt it was the only natural conclusion that kept faith with the show's essentially fatalistic view of life.'[iii]

Recalling the moment he learnt of his character's fate, Richard Wilson says: 'It was reaching the stage where scripts weren't as original as they had been. I knew David was finding it difficult to keep dreaming up ideas, and I was getting a bit tired of the character, trying to maintain a freshness. It was great that the show had remained popular for so long, but I agreed it was probably time to move on.'

Annette Crosbie, meanwhile, was saddened by the news. 'I would have liked it to run for ever because it was good and I enjoyed it so much. However, I knew it would have to come to an end eventually, and that it was becoming a burden for David, with people in the press constantly writing: "He'll never top the last one!" That kind of statement creates an unnecessary pressure.'

Now, Renwick had to decide how Victor would die. He'd toyed with the idea of him exiting a bookshop with a book on positive thinking, only for a piano to fall on his head. Although it was just a passing thought and didn't come to fruition, Renwick was determined to add an element of surprise to the script, and not pursue the expected path. While considering Victor's demise, he noted in his diary:

'Within a couple of hours of thinking about this final episode I'd conceived quite a good overall shape, I felt: two story strands, then and now, interwoven and mirroring each other. One an essentially comic Victor plot, the other showing Margaret coping with his demise six months down the line . . . This structure would avoid having to play the moment of Victor's exit in the traditional way. We never see the immediate response to his death, the moment of shock has long gone when we join the narrative, and it's all about Life After Victor, which I think will be more interesting. And not the route people are expecting you to take.'*iv*

He adds: 'I was less concerned with how Victor died than the fact that we must now draw down the curtain on him, finally and unequivocally. For as long as it had been my intention to kill him off, I'd always felt it should probably be in a road accident – mainly because I get so exasperated and angry about reckless driving, which just seems to be getting worse and worse. So I felt there was a minor comment to make there. Of course, once I started writing, the dramatic imperative took over. And although I would have loved to have got the knife into that whole yob element on the roads, it was more interesting to pull a switch at the end and reveal that the culprit was now actually Margaret's new friend. And so then you're not quite sure how to react, because you feel this great sympathy for Hannah Gordon's character, who was racing to the hospital where her own husband was near to death – and the story doesn't quite tie up in the way you expect it to. Obviously I didn't want Victor's exit to be in the form of a long, drawn-out terminal illness, or some other harrowing or depressing scenario. It needed to be fairly swift so that it didn't cast too bleak a shadow over the whole show and prevent you from enjoying the comedy.'

When Series Six finally aired, during the autumn and winter months of 2000, there was a noticeable absentee: director Susan Belbin. For the previous five series she'd headed the production team, and as the programme's popularity grew exponentially, her contribution to its success became immense. With her strength, drive, foresight, leadership skills and profitable relationship with Renwick, there was no one better

> *She'd been firing on all cylinders, so if you have a career like hers, I'm not sure many of us would have had the courage to give in. I'm convinced, though, that she made the right choice for herself, but was sadly missed because she was an excellent comedy producer and director.*
>
> GARETH GWENLAN, on Susan Belbin

to have guided the sitcom from birth to adulthood. But now, ill health forced a personnel change. Candidly, Belbin explained to me that she simply took on too much work. 'I was producing and directing *One Foot in the Grave* the same time as producing *Jonathan Creek*. It's impossible being in two places at once, and work took its toll.' Production schedules often clashed, increasing the pressure. 'The timing was appalling, but instead of me saying, "No, you can't have that one then because I'm already working on the other show," I worried that if I said "no" to something, people would think I couldn't cope and wouldn't ask me again. But I set a rod for my own back, found myself doing both at the same time, and getting it in the neck from either production for missing meetings.'

Belbin pinpoints the making of 'One Foot in the Algarve' as the beginning of her troubled period. 'It was the one time I asked the BBC for help. I'd never done a feature film before, which effectively it was. Psychologically it's different from going off on location and doing some film inserts. I thought that if I had a producer or a director, it would have worked out better, but that wasn't to be.' By now, the stress was becoming intolerable and physical symptoms were manifesting

We said we'd never do it without each other – it was rather silly, I suppose. But I certainly wouldn't have acted in it if David hadn't remained the writer. With Susie dropping out, the fact that Chrissie was very much her star pupil made it easier.

RICHARD WILSON

themselves, including panic attacks and chest pains. Belbin realised there was little alternative but to quit, for the sake of the programmes and, primarily, her health. 'I saw myself heading for a heart attack, so asked to be released from my position.'

Belbin called David Renwick on Wednesday, 23 April 1997 to break the news. Although aware she'd suffered high blood pressure, and had been confined to bed through exhaustion previously, he was still shocked. Belbin left the corporation on 31 May 1997, to the deep regret of her colleagues. Her former boss, Gareth Gwenlan, admires her for taking the decision. 'Her health hadn't been the best for some years. She made a lifestyle decision which was very brave. She'd been firing on all cylinders, so if you have a career like hers, I'm not sure many of us would have had the courage to give in. I'm convinced, though, that she made the right choice for herself, but was

sadly missed because she was an excellent comedy producer and director.'

For that year's Christmas Special, 'Endgame', Belbin's duties were divided, with Esta Charkham appointed producer and Christine Gernon director. But by the time the sixth series had been commissioned, it looked as if Belbin was fit enough to return as a freelancer to direct the final season. Having been associated with *One Foot* since day one, it would have been fitting for Belbin to bring it to a close, but it wasn't to be, despite her being formally offered the chance to produce and direct in January 2000. 'My husband Johnnie and I were living in Norfolk then, so it meant moving to London for the

Wilson's relationship with new director Christine Gernon was already well established.

period of filming and studio work. I discussed it with Johnnie and people like David, Richard and Annette before finally agreeing. David sent me scripts in advance and I began working on them, making notes as usual.' But her dream was shortlived. 'I lasted just two and a half days before the pains in my arms and legs returned. I travelled home and got off the train at Norwich, only for my husband to walk past me. I looked so dreadful he thought I was the bag lady! Driving to the house, I turned to him and said, "I'm not going back." He replied: "Great!" So I had to tell David Renwick that I was leaving not once but twice.'

For Series Six, Christine Gernon was appointed director while Jonathan P. Llewellyn wore the producer's hat. Picking Gernon, who'd not only directed 'Endgame' but worked as production secretary and production assistant on the show, seemed a logical decision, as Belbin explains. 'I'd regard her as stronger than me, inasmuch as I think her ability to say "no" is greater than mine. She's a little bit more single-minded and won't take any nonsense. I was very much of the old school – the programme at any cost. And the cost was me at the end of the day. Chris is a very talented girl, and being a good ten or fifteen years younger than me, had youth on her side. And everybody loves her, particularly Richard, so, yes, she was the obvious choice.'

Richard Wilson recalls entering into an informal pact with David Renwick and Susan Belbin some years before. 'We said we'd never do it without each other – it was rather silly, I suppose. But I certainly wouldn't have acted in it if David hadn't remained the writer. With Susie dropping out, the fact that Chrissie was very much her star pupil made it easier. It was sad that Susie left, but with it being Chrissie taking over, and David so hands-on anyway, it was possible to carry on.'

While Wilson regards the transition as virtually seamless, Annette Crosbie missed having Belbin leading the team. 'I enjoyed working with Chris but don't believe anyone could have done as good a job as Susie

did with David's scripts in the time we had. Working without her made me realise how tight a hold she had and how much she contributed to the show.'

Gernon and Wilson filming inserts for the final series in Dorset.

Renwick, too, was sad to lose Belbin, but felt there was no better replacement. 'Their styles were very similar because Chris, of course, had worked on so many shows with Susie over the years and had inherited that whole mature, more elegant approach. So it was just complete continuity, really. Obviously their personalities are very different, but Chris was always incredibly studious, professional and well-prepared, and I like to think we got on together quite effortlessly.'

'From day one, I had a huge affinity with David,' says Gernon. 'I like him enormously, but he's an incredibly complex man. With him, it's not a case of the glass being half full or half empty – there isn't a glass! He believes the worst will always happen, whereas I'm the complete opposite. I'd say, "Everything will be fine," and he'd reply, "No, it won't!" I think that's why we got on so well.

'He writes in such a rhythmical way, I'm convinced that if I had thirty scripts from different writers, I could pick out David's. Sometimes it's frustrating because he doesn't just say: "Here's the script, you take over and make it how you want." He has big ideas about how it should look – and rightly so. Therefore, you're not only doing what you think he wants you to do, but trying to insert some of your own ideas, too. We do, however, laugh a lot – although much of the time it's at his pessimism.'

During the period she's worked with Renwick they've developed a shorthand, which helps when preparing a show. 'I try to talk through everything first, so he knows what I'm thinking. That way, he can say if I've got the wrong end of the stick. It's a completely different way of working and I wouldn't do it with anyone else. It seems to work for us, though.'

When head of comedy Geoffrey Perkins asked Gernon to take over *One Foot*, she was preparing to direct another show, *Fun at the Funeral Parlour*, for BBC Choice. Despite this being a low-budget production, she was looking forward to the assignment. As far as Perkins was concerned, it was important a replacement for *One Foot* was found quickly, so Gernon was transferred immediately. 'It was hard leaving *Fun at the Funeral Parlour* because I was geared up to do it and excited by the project. Switching to *One Foot* was hard. And what I didn't know until I arrived on the show was that Victor would be killed.'

As thoughts switched to scheduling, it became apparent that the BBC wanted to transmit the final episode, depicting Victor's death, at Christmas. The thought horrified Renwick, who believed transmission over the festive period would set the wrong tone. He noted: 'It's almost as if, as broadcasters, we are glorifying his death. The context a show is presented in will have a huge impact on how it is received, and it's always been our policy to swim against the tide and resist the pressure to conform. It seems ironic – and depressing – to me that after deliberately avoiding the "obvious" approach in my script we are now facing a very "obvious" approach to the scheduling. If Victor dies at Christmas it's going to look like a naked push for ratings. The opposite is true: I want Victor's departure to be significant, but stripped of sensationalism.'[v]

If a Christmas transmission was imposed, Renwick decided he'd alter the script and omit the death scene. Renwick and Ellie were guests at Peter Salmon's table at the BAFTA awards ceremony on Sunday, 14 May, so during the evening Renwick tried conveying his concerns

regarding the closing episode's transmission. But feeling he'd failed to get his message across, he later wrote to Salmon. He explained how he'd written a sitcom that as well as delivering what one expects from a comedy, contained elements of surprise. He stated: 'Right from its inception *OFITG* has tried to subvert the form it appears to be part of. For me the struggle has been to maintain a broad appeal without compromising my own objectives: to produce an "anti-sitcom", stripped of the usual comic self-consciousness, that draws its rhythms and inspiration from reality, and occasionally has the power to disarm the viewer with material that is darker or more reflective than they are used to.'[vi] Although he acknowledged it was in everyone's interest to maximise the show's impact, he was worried that Victor's death over Christmas would be seen as a ploy to attract a large audience. He stated: 'Death, I would like us to say, may be tragic but it is commonplace, the eternal Truth. Let's not trumpet it, but place it simply and sparely before the public and let them make up their own minds. I would so like the feeling that we generate on the air to reflect the reality of death in life: most of the time it is a very quiet, private affair, generating little public attention: we grieve, and then somehow or other we just have to get on with things. I suppose at the risk of sounding squirmingly precious, I would like Victor to die with dignity.'[vii] The letter did the trick and within the month, Peter Salmon's reply confirmed that it was right to let Mr Meldrew die with dignity and, therefore, Christmas scheduling would be avoided.

It was Friday, 30 June, when everyone gathered at the BBC's Bridge Lounge for the read-through of all six scripts. Before long, laughter was echoing around the room, boosting Renwick's confidence. Nine days later, the cast and crew gathered at Bournemouth for the last time to film the exterior scenes. The wheels were well and truly in motion for the Meldrews' last six screen adventures, beginning with 'The Executioner's Song', which screened on 16 October. Its audience of just under 11.5 million was pleasing, considering it was pitching against *Who Wants to be a Millionaire?* on ITV. Again, critics were divided about *One Foot*, with the *Daily Telegraph* reporting that if the 'opening one [episode] was a guide, Victor's farewell might not prove the terrible blow it would once have been. Criticising

One Foot feels rather like attacking the Queen Mother. Even so, yesterday's programme was little more than an arbitrary sequence of implausible events, very few of which had the redeeming value of being funny.'[viii] Meanwhile, advocates included Nancy Banks-Smith at the *Guardian*, who classed the series as 'the last bottle in the cellar, something to be savoured'[ix], as well as contemporaries at the *Daily Express* and *Daily Mirror*. One journalist, Mark Simpson, contemplating life without Victor in a few weeks, claimed that 'when Victor finally draws his last, indignant breath, it won't just be Britain's most loveable old git that we lose, but an institution as important as, well, the *Nine O'Clock News*. For years now, it's been clear that the great British sitcom has also had one foot in the grave. Victor is its last gasp.'[x]

Although Renwick had struggled more than ever to write these final scripts, the second instalment, 'Tales of Terror', confirmed that he'd lost none of his ability to shock. Fans of the series realised long ago that tragedy is never far away when you're watching a Renwick show. Here, we saw some of the blackest moments, involving the garrulous Ronnie and Mildred. When a distraught Ronnie called the Meldrews to tell them his wife had committed suicide, they didn't expect to see her legs dangling in front of the living-room window. It transpired she'd been suffering bouts of depression, which ultimately led to her interrupting a game of Happy Families to end it all, and in doing so, 'totally exploding the myth that she and Ronnie are perennially and foolishly cheerful'[xi].

This powerful scene was one of the writer's attempts to shake the audience and enliven the product. 'It seemed to me quite nice to play with our preconceptions about Ronnie and Mildred: that they were basically just these two grinning simpletons who bored Victor and Margaret to tears. Having established them as, effectively, no more than cartoon characters it's all the more potent when you then introduce an element of tragedy and you're suddenly asked to relate to them on a more human level.' As with most of Renwick's controversial scripts, letters of complaint were soon winging their way to the BBC, including one from a viewer whose relative had recently hanged himself. 'I think it's important to note that at no point

in the show does anyone react in a comic way to Mildred's suicide,' says Renwick, while conceding there is an undercurrent of dark humour to the premise that is not unintended. 'I would never try to pretend we weren't looking for a laugh in the scene. The issue to me is whether you declare your comic intentions in an overt or self-conscious way as a programme maker. I would contend that we don't. Within the action the moment is treated with a sense of shock and gravity that is entirely appropriate. If you preserve the internal veracity and go with the drama, then the audience can react as they see fit.'

Not for the first time, the programme was referred to the Broadcasting Standards Council. 'Someone thought we were trying to get laughs out of hanging,' says Christine Gernon. 'The complaint wasn't upheld against us, but what saved us, I think, was a tiny bit of editing we did. There were a few chuckles from the studio audience that evening, which we decided to take out. The scene was transmitted in silence. But it's that old thing of people thinking a comedy is a comedy and has no place for tragedy, which isn't how David writes.'

The title for Episode Three, 'The Futility of the Fly', was inspired by an insect landing on Renwick one September afternoon. He used it as a metaphor for the 'futility of our own existence which begins to trouble Victor'[xii]. Compared against the high standards Renwick had set with previous scripts, the episode was noticeably weaker. Filming one scene in the episode forced the location manager to coordinate a PR exercise. A nighttime shot above a pier theatre was taken from a specially hired helicopter. Unfortunately, a play was being staged in the venue at the time and the hovering helicopter meant the audience couldn't hear the performance, resulting in the location manager having plenty of appeasing to do with the theatre's management.

Audience figures for the next two episodes were disappointingly low. 'Threatening Weather' was watched by less than nine million and 'The Dawn of Man' by under 9.5 million, the lowest figures since 'We Have Put Her Living in the Tomb' from the second series, ten years before. 'Threatening Weather' saw Victor and Margaret enduring a power cut on the hottest night of the year. Tempers were fraying owing to the intense heat and boredom. A restless Victor kept

Margaret awake, explaining her verbal attack the following day:

MARGARET: Some people grind their teeth in their sleep – you grind your buttocks.
VICTOR: Yes, all right!
MARGARET: Could have sharpened a pencil up there last night.
VICTOR: I said, all right! I don't want to be reminded about it, thank you very much.

It was an episode bursting with wonderful dialogue, including a scene where Victor remembered they'd got the 'dinner party from hell' the following night with Great Aunt Joyce and Uncle Dick. He contemplated whether it would be any grimmer than the last occasion.

MARGARET: I expect so, yes.
VICTOR: Knew we were in for a pleasant evening when he came in and said: 'Where shall I put the spittoon?' I told him to make himself feel at home so he took his false arm off, and said: 'Ah, that's better.' Didn't know where to look. He was using it as a back-scratcher at one point. [Silence for a while] Oh, do you remember . . .
MARGARET: [Annoyed because she's trying to read a book] Yes!
VICTOR: That's all you want to hear halfway through a meal, isn't it? 'Don't make her laugh too much, her glass eye's a bit loose.' Right in a plate of salad! And the eyesight's not that good in the other one. Shouting: 'It's all right, I've got it!' Thought we'd never prise that cherry tomato out of the socket.

The episode was recorded at low light levels, which Wilson and Crosbie thought had a detrimental effect. Christine Gernon recalls a conversation with Wilson. 'The point was, if you could see him all the time, there may as well not be a power cut. Richard said: "There are times when you can't see me!" I would agree, but told him that I knew he was funny. People didn't need to see his face to know what he was doing.'

Using low light was a deliberate ploy, Renwick says: 'Half the joy is picturing the expressions on Victor's face; the audience can do most of the work in their imagination.'

The only other character appearing in the episode was Mr Smedley. Originally envisaged for veteran actor Peter Jones, his untimely death meant a succession of actors was considered, including

Several hours in make-up were required to transform Roy Hudd into the super-obese Mr Smedley.

Hugh Lloyd, George Cole and Frank Middlemass, before Roy Hudd was offered the part. Playing the obese neighbour, who Victor sarcastically claims can cause a 'lunar eclipse by just passing the window', entailed donning a fat suit – but this time a more obvious outfit than that worn by Owen Brenman. The services of Neill Gorton were again required, and he recalls Hudd's reaction to wearing the suit. 'He was in hysterics. He's a comedian, of course, and was running around, having a ball. He had so much fun, he'd almost exhausted himself by the time of the recording. Although it's extremely flexible and light, the outfit gets hot, especially under studio lights. Roy was enjoying himself, bouncing about and doing silly walks, then it hit him. But he was fine after a brief rest.'

After the penultimate episode, 'The Dawn of Man' – which Renwick regards as his favourite in the series and was subsequently submitted when the show was, again, nominated for a BAFTA – was transmitted on Monday, 13 November, fans of *One Foot in the Grave* prepared themselves for the final visit to the Meldrews' world. As usual, not everything ran smoothly. Renwick was devastated when Jonathan Llewellyn, the producer, called early on Monday, 2 October to inform him that the *Daily Express* was carrying a story which 'blows the entire plot of the final episode, right down to the fact that Hannah's [actress Hannah Gordon] character was driving the car that killed Victor.'[xiii] When Victor's fate was announced earlier in the year, everyone associated with the

The Giant Tortoise coffee table was an idea Renwick had originally conceived for *Cosby*.

production was aware that the media would be pressing to know how he died. Despite initial reluctance, it was decided to disclose that Victor would be the victim of a hit-and-run driver, in the faint hope that the news would satisfy the media's insatiable appetite. Such was the concern that a leak might result in the fine detail of the plot being exposed by one of the national papers, a fake scene was even written to confuse the editors, with Victor appearing to be back in the land of the living. But the secret still got out and Renwick was furious. His immediate response was to call the *Express*. 'There was no way I could really respond, except to pick up the phone and shriek hysterically at some woman on the paper's news desk who took the call.'[xiv] He considered whether there was a way of re-editing the episode to reduce the impact of the revelation, but to no avail.

Recalling her role as Glynis Holloway, the

Hannah Gordon had already appeared in Renwick's *Jonathan Creek* mystery 'Black

woman responsible for Victor's death, actress Hannah Gordon says: 'One of the sad things about the part was that she was killing off Victor Meldrew!' She was, however, enamoured of the script. 'David got it right. He doesn't just write funny lines, he writes about actual life. So when someone is being killed, you do it for real. You can't make it funny because there's nothing humorous about the situation.' Gordon regarded the plot as 'very clever'. She explains: 'Glynis wasn't a careless driver as such. The background to how the accident happened was understandable: that night she had visited her husband, who was terribly ill, and was upset. Some people in her shoes might have acted the same: when she saw she'd knocked someone down, she decided to get the hell out of it. But her guilt and conscience is something from which she can't escape. As an actor, you fill in the background, and I love finding out what makes someone like Glynis tick. Why did she act that way? It was fascinating.'

Filming her character's big emotional breakdown was a difficult scene for Gordon because being on location meant little rehearsal time. She completed it, however, in one take. 'I'm not the sort of person who improves if I have to do it several times. Because it was such an emotional scene, I wanted to do it for real, to get the correct feeling. David likes getting it absolutely right because he's a perfectionist, but he was terrific. I'm not saying I was perfect, but he was sympathetic to the fact that we did the main thrust of the scene in one take.'

Hannah Gordon's performance impressed Renwick, who noted that 'she has fantastically strong, expressive eyes which say far more than my words can ever hope to.'[xv] And of the big scene, he wrote later: 'Hannah as professional and solid as ever, and her big emotional breakdown was, I think, incredibly powerful.'[xvi]

Richard Wilson regarded the final episode as a 'very good piece of writing' and 'wonderful to act', as did Annette Crosbie. The fragmented process of constructing an episode, however, means it's usually not until one watches the final product that its poignancy

is felt. Concerning filming the night scene where Victor was hit by the car, Christine Gernon says: 'When you're working on it, you're caught up in all the technicalities. It was a night shoot, which is never easy, and I remember Richard going to a nearby pub and having a couple of drinks because he was having to spend a fair bit of time lying on the pavement in the wet. At the time, it was just one of many location shots to complete.'

For a moment, Renwick felt a lump in his throat while watching the death scene being filmed. The image of Victor's arm falling into shot as his cap drifts away in a rivulet of rain was 'suddenly very chilling . . . and for just a moment I did feel the dramatic loss of a close friend'.[xvii] But by the time he arrived at Television Centre on Sunday, 17 September for the recording in front of the studio audience, he wasn't experiencing 'any sense of emotional transition or being present at a television landmark. It was just the usual torture of trying to address a load of stuff that wasn't working, so that by the end of the day we had something fit to transmit.'[xviii] He adds:

'We had a show to make. Its ending affects people in different ways: for me, it wasn't particularly emotional – life moves on.'

Victor's tragic death was only hours away.

After the recording, the BBC's Paul Jackson and Geoffrey Perkins passed on their congratulations. At the wrap party Janine Duvitski, who had been in the audience that evening, was in tears and emotions were running high. 'Richard of course very warm, all bear hugs and affection, and even Annette stayed on quite a while despite her declaration that it was "absolute purgatory". And as we kissed and hugged tightly on her departure she seemed quite moved and said, "Thank you for changing my life . . ."'[xix]

With the episode in the can, everyone awaited its transmission on Monday, 20 November. However, its screening was to coincide with the first contestant winning top prize on *Who Wants to be a Millionaire?* David Liddiment, formerly of the BBC before becoming ITV's director of programmes between 1997 and 2002, during which time he commissioned *Millionaire*, recalls the ruckus caused by Judith Keppell winning the same evening Victor Meldrew met his maker. 'It was total BBC paranoia,' says Liddiment. 'At the time, *Millionaire* was running on Monday, Thursday and Saturday. We have no control when contestants pop up and whether they do well and roll over to the next episode. As I recall, what happened was that Judith Keppell was on a Saturday edition and rolled over to the Monday; there was no way we could have known and done it as a deliberate ploy.' As Liddiment says, it was pure happenstance the way events unfolded. 'There was nothing we could have done to hold its transmission or move it – it just wasn't possible.'

What frustrated David Renwick most was ITV calling a press conference on the Monday morning, just a few hours before the transmission. 'That irritated me more than anything – and still does. The fact that they blew the result before the show went out: it was naked opportunism. Knowing it was our final episode and there would be more audience interest than usual there was no way they weren't going to declare their hand in advance. God knows, it was fearsome enough competition anyway, and they'd beaten us more often than not. You just think, wouldn't it have been more honourable to let the show go out in the normal way – apart from anything else they killed off any element of tension or surprise in their own programme – and then hold a press conference the day after. But that's me being naïve – television today is all about a cynical drive for ratings.'

Millionaire was the reason *One Foot's* audience figures were markedly lower than in previous seasons, and its likely fans, aware that Keppell was rolling over from Saturday evening, would have led to a sizeable audience, regardless of the press conference. 'Of course we did everything we could, without actually telling anyone, to get

people watching the show,' explains Liddiment. 'I think we did an on-air promotion.' Unnamed BBC sources questioned the authenticity of Keppell's victory, the same night as Victor's demise, but were soon issuing an official apology for suggestions that ITV had run a dirty tricks campaign to win the ratings battle. Liddiment says: 'Quite frankly, the BBC spin machine had got out of control.'

Although understandably frustrated about the affair, Renwick realised Keppell winning the million at that time was pure coincidence, recording in his journal: 'My response to it all is that the whole business is proof positive of Victor's basic tenet in life: that anything

Paul Merton, who played the barman, was a long-term fan of the series.

that can go wrong will. Expect the worst and you won't be disappointed.'[xx]

There were several elements of 'Things Aren't Simple Any More' which impressed Renwick, including Paul Merton's performance as the barman, which he felt 'could barely have been better: word perfect with a clear appreciation of and reverence for the lines'[xxi]. Renwick had always been appreciative of Ed Welch's music, but thought he'd surpassed his usual high standards in the final episode: 'searingly strong and moving where it mattered most'[xxii]. Of all the music Welch composed and recorded for the series, Renwick classes his first and final pieces as the best. 'His first cue was at the start of the second series when Victor revisits his old house and garden, and the ruins of his old apple tree, and Margaret takes his hand and leads him away, saying: "Come on, let's go off and plant another one." And they walk off up the road together, to this great emotional swell in the music, which is just the perfect ending.' Another score he admires accompanied the touching scene where Victor came upon an empty table at the reunion that never was. Old photos of the expected guests, former employees of the Lee Valley Dairy, where Victor worked some thirty years ago, decorated the table and Victor took a moment to walk around, admiring the portraits. It was a highly moving scene, beautifully executed by Wilson. 'Various members of the crew brought in photos of their fathers and grandfathers,' explains Renwick. 'I considered using one of my own dad, but knew I'd never be able to watch the scene without breaking up; it would have been too much. But, once again, what Ed provided for us at that moment really brought a lump to the throat.' Arguably the writer's favourite moment from the episode – which ironically he'd considered omitting from the script – found Victor believing he was the only person to turn up at the reunion, only to miss Limpy Briddock by a hair's breadth when he arrived seconds after Victor left the Stranger's Rest, the venue for the evening. Renwick dubbed it 'one of the most successful blends of comedy and tragedy I think I've ever achieved'[xxiii].

There is no denying the power and emotion emanating from the episode, which closed rather cryptically, typifying Renwick's love for the enigmatic and ambiguous. He regards it as much more stimulating to allow the viewers to make up their own minds.

Whether Margaret finally dropped paracetamols into Glynis' orange juice will remain a mystery. Renwick recalls Ellie trying her best to dissuade him from killing off Victor in the first place, then quizzing him about the ending. 'She asked what happened, saying that I must know because I wrote it, but I had to tell her that I didn't know and, what's more, didn't want to.'

Reflecting on an earlier exchange between an angry Margaret and a priest would help fuel the argument towards Margaret taking revenge in the gripping denouement. After he enquired as to how she was coping, Margaret retorted:

> You ask me how I'm coping, shall I tell you? Exactly how I'm coping? By clinging to the hope that one day they find the bastard who was at the wheel of that car because if they ever do, I swear to God I'm going to kill him, with my bare hands if necessary. Then they can do what they like with me. The trouble with the world nowadays is that nobody does anything about anything. Victor tried, God knows, and look where it got him. It's all speed and greed and he's probably best out of it.

Annette Crosbie delivered one of her best performances, which was recognised by Robert Hanks in the *Independent*. However, he felt her achievement was paired with a 'heavy-handed score and direction'[xxiv]. He also remarked on what he deemed 'flaws'[xxv] in the script, most notably 'transitions between now and then were clumsily signalled, and a number of Victor's catastrophes were related as drab anecdotes'[xxvi]. Overall, though, he applauded Renwick for his originality in announcing the death at the beginning of the episode instead of the end, and for 'the density of comic incident and its ambitious emotional range'[xxvii]. While James Walton at the *Daily Telegraph* believed the various flashbacks confirmed his opinion that 'the programme's patchiness always prevented it from moving beyond the unquestionably good to the ranks of the all-time greats'[xxviii], others were more positive in their reviews. Jaci Stephen in the *Mail on Sunday* viewed it as a 'dark, moving, yet often hilarious final episode'[xxix], singling out Crosbie's performance for particular praise, classing it as one of 'concentrated evil, resentment and hatred'*xxx*. Charlie Catchpole, meanwhile, noted that the sixth season had shown signs of tiredness, but that Renwick's 'brilliance in bringing pain, darkness, despair and – ultimately – death into the cosy world of the Britcom earns him a place in TV's hall of fame'*xxxi*. Long-term supporter of *One Foot*, Garry Bushell, wrote on the week that both Inspector

I'll miss malcontent Meldrew more than melancholy Morse. He was a great comic creation, a decent man caught in life's downpour without an umbrella . . . How can he be gone when there is still so much to moan about?

GARRY BUSHELL

Morse and Victor Meldrew were lost, 'I'll miss malcontent Meldrew more than melancholy Morse. He was a great comic creation, a decent man caught in life's downpour without an umbrella . . . How can he be gone when there is still so much to moan about?'*xxxii*

But he *was* gone. It was the end of an era, save for a brief scene Renwick wrote for Comic Relief 2001 after being badgered by Richard Curtis. 'I didn't want to do it,' says Renwick. 'Victor was dead so how could I bring him back? It was only Richard [Curtis] constantly going on that made me change my mind.' The sketch, titled 'Visiting Uncle Dick', was set in a hospital and had originally been considered for one of the earlier episodes. He crystallised his thoughts regarding his contribution to the annual event in mid-November 2000, noting: 'I had a good idea today to round off this Comic Relief piece in which Victor and Margaret visit Uncle Dick in hospital. The scene ends with Victor referring to a video of *The Sixth Sense*, and we realise retrospectively that he too has been a ghost throughout the scene.'*xxxiii* For Renwick, a man who likes the luxury of time to perfect his work,

contributing a sketch wasn't the most satisfying experience. 'Inevitably, you always want it to be as strong as possible. But we did that whole insert in such a rush, and although we did have a little bit of rehearsal beforehand, I know Chris [Gernon] was very unhappy that she didn't have time to prepare the shots the way she normally would. It ended up as a rather ramshackle effort that for my money was not the best memorial to Victor.'

Gernon agrees: 'It was the first and last time I'll ever attempt a multi-camera narrative piece (ten minutes long) with barely any rehearsal and no camera script. To call it chaotic would be an understatement and it's a memory that still haunts me!'

When it came to casting Uncle Dick, Renwick had originally considered Spike Milligan, before sadly discovering that he was too ill. 'Spike had rung me not long before we made the final series. I hadn't spoken to him for ages, and he basically just wanted to know if I could find a part for him somewhere. So when it came to the Comic Relief sketch, he seemed like a natural choice to play this decrepit old man in the bed, who never moves and has only two words to say. Just the sight of Spike lying there, with Victor pondering whether he's alive or dead, would have been very funny. But we were told he really wasn't up to it, and so we used Eric Sykes instead.'

If Renwick hadn't been aware just how his creation had become etched in the public's psyche, he would soon realise what *One Foot* meant to people when wreaths were being laid at the spot where Victor's life tragically ended. Even at the first anniversary of his screen death, fans were still arriving at the location in the village of Shawford, near Winchester, Hampshire, where the scene was filmed. One of the messages of condolence stated: 'Hope you've finally got some peace and quiet. Keep on moaning in heaven.' Renwick's pessimism once again came to the fore when he told me:

'Of course we have no way of knowing whether some journalist somewhere didn't ring up a few of the people originally involved, and say: "Do you realise it's a year to the day that Victor died? How do you feel about going down there again and laying another wreath? We'll be there to take a few photos – oh, and by the way, here's fifty quid." It may be that three people really went along and laid a few flowers. That's all a paper like the *Sun* needs to run a story. Had there been, say, fifty people, from different parts of the country, who'd all made a pilgrimage to the spot I would think it was significant to report. Otherwise, I'm afraid I do tend to take things like that with a huge pinch of salt. It's like the big front-page splash they ran about Victor's face being found in a constellation of stars – you know the facts are being very heavily massaged to generate a story.'

It's clear, though, that the name Victor Meldrew has entered the public consciousness. It's a name that has attained common currency in a way that a lot of sitcom names don't. Renwick is very gratified by this. Ironically, it's usually the least expected aspect of a programme that people remember, such as Victor's unintended catchphrase, 'I don't belieeeve it!' 'The sad thing for me is, it's always the aspects of the show you feel are the least significant, the least worthy of recognition, that everyone seizes upon. It's the fact that most people have Victor pegged as this terminally grumpy old git that's made him such an accessible commodity – because people want black and white, not shades of grey. I just think it's a shame that he'll for ever be remembered in such a two-dimensional fashion.'

Although an actor's life revolves around moving between characters, letting go after so many years in *One Foot in the Grave* was a wrench for all concerned, despite understanding the reasons behind the show's cessation. For Richard Wilson, the show marked the pinnacle of his career in terms of the exposure and opportunities it afforded. 'I enjoyed other shows I did, like *Tutti Frutti*, but *One Foot* opened everything up for me. Doing something that cultish means there is a price to pay, of course, inasmuch as sometimes

people find it difficult to cast you. Yes, it closed a few doors as well as opening them, but I feel extremely

> *It's like the big front-page splash they ran about Victor's face being found in a constellation of stars – you know the facts are being very heavily massaged to generate a story.*
>
> DAVID RENWICK

lucky to have played a character as popular as Victor Meldrew.'

Everyone is lucky to have been introduced to Mr Meldrew and the rest of the people living their lives in David Renwick's fictional world. God bless them all.

Silly season: five years on, Renwick's creation still refused to die.

EPILOGUE

While writing this book, I've interviewed a great many people about *One Foot*. During our conversations, the question of why David Renwick's sitcom became such a success, and remains an influential example of the genre to this day, was often posed. It's clear that the calibre of Renwick's scripts is the key but, of course, other factors come into play: wonderfully honed scripts can be destroyed by a weak acting performance, hence the importance of a cast of sufficient quality to deliver the writer's fine words. Undoubtedly *One Foot* had an estimable cast to achieve this, and an equally strong production team which, headed by Susan Belbin and, latterly, Chris Gernon, coordinated and delivered the show to our screens.

Here, a few of my interviewees share their thoughts about the success of *One Foot in the Grave*.

RICHARD WILSON

'I remember David [Renwick] saying: "We'd better enjoy this because it will never happen again." That's probably right, too. It was just the chemistry of all of us – David, Susie, Annette, Angus, Janine, Owen and Doreen – coming together that made it work. But mainly the show's success is down to David. His writing is so on the ball. I'm always saying at interviews that he's the sole cause, but that always spurs people to say: "No, it's Richard that made it funny." It was David, really – he was the catalyst.

'I never tried analysing the success too much. One of the reasons I originally resisted the role of Victor was that I thought it would become a series about older people – I wasn't particularly interested in that. I think, however, some older people didn't like it very much because of the title. They thought that "one foot in the grave" meant that you were finished, but the whole point about Victor was that he was out of his grave. The series became popular with young people – most of my fans are youngsters and students, which astonishes me. I think children liked it because Victor said things they wished they could, but were not allowed to. He spoke his mind. It was rich and inventive comedy, a sitcom that was different insomuch as it dealt with the tragic side of life from time to time. It was very real.'

ANNETTE CROSBIE

'I wouldn't say *One Foot in the Grave* was my favourite job of all time because for me there wasn't an awful lot of acting to be done. But I did love doing it, in a way that nothing else has provided. I enjoyed the discipline of the show and the sheer hard work involved in getting it on the screen, and I think that shows when you watch an episode. I like hard work and discipline, and when you get it right, it's so satisfying. Of course, most of the time we didn't get it right – or that's how it seemed!'

OWEN BRENMAN

'At the risk of sounding pretentious, I see *One Foot* as an existential comedy. Victor's story begins with him being sacked, thrown on the scrap heap and replaced by an electronic box. Everything that follows is his attempt to come to terms with this and make some meaning out of his life. This is, at times, tragic, funny and sad: the best kind of comedy. The brilliance of David's writing allows him to tackle powerful themes such as death, cruelty and love – normally the preserve of drama – but within the format of a mainstream sitcom. A stunning achievement.'

DOREEN MANTLE

'It was beautifully written, and a stroke of genius to cast Richard. I think people found themselves able to identify with Victor's quandaries. To this day, people say: "We have a Victor Meldrew in our home." The grumpiness and tetchiness of the character appealed, and people liked him because he always tried to do good – even if most of the time everything went wrong for him!'

ANGUS DEAYTON

'For me, one of the joys of *One Foot* is that David always had that slightly dark edge in his writing. But versatility is one of his greatest skills. In certain parts of the programme, he's able to suddenly enter into sketch land, almost – quite surreal areas which you think a lot of writers wouldn't be able to get away with. There was one scene where Victor hears someone talking about the bathroom being full of midges. He opens the door and we see a group of midgets. It's very unlikely and so surreal that you'd think in a conventional sitcom, supposed to be set in reality, that it would look completely implausible. Somehow, though, he gets away with it. But David can mix the surreal with a macabre side, a definite trait of *One Foot in the Grave*, which sets it apart from other shows. It has this gloss of looking very conventional on the surface, but there were a lot of sinister things going on.

'But there were a number of contributing factors to its success. Like other successful sitcoms, the audience had to be able to identify with it: it needed to be accessible, which I think it was. It always looked conventional even though it had this rather sinister underbelly. The writing had to be great, in terms of entertaining the audience, and the performances had to be driven, so viewers wanted to revisit the characters week after week. There were other elements as well, but those are the most crucial.'

JANINE DUVITSKI

'Success starts with the writing. It's what everyone is always looking for, and why David Renwick will always be in demand. When we used to sit around and read the scripts, we all loved what he'd written. People identified with the characters and the situations they found themselves in. I have days like Victor all the time: it's one thing after another. First you lose the car keys, then you're late for an appointment, which you subsequently miss, next the plumber doesn't arrive as expected and so on. Everybody's life is full of that, and we all want to take action sometimes like Victor does. It's pure identification.'

ANDREW MARSHALL

'*One Foot* is like a very dazzlingly polished, beautifully cut diamond with extraordinary sparkle and precision. Now and again I find it, just like a diamond, a little cold but that probably adds to its brilliance because it doesn't get bogged down in anything that would blur that wonderful clarity.'

DAVID LIDDIMENT

'*One Foot* was a great show. Like all the great sitcoms it had a strong central character, and Victor was a great archetype that we all recognise. Pretty much everyone in Britain would know someone as irascible as Victor, and beyond that his irritation and frustration with just getting through the day struck a very broad chord with the audience, because that's the experience of our lives. So it's universal on a number of levels.'

PETER SALMON

'It was a comedy of everyday life, including its blackness. You always felt that if something was going to go wrong, it would go wrong for Victor; he'd be frustrated and thwarted at every turn – it was delicious and done so inventively. It was perfect casting for the Meldrews, especially Richard Wilson, who found the role of a lifetime and made it his own. It marked the end of a golden period of British sitcom, which is now being revived. If I were offered it today, I'd commission it; I'd grab anything by David Renwick with both hands. Some writers just have that stamp of quality about them.'

Richard Wilson appeared in all episodes. Annette Crosbie appeared in every show except 'The Trial'.

SERIES 1
(Location scenes filmed between 18 September and 6 October 1989)

1: ALIVE AND BURIED
Recorded in studio: **Sunday, 15 October 1989**
Transmitted: **Thursday, 4 January 1990, 9.30 p.m.**
Audience figure: **9.28 million**
CAST:

Susie Blake	Mrs Inglis
Valerie Minifi	Mrs Jellis
Doreen Mantle	Mrs Warboys
Owen Brenman	Nick Swaincy
Simon Greenall	Police Officer
Nick Maloney	Garage Manager

Voice only: Joanna Phillips-Lane (Voice in Box); Colin Ward Lewis (Weatherman, Continuity Announcer and Chancellor) and Owen Brenman (Radio Show Presenter)

Extras: Russell Brook, Christian Barr, John Gallagher, Lillian Bravery, Iris Terry, Sylvia Victor and Jane Bisson

Synopsis:
Victor finds himself thrown on the scrapheap when he loses his job as a security guard. Facing the gloomy prospect of early retirement, the sixty-year-old is a victim of technology. He's given the company twenty-six years of his life but is now surplus to requirements thanks to the arrival of an inconspicuous little black box which, as Victor says, does everything except complain about the air-conditioning. Adjusting to his empty days is tough, with little to do but collect the plethora of empty crisp packets that are continually thrown into the Meldrews' back garden, but then their friend persuades him to dust off his conjuring routine and entertain the local WI. The trouble is, Victor thinks it's all a ruse and that his ex-work colleagues have organised a belated leaving do – but he's in for a disappointment. Worse still, his day ends in disaster when he's picked up as a suspected kerb crawler.

2: THE BIG SLEEP
Recorded in studio: **Sunday, 22 October 1989**
Transmitted: **Thursday, 11 January 1990, 9.30 p.m.**

Audience figure: **7.5 million**
CAST:

Fay McGuire	Girl Window Cleaner
Peter Corey	Mr Prout
Christopher Saul	Jehovah's Witness 1
David Peart	Jehovah's Witness 2
Kay Adshead	Keep Fit Instructress
Leonard Lowe	Len
Danny O'Dea	Michael
Helen Fraser	Dr Snellgrove
Hilary Mason	Elspeth
Pamela Lane	College Nurse
Lisa Bluthal	College Make-up Trainee

Voice only: Colin Ward Lewis (Radio DJ)

Extras: Michael Hanbury, Kay Woodgate, Ket Urah Sorrell, Judd Sollo, Sidney Kirsh, Kevin Matthews, Judy Cowne and Lee Towsey

Synopsis:
The vulnerability of life is highlighted when Victor learns that his cousin Geoffrey has died of a heart attack, shortly after taking early retirement at sixty. When he begins experiencing chest pains himself, Margaret enrols them both on a keep-fit class. The instructor appears to be a paradigm of good health, until she keels over and dies. What with this and his cousin's funeral on his mind, Victor soon believes that he's contracted every illness known to man and that death is knocking on his door. He decides to soak up the sun's warming rays and falls asleep in the garden, but before long the garden is enveloped by mist; when Victor awakes he believes he's arrived at the Pearly Gates.

3: THE VALLEY OF FEAR
Recorded in studio: **Sunday, 29 October 1989**
Transmitted: **Thursday, 18 January 1990, 9.30 p.m.**
Audience figure: **9.2 million**
CAST:

Doreen Mantle	Mrs Warboys
Peter Corey	Mr Prout
Gabrielle Blunt	Mrs Birkett
Christopher Ryan	Plumber
David Keys	Plumber's Assistant
Walter Sparrow	Beetroot George
Jonathan Kydd	Market Stall Holder
Donald Bisset	Bowls Player

| Jake Wood | First Yob |
| Joseph Wright | Second Yob |

Extra: Steven Downer

Synopsis:
After reading that adopting a hobby is the ideal way to relieve stress and tension, Victor buys a camera and sets out for Bluebell Wood to photograph badgers. Instead of badgers, he encounters a group of yobs who attack him. Tired of society's ills, including litter bugs and vandals, Victor convenes a residents' meeting. Now is the time for positive action in his crusade to curb the problems honest, law-abiding citizens are having to face on a daily basis. Prepared for action, he carries a starting pistol, while Mrs Warboys takes matters to the extreme and brings a grenade, but it's all to no avail.

4: I'LL RETIRE TO BEDLAM
Recorded in studio: **Saturday, 4 November 1989**
Transmitted: **Thursday, 25 January 1990, 9.30 p.m.**
Audience figure: **8.92 million**

CAST:

Rebecca Stevens	Iris
Norman Lumsden	Mr Parslow
Evie Garratt	Old Lady
Cecily Hobbs	Eye Clinic Nurse
John Bluthal	Mr Jellinek
Roger Hammond	Mr Gillespie
Joolia Cappleman	Cleaner
Victoria Hasted	TV Producer
Jim Barclay	Mr Davidson

Edward Harris	Dylan
Simon Bright	Elliott
John Cassady	Hospital Nurse
Heather Canning	Hospital Doctor
Tony Mathews	Tory MP

Extras: Joe Wenborne, Steven Palmer, Jean Morton, Leslie Adams, Liz Adams, David Bache, Lila Cherif, Paul Conway, Ernestine Hedge, Nicole Jackson, David Melbourne and Suzanne Walsingham

Synopsis:
Victor is full of the joys of spring but his joie de vivre is short-lived when he finds himself trapped with Margaret in his garden shed, thanks to a swarm of bees that decide to descend on the Meldrews' house. After more than three hours they escape their ordeal, thanks to the fire brigade, but just when Victor thinks his week couldn't get any worse, he wastes an entire day sitting in the waiting room at an eye clinic, and Margaret breaks the news that they're going to babysit their niece's two brats – but Victor has devised a plan to shut them up.

5: THE ETERNAL QUADRANGLE
Recorded in studio: **Saturday, 11 November 1989**
Transmitted: **Thursday, 1 February 1990, 9.30 p.m.**
Audience figure: **9.5 million**
CAST:

Angus MacKay	Art Teacher
Gillian Barge	Mrs Mauleverer
John Barrard	Harold Wharton
David Battley	Carpet Fitter
Peter Copley	Leonard

Synopsis:

When Victor gives Doreen, the nude model at his art class, a lift home, Margaret gets the wrong end of the stick, especially when she learns the divorcée has offered Victor a part-time job helping out at her house. Her suspicions deepen when she discovers an empty packet of condoms in Victor's jacket and he accepts another job when Doreen 'desperately needs a man's body'. Suspecting him of having an affair, Margaret cold-shoulders her husband, but when he returns home complaining about a bad back and that he doesn't think he's up to it anymore, she decides it's time to confront her suspicions.

6: THE RETURN OF THE SPECKLED BAND

Recorded in studio: **Saturday, 18 November 1989**
Transmitted: **Thursday, 8 February 1990, 9.30 p.m.**
Audience figure: **8.98 million**
CAST:

Doreen Mantle	Mrs Warboys
Clive Mantle	Electricity Man
John Cater	Mr Berenger
Lloyd McGuire	Garden Centre Manager
Willie Ross	Dustman

Extras: Glen Francis, Lisa Moreno, Barry Phelan and Laura Dixon

Synopsis:

The Meldrews are off on their hols but Victor's aversion to flying means he'd rather spend two weeks in a seaside guest house run by Pol Pot than climb into a plane. Athens is beginning to lose its appeal, even more so after the tactless Mrs Warboys has finished slating the place. Victor and Margaret eventually pack their suitcases and head off to the Greek sun, but they have an unexpected companion in their luggage – a gigantic python, which slithered into Victor's bag during a recent visit to the local garden centre.

SERIES 2

(Location scenes filmed between 1 July and 20 July 1990)

1: IN LUTON AIRPORT, NO-ONE CAN HEAR YOU SCREAM

Recorded in studio: **Friday, 3 August and Saturday, 4**

August 1990
Transmitted: **Thursday, 4 October 1990, 9.35 p.m.**
Audience figure: **8.86 million**
CAST:

Doreen Mantle	Mrs Warboys
Owen Brenman	Nick Swainey
Michael Robbins	Irate Neighbour
Doremy Vernon	Irate Neighbour
Peter Corey	Mr Prout
Michael Bilton	Mr Drewitt

Extras: Kenneth Coombs (Airline Captain), Gail Abbott and Serena Destouche (Air Stewardesses), April Ford (Waitress), Gary Forecast (Waiter), Leone Amis, Beverley Jennings, Penny Lambirth, Beatte Peter-Thomas, Michaela Welch, Fiona Williams, Dave Hampson, Lloyd Harvey, Teddy Massiah, Steven Eke and Patrick J. Ford (Holidaymakers), Joe Riordon, David Bache, James Delaney, Cy Town, Dick Hope, Kenneth Lawrie, Evan Ross, Leon Laurence, Tom Prentice, Mavis Wright, Elizabeth Hooper, Judy Szucs, Monique Briant, Joan Lovelace, Lisa Bergmayr and Muriel Wellesley (Party Guests)

Synopsis:

The Meldrews return from holidaying in Athens but Victor has the post-holiday blues, which deepen when he's forced to endure an intimate body search at Customs. To make matters worse, he sarcastically admits to the officials that he's 'fine except for the crack in my bottom'. There's worse news to come: their suitcases are lost by the airline and a fire has razed their house to the ground. Six months later, they're happily ensconced at 19 Riverbank and decide to throw a housewarming party – trouble is, the guests end up in the wrong house.

2: WE HAVE PUT HER LIVING IN THE TOMB

Recorded in studio: Saturday, 8 September 1990
Transmitted: **Thursday 11 October 1990, 9.30 p.m.**
Audience figure: **8.1 million**

CAST:

Doreen Mantle	Mrs Warboys
Sarah Mortimer	Jennifer
Andrew Powell	Barney (Sky TV Salesman)
Malcolm Frederick	Car Park Attendant

Extras: Lydia Henderson-Boyle (Jackie – age 5), Pat Worth (Aunty Norma), Arnold Chazen (Interflora Man), Liam McGuire and Gordon Williams (White Line Men)

Synopsis:

The Meldrews are proud that they've saved £90 by decorating the lounge themselves, but organisation was never one of Victor's fortes, which explains why they return home one day to find Stan, the decorator Victor should have cancelled, has ruined their five days of hard graft by stripping the paper they'd just hung. The next disaster on the menu involves the cremation of Kylie, their goddaughter's tortoise, which Victor accidentally throws on the garden fire. Confusion ensues when Margaret, trying to replace the creature without its owners being aware, takes around another tortoise. There's just one problem, though: their goddaughter's mother, Jennifer, already knows about the tortoise's demise and ends up burying the replacement. Talking of death, Mrs Warboys thinks Victor has taken an overdose and tries to revive him, while he continues to attract disasters like a magnet. An outing to the theatre

to celebrate the Meldrews' wedding anniversary is ruined when they realise they've turned up a year early.

3: DRAMATIC FEVER

Recorded in studio: Saturday, 11 August 1990
Transmitted: **Thursday, 18 October 1990, 9.30 p.m.**
Audience figure: **10.2 million**

CAST:

Fleur Chandler	Desirée Gibson
Terry Taplin	Jasper Gibson
Geoff Parry	Gerry
Dick Sullivan	Plumber
Billy Clarke	Plumber's Mate
Gareth Armstrong	Graham
Maggie Ollerenshaw	Hilary
Bill Monks	Martin
Mark Baxter	Postman

Voice only: Chris Emmett (Mr Gridley on phone and Voice in *Bergerac* on TV) and John Sessions (Gordon James on phone and Ulrich Eidel on phone)

Extras: Matthew King (Beefy Builder), Elaine Hopkins, Ellie Reece Knight, Maggie Mitchell, Paul Barton, Ray Martin and Joe Wells (Dinner Party Guests), Muriel Wellesley (Blur in Photos), Ryk Coleman, Waydon Croft, Jane Bisson, Steve Downer, Clade Edwards, Libby Louch, Les Clarke and John Wilson Goddard (People outside hardware shop)

Synopsis:

The smell of greasepaint fills the air in the Meldrews' household as Margaret returns to the world of amateur dramatics and Victor turns his hand to sitcom writing. Margaret's mother's unseen visit, meanwhile, to celebrate her eightieth birthday is memorable for all the wrong reasons, thanks to her mistaking wallpaper paste for bath salts and Polyfilla for Steradent, both with dire consequences. When his mother-in-law eventually returns home, Victor thinks he'll get some peace and quiet to finish his script, but it's interruption after interruption. And then there's the litter lout he spots in action, but confronting the offender is a bad move and Victor comes off the worse. They say revenge is sweet, but not in Victor's case.

4: WHO WILL BUY?

Recorded in studio: **Saturday, 18 August 1990**
Transmitted: **Thursday, 25 October 1990, 9.30 p.m.**
Audience figure: **10.66 million**
CAST:

Jimmy Jewel	Albert Warris
Owen Brenman	Nick Swainey
Janine Duvitski	Pippa
Angus Deayton	Patrick
William Vanderpuye	Toy Salesman

Voice only: Patricia Greene (Jill Archer on phone)

Extras: Mark Squires, Amanda Speed (Comedienne), Tony Grisilla, Paul Rutter, David Behennah, Rowland Collins, Clifford Predgen, Marcus Elliot, Alan Brown, Simon Fraser, Nigel Parkes-Davies and Avis Lilly (Concert Performers), Stephen Cookson, Teddy Massiah, Ed Meredith, Lance Craig, Nick Wilde, Andy Spiegel, Les Mills, Steve Perry, Ted Ludford, Mel Goodman, Suzy Lyle, Michelle Sansom, Lyndon McIntyre, Chloe Jerome, Suzie Mollet, Jay Mayson, Jane Sainsbury, Jakki Collins, Wendy Holker, Isaq Khan, Vaughan Pearce, Rakie Ayola, Astro Bash, Mark Richards, Seema Khan, Peter Lee Alexander, Robert Booker, Zamir Akram and Jeannie Scrancher (Concert Audience)

Synopsis:

Victor contemplates dusting off his dummy and returning to his hobby as a ventriloquist, news which pleases Nick Swainey, who persuades him to perform at a concert he's arranging to raise funds for the elderly. Margaret, meanwhile, befriends a blind man when she delivers flowers to his home. When she makes a subsequent visit, the front door being ajar rouses her suspicions, but nothing prepares her for the shock of finding Albert Warris murdered. There are no clues as to the identity of the murderer, but the Meldrews' next-door neighbour, Pippa, thinks she knows who committed the crime – Mr Meldrew!

5: LOVE AND DEATH

Recorded in studio: **Friday, 24 August and Saturday 25 August 1990**
Transmitted: **Thursday, 8 November 1990, 9.30 p.m.**
Audience figure: **10.24 million**
CAST:

Stephen Lewis	Vince Bluett
Georgina Hale	April Bluett
Leigh Samuels	Petra
Patricia Martinelli	Marie
Paul Mari	Policeman
Peter Burroughs	Rusty
Myrtle Devenish	Elderly Lady on Train

Extras: Michael Savva, Lloyd Harvey, Lorraine Ferraro, Tony Carlton and Lisa Clifton (Train Passengers), Peter Arnold, Hannah Dea Warner, Elaine Williams, Pearl Hawkes, Esme Dear, Peggy Bourne, Basila Sieff, Peter Finn, Robert Ashley Moore, Charlie Gray and Harry Klein (Boarding House Guests), Richard Travers, Glen Francis, Stephen Surrey, Laurie Stenning, Roger Hunt and David Medina (Fishermen on Pier)

Synopsis:

The Meldrews visit their friends Vince and April, who own a seaside guest house, but Victor isn't excited by the idea, especially as they have to sleep in the poky attic room where they have to open the fanlight to take off their vests. And Vince does little to cheer up Victor when he shows him the retirement present he's made for him: a headstone he's prepared for the day he finally pops off. The break wouldn't be complete without the usual chaos, which finds Victor rushed to hospital with a beer glass stuck on his forehead and a chance encounter with two Romanian girls in the bathroom resulting in Margaret getting the wrong end of the stick.

6: TIMELESS TIME

Recorded in studio: **Saturday, 1 September 1990**
Transmitted: **Thursday, 15 November 1990, 9.30 p.m.**
Audience figure: **10.7 million**
(No extra cast for this episode)

Synopsis:

Victor is suffering from insomnia and to top it all he has stomach ache, which he blames on his mother-in-law's dodgy pasta from the previous evening. He admits he knew he was embarking on a 'voyage of discovery' when she suggested he brought along a decent pair of secateurs. The hooting owls sitting directly above Victor's car are also a distraction, especially when they deposit on his roof. A milky drink does little to relax him and before long his leg cramps have returned, just as he was finally drifting off. Car alarms and a rotting hedgehog stuck on his foot ensure the Meldrews aren't going to enjoy a wink of sleep.

CHRISTMAS SPECIAL 1990
(Location scenes filmed between 10 and 18 September 1990)

WHO'S LISTENING?

Recorded in studio: **Friday, 28 September and Saturday, 29 September 1990**
Transmitted: **Thursday, 27 December 1990, 9.30 p.m.**
Audience figure: **10 million**
CAST:

Geoffrey Chater	Reverend Thomas Croker
Enn Reitel	Starkey
Janine Duvitski	Pippa
Angus Deayton	Patrick
Doreen Mantle	Mrs Warboys
Cathy Shipton	Mrs Burridge
Chase Marks	Adam Burridge
Bob Appleby	Ted

Extras: Jonathan Brook (Mr Burridge), Charlie Gray, Terry Duggan, Ignatius Temba, Charles Reynolds, Johnny Clayton, Jane Betterton, Ernestine Hedger, Kay Lyell, Elsie Percival, Irene Frederick, Doris Littlewood, Wym McLeod, Jimmy Morris, James Marston, Charles Phillips, Owen Hatchard, Darren Rapier, Astrid Dines, Bryan Coyle, Grant Wardrop, Jean Paul Orr, Susan Suleyman, Deborah Bundy, Andy Smart, Clive Cunningham, Bickers Clarke and Billy Moore (Down and Outs), Kristie Walker, Barbie Clarke and Lola Morice (Community Centre Helpers), Kerry Barratt, Gregory Ball and George Broad (Video Shop Customers), Bob Gorman, Gerry Gurr, Sandy Sinclair, Robert Frank, David Pelton, Colin Cleminson, George Egan, Bill Lyon, Gordon Williams, Nigel Parkes Davies, Eileen Gorman, Lee Ann Solo, Jane Quy, Juliette St James, Carole Leslie, Jane Perry, Pat Pelton, Sylvia Victor, Iris Terry, Barbara Stewart, Bridget Baugi, Elaine Hewitt, Melanie Gater, Jane Bisson, Rena Burton, Annette Bowers, Anna Farthing, Jo Bernard, Audrey Terrell, Maryloo Fontaine, Gary Mathews, Tony Birch, Terry Courtney, Bob Pearch, John Blake, Rogert Russell, Andy Hollywood, Waydon Croft, Tony Grisillo, Ben Spencer, James Spencer, Ayman Baugi, Dani Baugi, Mathew Williams, Amy Williams, Rebecca Gater, Melody Rockell, Adele Rockell, Jemma Truss, Jonathan Truss, Stephen Cookson, Liam McGuire, Diana Lauren and Nicola Maddock (Congregation)

Synopsis:

It's Christmas and Victor is becoming more like Scrooge with each passing year. He claims that 'all the miseries in the world seem a hundred times worse at Christmas' and proceeds to ban even a tree this year. His gloom isn't helped when 263 garden gnomes turn up on his doorstep when he's only ordered one, and the company has the audacity to suggest he returns the extras. But the arrival of an expensive bottle of wine lifts his spirits for a while; thinking it's a present, the Meldrews delight in the wine's smooth, silky finish only to discover, to their horror, that this £850 offering was for Pippa's father and the courier only delivered it to the Meldrews for safe-keeping. Even when Victor willingly does a good turn, like giving up his Christmas Day to help the local vicar dish up dinner to vagrants at the community hall, life conspires against him and he ends up being held at gunpoint by the deranged Mr Starkey – that is until a brave-hearted Pippa stands up to the gun-wielding vagrant. Christmas turns out to be the most depressing ever for the Meldrews, but for some there's a happy ending, though not for the garden gnomes.

CHRISTMAS SPECIAL 1991
(Location scenes filmed between 23 September and 18 October 1991)

THE MAN IN THE LONG BLACK COAT
Recorded in studio: **Sunday, 3 November 1991**
Transmitted: **Monday, 30 December 1991, 9.00 p.m.**
Audience figure: **10.84 million**
CAST:

Angus Deayton	Patrick
Janine Duvitski	Pippa
Owen Brenman	Nick Swainey
Eric Idle	Dr Mervyn Whale
Michael Robbins	Mr Killick
Cecily Hobbs	Surgery Receptionist

Extras: Adrian Hammond, Neville Denton, John Lewery, Graham Gadd, Gloria Wise, James Miles, Melanie Parr, Horace Carter Allen, Ignatius Temba, Mark Breckon, Anthony Owen, Sylvester Salmon, Muriel Hunte, Ilana Barry, Nancy Adams, Kay Lyell, Inga Daly, Veronique Chomilo-Edwards, Shireen Anwar, Fiona Moyes, Mike Mulloy, Carlo Borelli, Collette Walker, Kathy Eu, Mary Ten Pou, Sonja Kristina, Helena Clayton, Eileen Winterton, Eufa Taylor, Julia Bolden, Ali Ashgar, Dianna Keene, Sarah Gardener, Ernestine Hedger, Keith Ferrari, Charabala Chokshi, Justin Keilty, Lesley Wilson, Irene Frederic, Andy Spiegal, Graham Brooks, Richard Travis, Phoebe Drayton, Gemma Eglington, Poppy Drayton, Sanjay Patel, Scott Luke, Jack Carrivick, Neil Chopra, Jordon Daniel and Daksha Gohil

Synopsis:

It's seven months since Patrick mowed down Victor's garden gnomes with a machine gun and the pair are still not talking. Such is the bitterness Victor feels towards his neighbour that he's been trying to teach Mrs Lacey's cat to vomit on Patrick's rockery. Patrick has another reason to complain, like many other neighbours, when a man in a long black coat sells a pile of manure to the Meldrews but dumps it on their path, not in the allotment. No sooner is it shifted than Dr Whale, from the borough council's Health and Public Safety Department, appears to tell Victor that his manure isn't all that it seems. There's a certain glow about it. And while Victor worries about his dung, Pippa's discovery that she's pregnant is short-lived when she's involved in an accident while driving a bus, resulting in hospitalisation. In one fell swoop she loses her baby, job and licence for drink-driving.

SERIES 3
(Location scenes filmed between 23 September and 18 October 1991)

1: MONDAY MORNING WILL BE FINE
Recorded in studio: **Sunday, 17 November 1991**
Transmitted: **Sunday, 2 February 1992, 9.05 p.m.**
Audience figure: **14.75 million**
CAST:

Tony Millan	Jack Aylesbury
Jan Ravens	Pat Aylesbury
Richard Davies	Billy
Diana Coupland	Meg
Jonathan Kydd	Chippie Joe
James Hickish	Detective Gannis
Nick Ball	Detective Diller
Helen Patrick	Sales Assistant
Angus Deayton	Announcer

Extras: David Madiana, Colette Appleby, Susan Goode, Peggy-Ann Fraser, Ray Martin, George Raymond, Carina Roma, Joann Allchin, Michael Brown, Nick Davion, Treacle, Danny Lawrence, Noreen Phillips, Karen Bourne, Joanna Garcis, Prince Morgan, Doris Littlewood, Ellen Miller, Charlie Rayford, Sharon E. Robertson, Phil Downes, Judy Cowne, Rab McClintock, Eric Kent, John Buckland, Terry Cavanagh, Barbie Clarke, Graham Davies, Frank Jakeman, Denise Mansfield, Eniye Osifo, Jon Raymond, Avril Kaye, Roy Ashby, Don Bachurst, Ken Field, Graham Ackman, Kathleen Heath, Barbara Jaeson and Bickers Clarke

Synopsis:

The Meldrews had only popped out for an hour and return to find they've been burgled. To make matters worse, if their neighbours across the road, the Aylesburys, had been more vigilant they could have reported the incident instead of mistaking them for removal men and making them a cuppa. One of their greatest losses is the television, leaving Victor and Margaret twiddling their thumbs and struggling to pass the time. Victor decides to visit his local pub, where he bumps into an old school pal. Confusion ensues, though, when his school mate, Billy, gets Victor confused with someone else and proceeds to insult this guy he remembers from school called Victor Meldrew!

2: DREAMLAND

Recorded in studio: **Sunday, 10 November 1991**
Transmitted: **Sunday, 9 February 1992, 9.05 p.m.**
Audience figure: **14.5 million**
CAST:

Doreen Mantle	Mrs Warboys
Owen Brenman	Nick Swainey
Barbara Grant	Lady 1 in Tea Shop
Annette Kerr	Lady 2 in Tea Shop
Damaris Hayman	Elderly Lady
Enn Reitel	Tramp
Julie Hewlett	Policewoman

Extras: Kit Hillier (PC), June Hammond and Sarah Gardner (Women at Victor's), Denise Harland and Thea McIntyre (Tea Shop Customers), Lynden McIntyre (Waitress), Richard Bond Andrews, John Gallagher, Roy Baker and John Fernley (People at Fête), Ron Williams and Roy Selfe (Dog Handlers), Julie Morgan (WPC) Also: Margaret Shore, Jeannette Arke, Nina Downey, Gordon Williams, Pat Fincham, Pat Douglas, Chris Abbott, Jane Quy, Dave Jackman, Ethel Vaudrey, Wendy Walsh, Sylvia Victor, Marlene Rabin, Mike Mungarven, Ruth Stewart, Shirley Morgan, Mave Morgan, Annet Peters, John Jones, Derrick Fincham, Vanessa Newbury, Alexander Lyon, Gail Rowney, Margaret Turner, Sue Batchelor, Penny Perfect, Ernestine Hedger, Pat Le Clerc, Marjorie Maxted, Eric Courtney, Elaine Hewitt, Roger Hunt, Mary Courtney, Penelope Goddard, Martin Daniels, Susie Lyle, Sallie Francis, Angela Bee, Patricia Varley, Audrey Joke, Pamela Foa and Mark Brett

Synopsis:

As Mrs Warboys informs a couple of strangers in the local café, Margaret Meldrew has been having a recurring nightmare where she's waiting to hang for battering to death a balding old man, and although she's given a last-minute reprieve she doesn't want to leave her cell. While Victor decides to attend Nick Swainey's fête, purely because the blonde with the pouting lips from that coffee commercial is the special

guest, Margaret causes a panic when she doesn't arrive for work. A fretting Victor calls the police, but when a coat like Margaret's is found on the canal towpath, he fears the worst and begins contemplating a life alone. Then his wife walks through the door, to Victor's immense relief. Needing some space, en route to work one day she booked an impromptu coach trip to Margate. Victor later attends the Action for the Elderly annual fête but is disappointed when the special guest doesn't turn up and he gets caught up in some monkey business.

3: THE BROKEN REFLECTION

Recorded in studio: **Sunday, 1 December 1991**
Transmitted: **Sunday, 16 February 1992, 9.05 p.m.**
Audience figure: **14.5 million**
CAST:

Angus Deayton	Patrick
Janine Duvitski	Pippa
Paul Courtenay Hugh	Chinese Youth
John Shin	Chinese Customer
Vincent Wong	Chinese Chef
Su-Lin Looi	Chinese Girl
Jim Sweeney	Sales Representative
Richard Pearson	Alfred
Ruth Burton	Young Mother
Michael Jones	Young Toddler
Peter Heppeltwhaite	Workman

Extras: Juliette St James (Mother's Friend), John Packham, Dennys Hackett and Norman Wheeler (Pipe Smokers). Also: Jack Curtis, Eddie Hicks, Yvonne Highton, Sheila Williams, Bill Butcher, Mick J. Gutteridge, Andy Sanderson, Rosemary Warwick, Vicki Maxine, Stella Duffy, Clea McIlraith, David Bowles, Katharine Reeve, Diana Keene and Michael Ho

Synopsis:

Victor's brother, Alfred, visits from New Zealand but although he hasn't set eyes on his brother for over two decades, Victor's far from happy and feels they haven't anything in common any more. And if he hasn't got enough on his plate having to reminisce about the old days, he's got to water Pippa and Patrick's house plants while they're on holiday. Alfred's peculiar ways and deafness grate on Victor but an unfortunate incident results in his brother packing his bags and returning home. It seems Victor can't get anything right because when he sees a young girl throwing a beer can into his garden, he seeks revenge by dropping litter through her family's letterbox. The trouble doesn't stop there, though, and the neighbours stuff a hosepipe through the letterbox and flood the house – except they've picked the wrong property, dampening Pippa and Patrick's mood when they return.

4: THE BEAST IN THE CAGE
Recorded in studio: **Sunday, 24 November 1991**
Transmitted: **Sunday, 23 February 1992, 9.05 p.m.**
Audience figure: **15.6 million**
CAST:

Doreen Mantle	Mrs Warboys
Trevor Byfield	Mr Salmon
Louise Duprey	Lisa
Tish Allen	Carol

Extras: Barbara Desmond, Eric Courtney, Jay Roberts, Keith Steele, Katherine Loeppky, Mike Pruden, Ben Lester, Dallas Dee, Jenny Roberts, Alan Hankinson, Frank Curtis, Miriam Humphries, Ray Brooks, Rebecca Campbell, Mary Courtney, Weston Hayles, Neville Clark, Llewellyn Williams and Adam David

Synopsis:
Victor, Margaret and Mrs Warboys have been stuck in bank holiday traffic for over four hours and tempers are starting to fray. With temperatures soaring, and Victor promising to book a couple of seats in a bread oven next bank holiday, his mood deteriorates because of the constant electric shocks he's receiving from the car. Margaret's suggestion that he wears rubber shoes next time is rebuffed with the comment that it's so bad he'll insert a lightning rod up his trousers. And to make matters worse, Mrs Warboys has forgotten to buy Victor some smoky bacon crisps. Whoever came up with the stupid idea of setting foot inside the car on a bank holiday?

5: BEWARE THE TRICKSTER ON THE ROOF
Recorded in studio: **Sunday, 15 November 1991**
Transmitted: **Sunday, 1 March 1992, 9.05 p.m.**
Audience figure: **16.16 million**
CAST:

Angus Deayton	Patrick
Janine Duvitski	Pippa

Owen Brenman	Nick Swainey
Britt Morrow	Young Wife
Hilda Braid	Mrs Skimpson
Steve Perry	The Cyclist
Peter Aubrey	Mr Tildsley
Louise Kerr	Wife

Voice only: John Challis (Jack the Burglar)

Extras: Cynthia Powell and Keeley Marshall (Jehovah's Witnesses), James Harvey and David Foster (Husbands), Carole Garcia (Wife), John Dodd (Resident), Mike Mungarven and Pat Le Clerc (Poilcemen), Carol Church (WPC), Terry Dallison and Keith Nicholas (Ambulancemen) and Benjamin Dimmick (Little Boy). Also: Celia Maslin, Gay Pulman, James Hendry, D. Maslin, Ann Gillham, Ray Ash, Mike Benjafield and Dianne Ash

Synopsis:
Patrick and Pippa are placing their house on the market but are worried that Victor's antics next door, including escapades with a dismembered teddy and Margaret's problem with a cow, will put prospective purchasers off. Nick Swainey, meanwhile, returns from his North African jaunt bearing a holiday gift: a dead scorpion paperweight, which according to local custom is supposedly unlucky to its owner. Victor doesn't believe in such nonsense, but when a taxi they ordered fails to arrive and a storm leads to a leaking roof, it seems there could be some truth in the curse of the scorpion.

6: THE WORST HORROR OF ALL
Recorded in studio: **Sunday, 8 December 1991**
Transmitted: **Sunday, 8 March 1992, 9.05 p.m.**
Audience figure: **16.2 million**

happiness when Victor is offered a full-time job as a doorman at the Norfolk Royale Hotel. His period of employment is short-lived, though, when he argues with a toffee-nosed couple and gets to grips with a toupee. If Victor thinks the day couldn't get any worse, he's wrong, because he hadn't anticipated the arrival of Ronnie and Mildred, armed with photographs and a tin of assorted biscuits.

SERIES 4
(Location scenes filmed between 13 September and 11 October 1992)

1: THE PIT AND THE PENDULUM
Recorded in studio: **Sunday, 13 December 1992**
Transmitted: **Sunday, 31 January 1993, 8.55 p.m.**
Audience figure: **17.3 million**

CAST:

Doreen Mantle — Mrs Warboys
John Rutland — Wilfred
Harold Goodwin — Window Cleaner
Gordon Peters — Ronnie
Jean Challis — Mildred
William Chubb — Man in Taxi
Rowan Suart — Woman in Taxi
Geoffrey Fordham-Barnett — Man in Wheelchair

Extras: Jill Goldston, Della McCrae and Sally Sinclair (Nurses), Maria Rice-Mundy (Hotel Guest on Steps), David Fowlds (Porter), Kay Langfield and Wendy Holker (Hotel Guests) and Vaughan Collins (Haughty Hotel Guest). Also: Carrie Leigh, Jane Perry, Nick Wild, Sally Horsley, Andy Coombes, Keith Swaden, Janine Cook, Cherrie Marshall, Caroline Lyndsey, Eric Jack, Lysette Symonds, Helen Kelly, Anthony Owen, Martin Miller, Paul Rutler, Ross Gibbins, Ken Coombs, Philip Ticehurst, Kay Lyell, Zamir Akram, Kelvin Suaquan, Yvonne Allard, Odette Smith, Jenny Crome, Tony Snell, Roger Weightman, Lee Harington, Gertrude Shilling, Tony O'Leary, Fred Loe, Davinda Kaur, Laura Kingsman, Lucia Abdalla, Juanita Dinham, Billy Kelly, Daisy May Mulcahy, Jean Oringe, Graham Mason, Beatrice Young, Kathy Thomas, Jessica McDonald, Ashley Daly, Bonnie Pang, Mike Brown, Ian Gledhill, Clive Hopkins, Simon Joseph, Peter Steiner, Huw Prall, Donald Allard, Amber MacDonald and Nicola Kingsman

Synopsis:
Another eventful week in the life of Victor Meldrew: he visits the local casualty department when the garden shed collapses on him and ends up being scrubbed with turps, and arrives home scratching because he's caught fleas from Mrs Lacey's cat. But there's one moment of

CAST:

Angus Deayton — Patrick
Janine Duvitski — Pippa
Daniel Peacock — Mr Kazanzi
Sarah Bolden — Mr Kazanzi's daughter

Voice only: Katharine Page (Margaret's Mother)

Extras: Tishaka Jackson, Greta Lange and Louise Ling (Schoolgirls)

Synopsis:
Tangling with Mr Kazanzi, alias The Hairy Man, isn't advisable as Victor soon discovers. When Patrick's outsized cherry tree invades Victor's rockery and begins throttling his junipers, he hires Kazanzi to help repair the damage. But instead of hard graft it's idling that the hairy creature seems more qualified in, chatting up Pippa and entertaining passing schoolgirls with his chainsaw act. Later, when Victor stumbles across Mr Kazanzi and a girl in his house, he gets the wrong end of the stick and ends up being planted up to his neck inside the chasm Kazanzi has dug in the garden. When Margaret returns home, she hasn't time to start shovelling before the phone rings and she receives shocking news: her mother has died.

2: DESCENT INTO THE MAELSTROM
Recorded in studio: **Sunday, 20 December 1992**
Trasmitted: **Sunday, 7 February 1993, 8.55 p.m.**

Audience figure: **16.67 million**

CAST:

Doreen Mantle	Mrs Warboys
Owen Brenman	Nick Swainey
Stephen Ley	Unemployed Man
Helen Lederer	Andrea Temple
Ben Perkins	Baby Boy
Joanna Bacon	Woman
Laura Cox	Mrs Ashcroft

Extras: Richard Kennedy-Valentine (Baby Boy), Amritpal Notay (TV Engineer), Roger Trim (Mr Ashcroft), Connor Donegan (Stand-by Baby Boy for Studio).

Synopsis:

Margaret collapses and is confined to bed. Nervous exhaustion building up over the last thirty-five years is to blame, but there's little chance of a speedy recovery with Victor acting as nursemaid. With his wife bed-bound, Victor has to attend cousin Roger's sixtieth birthday bash on his own, but that's looking unlikely when a mix-up at the dry cleaner's leaves him with little choice of suits: it's either a mix-and-match outfit or a gorilla costume! Gradually Margaret regains her strength, boosted by the arrival, one day, of a face from the past. Andrea Temple, who used to live behind the Meldrews, visits to show off her new baby, but not everything is as it seems.

3: HEARTS OF DARKNESS

Recorded in studio: **Sunday, 3 January 1993**
Transmitted: **Sunday, 14 February 1993, 8.55 p.m.**
Audience figure: **17.48 million**

CAST:

Owen Brenman	Nick Swainey
Doreen Mantle	Mrs Warboys
Bill Gavin	Mr Gorshin
Arabella Weir	Sonia
Janet Henfrey	Miss Lander
Melody Brown	Rachel
Nick Scott	Martin
Katharine Page	Mrs Endicott
Seymour Matthews	Official
Marcia Myrie	Official

Extras: Simon Sands (Man with Burger), Paul Slade (Park Keeper), Robert Powers (Boat Keeper), Kevin Hudson (Man in Boat), Pat Le

Clerc (Policeman), Marianne Bergin (Policewoman), Kristopher Shaw, Karly Shaw, James Spencer, Ben Spencer and Matthew Williams (Children); Paul Rutter, Marc Raymond and Gary Brown (Yobs), Paul Bannon, Wendy Lowder, Chris Fennell, Jane Bisson, Gary Mathews, Pat Pelton, David Pelton, Simon King, Nick Wilde, Mark Squires, Colin Cleminson and John Jones (Pub Customers), Adam Poulton, Melita Clarke, Deborah Perry, Joe Wenbourne, Tricia Darns, Patricia Hall, Jackie Avey, Ever Green, Pauline Green, Martin Garfield, Sally Sinclaire, Lee Field, Stephen Hunter, Joanna Marshall, Lisa McHugh, Carlo Borrelli, Micky Winston, Kay Lyell and Wyn McLeod (Daytrippers), Eileen Winterton, Carlo Borrelli, Muriel Wellesley, Madge Ward, Douglas Coates, John Dodd and Kay Lyell (Residents), Lisette Simmonds, Lyndon McIntyre, Annet Peters and Waydon Croft (Scarecrows), Andy Coombs and Zena King (Doubles for Officials). Also: Sydonie Platt, Max De Nett, James Grimes, Lindsey Chamier and Simone Dawson

Synopsis:

It was supposed to be a pleasant day trip in the Norfolk countryside for the Meldrews – they've even asked Mrs Warboys and Nick Swainey along. As he's inclined to do, Victor spoils the fun by sporting a bloody nose after an altercation with yobs and an encounter with a guy at the pub. It's certainly an eventful day because a gentle row on the water finds the party marooned in the middle of nowhere. Victor's cries of help are futile and end up aggravating his nosebleed again, but if only they had known earlier that the river is only knee-deep. Back on dry ground, they trudge through thick woodland before Victor and Mrs Warboys put their feet well and truly in it! As a last resort, Victor heads off alone to summon help and stumbles across a retirement home – but it's more like a rest home from hell. A valiant Victor prepares to come to the rescue of the aged.

4: WARM CHAMPAGNE

Recorded in studio: **Sunday, 10 January 1993**
Transmitted: **Sunday, 21 February 1993, 8.55 p.m.**
Audience figure: **17 million**

CAST:

Angus Deayton	Patrick
Janine Duvitski	Pippa
Anthony Watson	First Boy
Simon Long	Second Boy
Alan Cooke	Ambulanceman

Susan Barnard	Ambulancewoman
Georgina Beer	Mrs Staveacre
Tristram Jellinek	Ben

Extras: Denny Lee (Man Driving Van), John Stacey and Jay Mayson (Ambulancemen), Stuart Myers (Maitre d'Hotel), David Garry (Wine Waiter), Peter Cooney (Waiter), Peter Ripley, Paul Kirby, Ray Severn, Peter Jessup, John Baker, Frances Ward-Smith, Carole Garcia, Leah Foly, Melita Clarke, Ronald Markham, Patricia Turton and Carole Careford (Diners), Patients: From Highcliff Day Centre

Synopsis:

The Meldrews return from holiday to be greeted by the usual display of graffiti on the walls and a smashed window, and no sooner has Victor walked through the door than he's shouting and complaining about society's ills. Margaret is suffering from post-holiday blues, too, and is tempted to phone Ben, someone she took a shine too while away. Her hesitation is resolved when he calls instead. She surreptitiously arranges a rendezvous but her liaison is short-lived when, despite all his foibles, she realises it's Victor she loves — although she's in for a shock when she arrives home and finds her beloved unknowingly climbing into bed with a mystery woman.

5: THE TRIAL

Recorded in studio: **Sunday, 29 November 1992**
Transmitted: **Sunday, 28 February 1993, 8.55 p.m.**
Audience figure: **18.39 million**
CAST:
(Only Richard Wilson appeared in this episode.)

Synopsis:

Victor is summoned for jury service but five days have passed and he's yet to set foot inside the courtroom. He's bored stiff hanging around, like a prisoner in his own home, waiting for the phone to ring. To help pass the time he browses through a medical dictionary until he believes he's got every ailment under the sun, thinks a growing crack on the wall means subsidence and also finds time to shout at the manager of the local garden centre when a yucca is delivered and firmly planted in the toilet pan. But being abusive to some Jehovah's Witnesses who came calling the previous week comes back to haunt him and he finally gets his turn in court — not as a witness, but as the accused.

6: SECRET OF THE SEVEN SORCERERS

Recorded in studio: **Sunday, 17 January 1993**
Transmitted: **Sunday, 7 March 1993, 8.55 p.m.**
Audience figure: **17.99 million**
CAST:

Doreen Mantle	Mrs Warboys
Chris Walker	Fire Officer
Owen Brenman	Nick Swainey
John Cassady	Window Cleaner
Angus Deayton	Patrick
Janine Duvitski	Pippa
Simon Fisher-Becker	Magician
Vincent Leigh	Fire Officer (2)

Voice only: David Renwick (Radio Presenter)

Extras: Ann Bryson (Mimsy), Adam Poulton (Café Owner), Ken Flory (Customer), Alan Thompson-Jones (Mr Matthews, the Magician), Laurence Hawsley, Geoff Strum and Ricky Galahad (Firemen), Charles Reynolds, Roy Seeley, Steven Rose, Danny Lawrence and Harry Klein (Magicians)

Synopsis:

Mrs Warboys' world is thrown into turmoil when she suspects her husband, Chris, of having an affair with a woman further down the street. Her suspicions are aroused when a pillow case from the woman's washing line blows into her garden and she notices upon examination stains similar to those Chris has on his shirts, courtesy of his acne gel. Hiring a private eye is the only answer. Victor, meanwhile, has started a new job as a lollipop man at a local school, but he's worried about his chances of turning the job into a long-term assignment, especially as the previous incumbent gave his life in the line of duty. Later on, there's high drama at Victor's weekly meeting of the Magic Club when one of the magicians suffers a suspected heart attack, but the wrong person is carted off to hospital while the poor patient is stuck inside a trunk for an agonising five hours. Amid all the chaos, Patrick and Pippa arrive for a meal, comparing the event with an evening spent at the Munsters' because 'you don't know what nameless horror you're going to come across next'. Meanwhile, Mrs Warboys has her heart broken when her hubby ditches her for another woman — to Jean's dismay, it's the private detective she hired.

COMIC RELIEF SPECIAL 1993
VICTOR IN THE BATH
Transmitted: **12 March 1993**

CHRISTMAS SPECIAL 1993
(Location scenes filmed between 8 May – 26 June 1993)

ONE FOOT IN THE ALGARVE
Transmitted: **Sunday, 26 December 1993, 9.05 p.m.**
Audience figure: **20 million**
CAST:

Doreen Mantle	Mrs Warboys
Peter Cook	Martin Trout
Wilfred Grove	Ticket Collector
Joan Sims	Lady on Plane
Edward De Souza	Afonso
Louis Mahoney	Humphrey Lennox
Eamonn Walker	Hugo Lennox
Louise Duprey	Shirley Lennox
Craig Ferguson	Glaswegian
Anna Nicholas	Isabella
Clare Porter	Girl by Pool

PORTUGUESE CAST:

Benjamin Falço	Old Man at Tavern
Augusto Portela	Policeman
Eduardo Viana	Policeman
Jose Gomes	Farmworker
Jorge Parente	Farmworker
Andre Maia	Fisherman
Jorge Sequerra	Coastguard
Joço D'Avila	Mortuary Attendant
Maria D'Aires	Mortuary Assistant
Luis Zagalo	Photo Shop Owner
Lidia Franco	Maria
Joço Lagarto	Cabbie
Margarida Rodrigues	Waitress

Synopsis:

Romance is in the air for newly divorced Mrs Warboys who, after thirteen years of writing, is finally meeting her Portuguese pen pal, Afonso, who's also lost his partner. She probably wishes that she'd left Victor behind when she jets off to the Algarve, because his plans for a quiet sunshine break are shattered when he becomes innocently embroiled in a plot to discredit a well-known national figure. A mix-up back in England results in paparazzo Martin Trout believing his would-be headline-hitting roll of film has been mistakenly picked up by the Meldrews, forcing Trout to head for Portugal in pursuit of his snaps. While Victor's aftershave is attracting unwanted attention from four-legged creatures, Mrs Warboys is hoping her perfume doesn't repel Afonso, by whom she's rather smitten. But there is more to his story of his wife's disappearance two years previously: why has no body been found? And why aren't there any photos of his beloved around the house? Their eventful trip continues when Victor believes Jean has fallen off the cliff, but surely the severed foot found in a shark's stomach isn't all that's left of the Meldrews' long-standing friend? Fortunately it's a case of mistaken identity as far as the foot is concerned, and Mrs Warboys is found in hospital, although she's perfectly fit. Later, just as Afonso proposes to Jean, she stumbles across Afonso's wife's shoes and soon discovers the truth about his wife of twenty-six years. At least she's got her holiday snaps to help her remember this memorable trip to the sun, or so she thought.

SERIES 5
(Location scenes filmed between 9 October and 13 November 1994)

1: THE MAN WHO BLEW AWAY
Transmitted: **Sunday, 25 December 1994, 9.00 p.m.**
Audience figure: **15.14 million**
CAST:

Janine Duvitski	Pippa
Angus Deayton	Patrick
Brian Murphy	Mr Foskett
Daniel Smith	Ian Grimwade
Ryan O'Leary	Neil Grimwade

Extras: Vaughan Collins (Leibnitz), Denis Matsuki (Wang), Paula Hartigan (Mrs Bithery). Also: Rojer Weightman, Matthew Day, Cliff Eddleston, Yasmin Asar, Geoff Lewis, Helen Kirby, Ann Chapman, Karen Banning, Gordon Williams, Angela Taylor, Thomas Chapman, June Simmonds, Mark Chapman, Petra Taylor and Nicola Maddock

Synopsis:

Victor's weekend is a washout long before it's even started, thanks, partly, to the news that the notorious heap of metal passing as his car is found after three months, shattering dreams of claiming off the insurance and investing in a newer model. Adding to his misery, the Meldrews' neighbours are having one of their rowdy parties again. The music is still blaring at 2.30 a.m., keeping him awake. Just when the Meldrews realise it's Sunday and they won't have to surface before lunchtime, an unexpected phone call from Mr Foskett, whom the Meldrews met whilst holidaying at Weston-super-Mare, puts paid to their plans of a lie-in. The Meldrews are kicking themselves for politely suggesting that if he's ever in the neighbourhood, he should pop in. It's a troubled Mr Foskett, though, who arrives on their doorstep.

2: ONLY A STORY

Transmitted: **Sunday, 1 January 1995, 9.00 p.m.**
Audience figure: **16.34 million**
CAST:

Doreen Mantle	Mrs Warboys
Owen Brenman	Nick Swaincy
Steve Humphrey	Reporter

Synopsis:

Since Mrs Warboys' flat was flooded, she's been lodging with the Meldrews. Surprisingly, having the eccentric Jean staying isn't bothering Victor in the slightest. In fact, it's Margaret who bridles while her husband – Mr Impatient himself – is unusually placid and remains a picture of serenity. His calmness is the result of stress-relieving therapy at a reflexologist's. He's more able to cope with the problems life throws at him, that is until events decide to gang up against him, including puncturing his bum, being mistaken for the editor of the local rag, finding himself locked out of his house in the pouring rain and having to endure Nick Swaincy's annual jolly with the *Dixon of Dock Green* Appreciation Society. Perhaps spending out on a stress-relieving course isn't such a good idea after all, especially when Margaret informs him that his so-called reflexologist is, in fact, a prostitute who's been using more than her little finger to stroke Victor's feet!

3: THE AFFAIR OF THE HOLLOW LADY

Transmitted: **Sunday, 8 January 1995, 9.05 p.m.**

Audience figure: **11.7 million**
CAST:

Doreen Mantle	Mrs Warboys
Barbara Windsor	Millicent Miles
Nick Maloney	Mr Laverick
Edna Monterel	Woman in Hospital
Richard Lumsden	Nurse

Extras: Irene Frederic, Nigel Parkes Davies, Michelle O'Brien, Jean Price, Jane Quy, Mike Newbold, Jamie Spencer, Nadger Webb, Emily Holker, Janet Richards, Michelle Ballentyne, Paul Rutter, Sheila Currie, Alan Musgrave-Scott, Debbie Lamb, Cliff Eddleston, Ian James, Mike Beryafield, Madge Ward, Maretta Sibley, Hugh Gallagher, Yvonne Greenslade, Peter Price, Francesca Irwin & children, Eric Billingham, Jane Bisson, Gay Pulman, Wendy Holker, Katie Austen, Christine Lee, Mark Davis, Adrian Hammond, Sue Woods, Mickey Winston, Lucy Simmons, Lorna Rosslyn, Lisa Madkins, Brian Ward, Donald Austen, Chandana, Sarah Jane D'Or, Femi, David Howell, Bryan Jacobs, Sara Neighbour, Richard Francis, John Godwin, Charles Benard, Rachel Chaney, Frances Ward, Harjit Singh, Fed Whitham, George Bailey, Chris Connor, Ricky Ellis, Lorraine Gunnery, Daviner Kalrer, Joanna Marshall, Tony Poole, Richard Hall, Patrick Courteney, Barbara Smith, Polly Allen, Judd Solo, Jennifer Storey, Kevin Sumner, Jane Bishop, Dot Cosgrove, Tania Emery, Cassie Hatton, Roland Kitchen and Della McCrae

Synopsis:

Margaret's need for vegetables for that evening's casserole means Victor will have to fend off red-haired Millicent Miles at the local greengrocer's, who'd love to get her claws into Victor. Before he leaves the house, the Meldrews are confronted with two pieces of bad news: their drive to tighten up on household security is fruitless when they find their fridge has been stolen whilst they're in the house, and a phone call informs them that Mrs Warboys has had a car accident while returning from her sister's in Blackpool. Later, a brief encounter with flirty Millicent results in Victor being locked in her delivery van and, therefore, missing an important football match he was planning to attend. But then the offer to watch it at Millicent's comes his way.

4: REARRANGING THE DUST

Transmitted: **Sunday, 15 January 1995, 9.05 p.m.**
Audience figure: **10.91 million**

CAST:

Antony Sher	Businessman
Damaris Hayman	Receptionist
Valerie Minifie	Woman
Laura Cox	Woman

Voice only: David Renwick (Solicitor)

Synopsis:

The Meldrews are planning to make a will but have been waiting so long to see their solicitor that Victor comments sarcastically that his buttocks are turning into 'fossilised fuel'. A series of mishaps, including getting chewing gum stuck all over his fingers, knocking the barometer off the wall, finding bird's muck on his nose and nearly demolishing the glass-topped table with his foot, adds to his misery. While an exasperated Margaret tries desperately to retain her sanity, Victor is handed a notice by the secretary informing him that he's being sued for damages for an alleged assault on a pit bull terrier with a coconut meringue.

5: HOLE IN THE SKY

Transmitted: **Sunday, 22 January 1995, 9.05 p.m.**
Audience figure: **10.87 million**

CAST:

Angus Deayton	Patrick
Janine Duvitski	Pippa
Christopher Ryan	McKendrick Twins
Michael Fenton Stevens	Geoffrey Croker
Hilary Mason	Mrs Stewkley
Peter Tuddenham	Mr Stewkley

Synopsis:

Margaret and Pippa's attempts to restore neighbourly relations between their husbands backfire when they book a table for them at an Armenian restaurant where no one speaks English and they're regarded as secret lovers, thanks to Pippa's request for an intimate table where they can discuss private affairs. The following morning, the Meldrews are preparing their loft for the arrival of the notorious McKendrick twins whom Victor has hired to carry out the loft conversion, and Margaret thinks her luck might be changing when she finds £80 at the greengrocer's. Unfortunately, Victor has got his conscientious hat on and thinks it should be returned. Via a receipt, he learns it's a

Mr Croker's money; Croker turns out to be Pippa's brother. When Victor later spots Pippa and her brother kissing, he suspects his neighbour of having an affair.

6: THE EXTERMINATING ANGEL

Transmitted: **Sunday, 29 January 1995, 9.05 p.m.**
Audience figure: **10.39 million**

CAST:

Owen Brenman	Nick Swainey
John Bird	Lewis Atterbury
Anita Chellamah	Tania
Gordon Peters	Ronnie
Barbara Ashcroft	Mildred
Ronald Leigh-Hunt	Roy
Annette Kerr	Ruth
Jennie Stoller	Dentist

Extras: Sarunit Kaur (Nurse), Philip Jay (Businessman). Also: Annet Peters, Penny Perfect, Carole Leslie, Vanessa Newberry, Jane Perry, Barbara Whatley, Thea McIntyre, Kay Renner, Jodie Jackman, John Dodd, Eric Courtney, David Weller, Andy Coombes, Martin Daniels, Rhoda Lappage, Angela Bee, Mary Courtney, Denise Harland, Debbi Lloyd, Lynda Leith, Lyndon McIntyre, Sharon Wildern, Peter Kemp, John Gallagher, Neville Denton, Stephen Cookson, Daniel Jackman, Waydon Croft, Suzi Mollet, Christine Gallagher, Wendy Lowder, Lisette Simmonds, Pat Pelton, Penny Goddard, Diana Lauren, Suzy Lyle, Dave Jackman, George Egan, Rupert Webb, Dave Cole, Philip Ticehurst, Robert Crake, Kevin Hudson, Steve Greer, David Hayley, Tim Wallace Abbot, Terry Courtney, Clarke Johnson, Rodney Wood, Melanie Gater, Gaynor Morgan, Chris Lloyd, Tony Birch, Richard Morgan and Sydonie Platt

Synopsis:

While Nick Swainey has fallen for the nurse caring for his mother but is too shy to ask her out, Victor receives a call from Lewis Atterbury with an offer of work: acting as his chauffeur, ferrying him around in either his Merc, BMW or Jag. But his appointment is nearly over before it's started when on his first day one of the car's aerials tangles with the carwash, and he infuriates a group of rugby players who retaliate by tipping the Merc on its roof. Everyone is entitled to make one mistake, but the trouble with Victor is that his bouts of misfortune tend to gang up on him. Visiting Ronnie and Mildred is never a good idea, especially when he decides to drive Mr Atterbury's BMW, only to discover, to his horror, that their garage is floorless. And surely Victor should have expected a tank to come crashing through a hedge in the exact spot he's parked his employer's treasured Jag. It's the last straw for his employer, who gives Victor his cards. But it's not just Victor's day that has been ruined: Nick Swainey faces sad news about Tania, the nurse he'd set his heart on.

CHRISTMAS SPECIAL 1995
(Location scenes filmed between 27 September and 16 October 1995)

THE WISDOM OF THE WITCH
Transmitted: **Monday, 25 December 1995, 9.00 p.m.**
Audience figure: **17.77 million**
CAST:

Angus Deayton	Patrick
Janine Duvitski	Pippa
Phil Daniels	Melvin
Rachel Bell	Lorna
Joanne Engelsman	Christine
Bruce Byron	Tunstall
Peter McNally	Gridley
Peter Terry	Postman
Virginie Gilchrist	Party Guest
Tony Sibbald	American
Boris	Edwin

Voice only: Dick Vosburgh

Extras: David Garry, Jennifer Storey, Steve Rome, Rachel Bond, Philip Phedonos, Tracey Merrit, Ash Boxall, Ivan Lee, Richard Shidhu, Sehtjin Woo, Richard Francis, Clive Thompson, Sue Goode, Jane Ellison, Sara France, Martin Garfield, Penny Rigden, Sherryn Salmon, Tommy Walsh, Gillian Duxury, Alan Macaulay, Violet Leeown, Jenny Vim, Sharon Tan, David Lloyd Fisher, Keith Connolly, Denise Powell, Anita Green, Robin Marchal, Maurice McParland, Pearl Richie, Jason Paul, Frances Ward, Jackie Hall, Julian Sua, Sandra Tan, Richard Tharp, Paul Ellison, Robert Crake, Maggie Greenwood and Suzanne Grala

Synopsis:
Margaret writes to relatives informing them of the sudden death of cousin Ursula and the nightmare that was to take hold of their lives three weeks ago while the Meldrews prepared to celebrate their thirty-seventh wedding anniversary. We drift back in time to the point where Victor has secured part-time work on a farm –

but by 6 p.m. trouble is brewing. Margaret explains to Victor during a meal at a Chinese restaurant that an unexpected meeting with a witch has left her worried. While she predicted Margaret enjoying a long and peaceful life, Victor would be visited by a plague of devils. It's later discovered that Victor's life will meet a sudden end and that he should avoid, at all costs, making long journeys. Unfortunately that's something he can't do because cousin Ursula's death while watching *Telly Addicts* means the Meldrews have her rambling house in the country to sort out, resulting in a 100-mile trip for Victor. When a blizzard sets in and he ends up abandoning the car just half an hour from Ursula's house, he suddenly discovers Patrick locked in the boot. Having finally sold their house and seemingly ridding themselves of Mr Meldrew, Patrick, thanks to his new secretary and her jealous thuggish boyfriend, finds himself having to spend the weekend fetched up with Victor. Then there's the added problem of the maniacal boyfriend, the lost furniture and the dreaded Edwin.

CHRISTMAS SPECIAL 1996
(Location scenes filmed in September and October 1996)

STARBOUND
Transmitted: **Thursday, 26 December 1996, 9.00 p.m.**
Audience figure: **17.47 million**
CAST:

Owen Brenman	Nick Swainey
Elizabeth Chambers	Dog Owner
Lucy Davis	Mrs Blanchard
Angus Deayton	Patrick Trench
Janine Duvitski	Pippa Trench
Rula Lenska	Fenella Fortune
Doreen Mantle	Mrs Warboys
Roli Okorodudu	Primary School Teacher
Ray Winstone	Vagrant and Millichope

Extras: Michael Kenton (Uncle Louie), Robert Crake (Policeman), Sheila Rennie (Woman with Truss), Lucy Hewlett, Lottie Etwell and Lucy White (Giggling Girls at Bus Stop), Henry Cole, James Harvey, Phillip Jay and Mike Mungarvan (Businessmen), Paul D'Monaco and Jo Eastman (Police Officers)

Synopsis:
While Nick Swainey's mother is convinced she's being

abducted each night by aliens, Victor is not himself either: not only does his house become a dumping ground for the local area's unwanted surgical appliances and artificial limbs but he's remaining calm about the so-called vagrant who's decided to squat in the Meldrews' garden shed. Victor has even taken to keeping him in supplies of biscuits. Meanwhile Patrick, whose job is on the line, is doing all he can to impress his new man-eating boss, Fenella Fortune, including letting himself be molested on a bed of tomatoes. Patrick can't believe his eyes, though, when he realises Victor is being employed at Fenella's sumptuous home as a gardener. But while Nick's mother now thinks she's being kidnapped and taken to Neptune, Margaret looks to the heavens to try and understand why Victor is full of the joys of spring after just one day gardening. He's even started telling Margaret that she 'looks lovely' – most unlike him. Could it really be forces from another world that are to blame for Victor's strangeness, or could it be something to do with the so-called tramp and the powder he's been mistaking for plant food?

CHRISTMAS SPECIAL 1997
(Location scenes filmed between 20 and 30 October 1997)

ENDGAME
Recorded in studio: **Sunday, 16 November 1997**
Transmitted: **Thursday, 25 December 1997, 9.00 p.m.**
Audience figure: **15.76 million**
CAST:

Tim Brooke-Taylor	Derek McVitie
Marian McLoughlin	Betty McVitie
Owen Brenman	Nick Swainey
Usha Patel	Mrs Khan
Norman Eshley	DI Rickles
Ian Redford	Archie
Robin Davies	Rambler
Christopher Robbie	Dr Clarke
Regina Freedman	Doctor
Arif Hussein	Mr Khan
Matthew Whittle	Doctor
Alisdair Ross	Beggar
Nicholas Moore	Painter
Ian Swann	Airport Attendant

Voice only: Eiji Kusuhara (Answerphone Instructions)

Extras: Lydia Cox, Ben Cox, Sarah Arnold, Danielle Howe, Sophie Briggs, Rachel Briggs, Shyan Sawney, Ram Sawney and Raya Parveen (Children). Also: Clive Berry, Lynn Boxall, Rachel Chaney, Tricky Colwell, Malcolm Cooper, Herbert Crook, Nick Dodge, Steve Duffy, Bob Earle, Matthew Giles, John Hocking, Erik Jack, Coral Lorne, Gerald Luers, Ronald Markham, Ray Martin, Colin Mason, David Mason, Terence Nelson, Laxmi Patel, Mrs S. Patel, Sitaben Patel, Crozier Paul, Mark Powis, Timothy Pragnell, Harry Preston, Paul Rutter, Robert Sansom, Mike Sherwood, David Sutcliffe, Dave Stones, Pete Whittear, Rebecca Adlard, Zamir Akram, Janet Allen, Yasmin Asar, Ron Baker, Andrew Bell, Chantele Bindon, Georgina Briggs, Andrew Bullivant, Kirsty Calder, Tasha Calder, Jade Candis, Nirmal Chaudhri, Diana Clay, Andy Cox, Liz Cox, Nick Crook, John Curry, Ken Dee, Heather Gadd, Tyer Ghani, Craig Gilman, Carol Gilpin, Gadd Graham, Charlotte Horton, Pat Horton, Juliet Hornsby, Janet House, Paul House, Peter House, Rita House, Mark Howe, Roger Hunt, Colin Idiens, Amanda Jane, Ian Jennings, Michael John, Beth Kepney, Jill Lamede, Dave Lea, Amid Mikhta, Richard Moody, Akhtar Naseem, Sarah Neale, Bleary O'Legless, Abder Parveen, Babuchiou Patel, Bhanu Patel, Bhawnita Patel, Chiman Patel, Dipesh Patel, L.U. Patel, Monanchai Patel, Nilam Patel, Panna Patel, Sangha Patel, Savita Ban Patel, Sitaben Patel, Unka Patel, Chrissie Peart, Frasier Perry, Hanna Perry, Annet Peters, Deborah Peters, Simon Peters, Robert Pitman, Richard Pratt, Roy Rahaman, Steve Read, Tom Rolfe, Peter Sanghera, Meena Sawney, Raj Sawney, Carlton Sewell, Catherine Shaw, Michael Shute, Mano Sol, Paul Street, Adrian Tankard, Dulcie Wellard, Samantha Weston, Fay Williams, Guy Winfield and Gloria Wys

Synopsis:
Margaret bumps into her new neighbour, Betty McVitie, who's looking forward to having them over for a meal. Victor's day, however, is as chaotic as normal: he's roped in to partake in an identity parade because a man is indecently exposing himself, the painter he hires isn't what he's expecting, he can't fathom out his newly purchased answerphone and the dilapidated caravan he's bought doesn't impress Margaret, who refuses to go anywhere in the 'tin box'. After a seemingly successful meal at their neighbour's home, Margaret hopes they'll remain friends, but Victor has more important matters on his mind: Nick Swainey has shown him the front page of the *Psychic News* carrying the headline: 'Hell-home on Wheels Heads South'. To his dismay, it seems he's just acquired the most haunted caravan in Britain,

containing the spirit of a Satan worshipper. Victor unknowingly adds to his worries when, as a favour for Nick Swainey, he agrees to collect an old lady from the airport. The problem is, he picks up the wrong one, a wealthy mother of a millionaire businessman, and finds himself caught up in a suspected kidnapping case. By the time he ends up caravanning alone in Dorset, it looks like his marriage is well and truly on the rocks. But when he finally returns home he's hit with the news that Margaret has suffered a heart attack. At her bedside, memories of many blissful moments with his wife come flooding back, reminding him of just how lucky he is.

SERIES 6
(Location scenes filmed between 9 July and 4 August 2000)

1: THE EXECUTIONER'S SONG
Transmitted: **Monday, 16 October 2000, 9.00 p.m.**
Audience figure: **11.41 million**
CAST:

Angus Deayton	Patrick
Janine Duvitski	Pippa
Rae Baker	Sally
Stephen Bateman	Mr Jefferson
John Harding	Warren
Cliff Kelly	Roger the Policeman
Lorraine Kelly	Herself
Hassani Shapi	Rajeev Jamal
David Renwick	Derek Pangloss
Auriol Smith	Mrs Fairley
John Hales	Workman

Extras: In-Sook Chappell (Chinese Waitress), Julian Sua (Client In Brothel), Leilani (Topless Prostitute), Tina Bunnag (Topless Prostitute), Stewart Sharman (Middle-Aged Man in Chinese Restaurant), Janet Lisa House (Prostitute), Rob Sellers (Workman), Peter House (Barman in Chinese Restaurant), Jonathan P. Llewellyn (Client in Brothel), Roger Goold, Karen Harris, Debbie Lloyd, Derek Parkes and Marie Sutherland (Clients in Therapy Clinic) and Mark Johnson (Man in Chinese Brothel)

Synopsis:
The Meldrew household seems in a state of relative equilibrium with Margaret working as a part-time care assistant and Victor having a splashing time on his window-cleaning round. It's just a shame that former neighbour Patrick is suffering from stress, induced by years of living next door to Victor, and is attending therapy classes to help. It's understandable, therefore, that he's reluctant to join his wife and the Meldrews for a meal. Margaret isn't too sure, either, because she's heard bad reports about the restaurant Victor books, and begins wondering whether the misprint on the menu – The Shaghai Express – is indeed apposite. As it transpires, the food has seen better days, a trip to the loo finds Victor being transported into an underground brothel and Pippa has a brief encounter with Warren, a man she meets while waiting for a taxi. So Patrick's birthday is far from rosy, especially when the Meldrews deliver their present. Patrick may be an advocate of modern art, but a piece of rubbish from a dismantled aviary is pushing the boundaries of abstract painting too far!

2: TALES OF TERROR
Transmitted: **Monday, 23 October 2000, 9.00 p.m.**
Audience figure: **10.94 million**
CAST:

Owen Brenman	Nick Swainey
Leila Hoffman	Mrs Impey
Ann Wenn	Lindsey
Andrew Hilton	Mr Dineage
Doreen Mantle	Mrs Warboys
Gordon Peters	Ronnie
John Rutland	Cousin Wilf

Extras: Daphne Neville (Stuffy Woman), Martin Neville (Stuffy Man) and Valerie Carroll (Mildred)

Synopsis:
Victor only wanted some crazy paving in the front garden but all Mr Blisset does is deliver a pile of bricks. His new barbecue isn't working either, but complaining backfires in a big way. Bad news is in plentiful supply: not only are Ronnie and Mildred keen to meet up again, but Mrs Warboys pops round with her cousin Wilf and the bizarre palm-top voice synthesiser he's been using since suffering a stroke. He's yet to master it, though, irritating Victor no end. Nick Swainey, meanwhile, has persuaded Victor to play the lead in his production of *Nosferatu the Vampire*, but surely this isn't

the reason the doctor is concerned about Victor's test results for an irritable bowel? If Victor thought he had problems, they pale into insignificance compared to poor old Ronnie who phones to say his wife, Mildred, who'd been suffering depression, decided to end it all while playing Happy Families.

3: THE FUTILITY OF THE FLY
Transmitted: **Monday, 30 October 2000, 9.00 p.m.**
Audience figure: **10.58 million**
CAST:

Doreen Mantle	Mrs Warboys
Katy Carmichael	Katy
Paul Clayton	Mitch Werner
Richard Evans	Hilton
Sarah Leung	Receptionist
Toshie Ogura	Jackie Tang
Jean Trend	Ruthie
Arturo Venegas	Enrico

Voice Only: David McKail (Voice Rec for Hilton) and Mark McLean (Voice Rec for Jehovah's Witness)

Synopsis:
Another hub cap in the marigolds, emerging from a cloud of steam to climb into the bath with Mrs Warboys and a deep-fried finger in Jean's chips – it's another eventful day in the life of Victor Meldrew. Enrico, the local chippie, invites himself round for lunch to express his gratitude that his lost digit has been found. But when Jean later reads a letter from Enrico, she's in for a shock, and an even bigger shock when she ends up with a tattoo. And Victor doesn't escape, either, because he's in for a surprise when he collects a mysterious parcel.

4: THREATENING WEATHER
Transmitted: **Monday, 6 November 2000, 9.00 p.m.**
Audience figure: **8.94 million**
CAST:

Roy Hudd	Mr Smedley

Synopsis:
It's the hottest night of the year and the Meldrews are enduring a power cut. They can't even open the windows for fear of mosquitos eating them alive, all resulting from a neighbour's ornamental pond, which turns into a public health hazard. With no television and the three heavy-duty electric fans Victor bought that day out of action, he has more time to bemoan society and mankind, such as the length of time – four hours – he wasted trying to assemble the grass box for his new lawnmower. At least the power cut means Victor doesn't have to sit through the weather forecast. As he says, if you hear that it's going to rain in the afternoon, it will only stop you enjoying the sun in the morning. It may be hard work idling away their evening without the comfort of telly, but Victor didn't want a visit from their corpulent elderly neighbour, Mr Smedley, whom he nicknames 'The Hindenberg Disaster on Legs', claiming he can cause a lunar eclipse by just passing the window.

5: THE DAWN OF MAN
Transmitted: **Monday, 13 November 2000, 9.00 p.m.**
Audience figure: **9.45 million**
CAST:

Stewart Harwood	Shopkeeper
Nick Frost	Mr Gleeson
Geoffrey Perkins	Nigel
Owen Brenman	Nick Swainey
Angus Deayton	Patrick
Janine Duvitski	Pippa

Voice only: John Rye (Voice Rec for Skip Hoberman)
Extra: Jan Mark (Mrs Gleeson)

Synopsis:
First of all there was the curious case of the American news reporter who bore an uncanny resemblance to Nick Swainey, puzzling Margaret, but having an even more peculiar effect on Nick himself. Meanwhile, Pippa endures the challenging three-week visit by Patrick's gay brother, Nigel, which leaves her feeling physically and mentally exhausted. Perhaps a nice glass of wine could soothe her mind, although she is soon to rue the day she sets foot inside the off licence. But not as much as Victor regrets the day he visits the corner shop – what can you expect when the proprietor's name is Dodgy Douglas? He's regretting even further his altercation with a vicious yob which results in Victor tipping a dish of maggots onto the man's meal, especially when the guy turns out to be a prospective

purchaser of Nick Swainey's house. Is this the arrival of the neighbour from hell?

6: THINGS AREN'T SIMPLE ANY MORE

Transmitted: **Monday, 20 November 2000, 9.00 p.m.**
Audience figure: **12.84 million**

CAST:

Hannah Gordon	Glynis
Howard Attfield	Blind Man
Jonathan Cecil	Mr Gundry
Jean Challis & Ed Welch	Cabaret
Paul Merton	Barman
Jeanne Mockford	Catholic Woman
William Osborne	Father Blakey
Joanna Scanlan	Gillian

Extras: Monty Charkham, Vivienne Jay, Joan Lovelace, Patricia Varley, Phyliss Roe and Bob Hawkes (Joggers), Eddie Evans (Limpy Briddock), John Walker and John Carney (Cab Drivers), Hannah Gould (Barmaid), Lenny Fowler, Maxwell Laird, Malcolm Dixon, Mark Lisle and Jason Tompkins (Santa's Elves); John J. Moore (Father Christmas), Tessa Ellis (Daughter); Margaret Holmes-Drewry (Mother), David Milnes (Father), John Stanghon (Son), Judy Cowne (Nurse), John Dickie and David Holmes (Stretcher Bearers), Norman Holmes (Old Man) and Big George Webley (Musical Director)

Synopsis:

How will the world cope without Victor Meldrew trying desperately to steer it in the right direction? Margaret is putting on a brave face but beneath the surface she is brimming with anger, sadness and grief. It's five months since her husband's life was snuffed out at the hands of a hit-and-run driver, and Margaret's fury finds her telling the vicar, when he enquires as to how she's coping, that if they find the driver, she's going to kill him. When Glynis Holloway, Margaret's new soulmate, who's also facing her own personal tragedy, remarks that problems don't seem to go away, Margaret states they never did, before reflecting on memorable moments with her late husband, concluding with the evening he headed off to a reunion for people who'd worked at the dairies, where Victor was employed some thirty years ago. Margaret is feeling pangs of regret because she almost begged him to attend – it was the evening he was killed. He was all alone on that cold, wet evening, having given up on the reunion party because he was the only one who turned up. Sadly, he never realised Limpy Briddock arrived late. At Glynis' home, Margaret inadvertently stumbles across Glynis' photo album containing cuttings regarding Victor's death. Has she been in the company of Victor's killer all this time? Suddenly, popping pills to give Glynis for her migraine has a deeper significance.

COMIC RELIEF SPECIAL 2001
VISITING UNCLE DICK
Transmitted: **Friday, 16 March 2001**

PRODUCTION TEAM

(NOTE: Only those people acknowledged in the closing credits of the television episodes have been listed.)

All episodes written by David Renwick.

PRODUCER
Susan Belbin (Series 1–5 and Christmas Specials 1990, 1991, 1993, 1995 & 1996); Jonathan P. Llewellyn (Series 6); Esta Charkham (Christmas Special 1997)

DIRECTOR
Susan Belbin (Series 1–5 and Christmas Specials 1990, 1991, 1993, 1995 & 1996); Christine Gernon (Series 6 and Christmas Special 1997)

CASTING ADVISOR
Rebecca Howard (Series 1); Judy Loe (Series 2, Episodes 1–5; Series 3, Episodes 2–6; Series 4, Episodes 1–4 & 6 and Christmas Specials 1995 & 1996); Tracey Gillham (Series 6, Episodes 1–6 and Christmas Special 1997); Kika Felix da Costa (Christmas Special 1993 Portugal)

FILM CAMERAMAN/
DIRECTOR OF
PHOTOGRAPHY
Keith Burton (Series 1); John Record (Series 2, Episodes 1–5; Series 3, Episodes 1–6 and Christmas Specials 1991, 1995, 1996 & 1997); John Rhodes (Series 4 and Christmas Special 1993); Peter Loring (Series 5, Episodes 1–3 & 5–6); Rex Maidment (Christmas Special 1990); Geoff Harrison (Series 6, Episodes 1–3 & 5–6)

FILM SOUND
John Hooper (Series 1; Series 5, Episode 5 and Christmas Special 1995); Ron Keightley (Series 2, Episodes 1–5); John A Parry (Series 3; Series 4,

Episodes 1–2 & 4–6 and Christmas Special 1991); Clive Derbyshire (Series 5, Episodes 1–3 & 6); Colin March (Christmas Special 1990); Terry Elms (Christmas Special 1996)

FILM EDITOR
Mike Houghton (Series 1; Series 3, Episode 4; Series 4; Series 5, Episodes 1–3 & 5–6 and Christmas Specials 1995 & 1996); John Dunstan (Series 2, Episodes 1–5; Series 3, Episodes 1–3 & 5-6 and Christmas Specials 1990 & 1991); Jeff Gay (Christmas Special 1993); Bronwen Jenkins (Christmas Special 1997)

MAKE-UP DESIGNER
Jean Steward (Series 1; Series 2; Series 3; Series 4 and Christmas Specials 1990 & 1991); Vanessa White (Series 5; Series 6 and Christmas Specials 1995 & 1996); Rebecca Walker (Series 6, Episodes 1 & 6); Viv Riley (Christmas Special 1993); Christine Powers (Christmas Special 1997)

COSTUME DESIGNER
Richard Winter (Series 1–5 and Christmas Specials 1990, 1991, 1993, 1995 & 1996); Jacky Levy (Series 6); Pam Maddox (Series 6, Episodes 1 & 6); Karen Beale (Christmas Special 1993); Val Metheringham (Christmas Special 1997)

GRAPHIC DESIGNER
Pete Wane (Series 1; Series 2 and Christmas Special 1990)

PROPERTIES BUYER
Amanda Smith (Series 1); David Hayden (Series 2 and Christmas Special 1990); Barbara Horne (Series 3 and Christmas Special 1991); Sue Claybyn (Series 4); Nick

Barnett (Series 5 and Christmas Special 1993); Amanda George (Christmas Special 1995); Pauline Seager (Christmas Special 1996); Ian Tully (Christmas Special 1997); Nicola Burrough (Series 6)

VISUAL EFFECTS DESIGNER
Colin Mapson (Series 1); Chris Lawson (Series 2, Episodes 1–3 & 6; Series 3, Episodes 1–3 & 5–6; Series 4; Series 5; Series 6 and Christmas Specials 1990, 1991, 1993, 1995 & 1996); David Viles (Series 2, Episode 5); Martin Neill (Series 3, Episode 5); Paul Mann (Christmas Special 1997)

TECHNICAL/STUDIO RESOURCE MANAGER
Philip Quinn (Series 1; Series 2; Series 3, Episodes 1–3 & 5–6; Series 4, Episodes 1–2 & 4–6; Series 5 and Christmas Specials 1990, 1991, 1995 & 1996); Terry Wild (Series 1, Episode 5); Mark Sanders (Series 6, Episodes 1–3 & 5 and Christmas Special 1997); Andrew Breaks (Series 6, Episodes 4 & 6)

VISION MIXER
Sue Collins (Series 1; Series 2; Series 3, Episodes 1–3 & 5–6; Series 4, Episodes 1–2 & 4–6; Series 6, Episodes 1–5 and Christmas Specials 1990, 1991, 1995 & 1996); Heather Gilder (Series 5 and Christmas Special 1997)

CAMERA SUPERVISOR
Roger Goss (Series 1; Series 2, Episodes 2, 3 & 6; Series 3, Episodes 1, 3, 5 & 6; Series 4, Episodes 1–2 & 4–6 and Christmas Specials 1990 & 1991); Alan Bayley (Series 2, Episodes 1 & 5; Series 3, Episode 2); David Short (Series 2, Episode 4); Duncan Unsworth (Series 5; Series 6, Episodes 1–5 and Christmas Specials 1995, 1996 & 1997)

PRODUCTION SECRETARY/
PRODUCTION SUPERVISOR
Christine Gernon (Series 1); Fiona Strachan (Series 2;

Series 4, Episodes 1, 2 & 4–6 and Christmas Special 1990); Samantha Frith (Series 3 and Christmas Specials 1991 & 1993); Charlotte Simmonds (Series 6, Episodes 1, 2, 5 & 6); Viki Margerum (Series 6, Episode 3); Linda Hearn (Series 6, Episode 4); Marta Azevedo (Christmas Special 1993 – Portugal); Lesley Hardstaff (Christmas Special 1995); Vicky Ransom (Christmas Special 1997)

ASSISTANT FLOOR MANAGER
Adam Tandy (Series 1); Charles Whaley (Series 1, Episodes 5 & 6); Jenny Penrose (Series 2 and Christmas Special 1990); Nick Wood (Series 3 and Christmas Special 1991); Simone Dawson (Series 4, Episodes 1, 2 & 4–6); Kate Carrol (Series 5); Jo Cole (Christmas Special 1995); Rebecca Hewitt (Christmas Special 1996); Charlene Farrell (Christmas Special 1997)

PRODUCTION ASSISTANT
Amita Lochab (Series 1); Jane Wellesley (Series 2 and Christmas Special 1990); Susan Silburn (Series 3 and Christmas Special 1991); Gail Evans (Series 4, Episodes 1, 2 & 4–6); Christine Gernon (Series 5 and Christmas Special 1995); Gabriel Moniz (Christmas Special 1993 – Portugal); Teresa Ramos (Christmas Special 1993 – Portugal); Pedro Sá Santos (Christmas Special 1993 – Portugal); Jane Sprague (Christmas Special 1996)

VIDEOTAPE EDITOR
Chris Wadsworth (Series 1; Series 2; Series 3, Episodes 1–3 & 5–6; Series 4, Episodes 1–2 & 4–6 and Christmas Specials 1990, 1991 & 1993); Mark Lawrence (Series 5, Series 6 and Christmas Specials 1995, 1996 & 1997); Phil Southby (Christmas Special 1996)

STUDIO SOUND/SOUND SUPERVISOR
Mark Holland (Series 1); Martin Deane (Series 2 and Christmas Special 1990); Laurie Taylor (Series 3, Episodes 1–3 & 5–6; Series 4, Episodes 1–2 & 4–6;

Series 5, Episodes 1, 5 & 6 and Christmas Specials 1991 & 1997); Nick Roast (Series 5, Episodes 2–4; Series 6, Episodes 1–5 and Christmas Specials 1995 & 1996); Dave Wagner (Series 6, Episodes 2–4 and Christmas Special 1997); Geoff Moss (Series 6, Episodes 1 & 5); Jem Whippey (Christmas Special 1997)

STUDIO LIGHTING/LIGHTING DIRECTOR
Christopher Kempton (Series 1; Series 2; Series 3, Episodes 1–3 & 5–6; Series 4, Episodes 1–2 & 4–6; Series 5; Series 6 and Christmas Specials 1990, 1991, 1995, 1996 & 1997); Will Charles (Series 6, Episodes 1, 2 & 5 and Christmas Special 1996); Julia Smith (Series 6, Episodes 3 & 4); Martin Kempton (Christmas Special 1995 & 1996)

PRODUCTION MANAGER
Gavin Clark (Series 1; Series 2, Episodes 1–5); Duncan Cooper (Series 2 and Christmas Special 1990); Murray Peterson (Series 3 and Christmas Special 1991); Nick Wood (Series 4, Episodes 1–2 & 4–6; Series 5); Francis Gilson (Series 6); Nick Page (Christmas Special 1993 – Portugal); Lesley Bywater (Christmas Special 1995); Jenny Penrose (Christmas Special 1997)

DESIGNER
Nick Somerville (Series 1; Series 4 and Christmas Special 1993); John Asbridge (Series 2 and Christmas Specials 1990, 1995 & 1996), Chris Hull (Series 2, Episode 2 and Christmas Special 1990); John Bristow (Series 3 and Christmas Special 1991); Linda Conoboy (Series 3, Episode 4; Series 5, Episodes 4–6; Series 6 and Christmas Specials 1996 & 1997); Laurence Williams (Series 5)

TITLE MUSIC written and performed by Eric Idle, arranged by John Du Prez and produced by André Jacquemin. Idle also sang the 'Car Mechanics Song' in Series 3, Episode 4.

INCIDENTAL MUSIC composed by Ed Welch from Series 2 but only credited from Series 3.

NOTE: The following jobs were only credited as shown

FLOOR MANAGER
Amita Lochab (Series 5, Episodes 4, 5 & 6)

GRIPS/CAMERA GRIP
James Grimes (Series 3, Episode 4; Series 4, Episode 3 and Christmas Specials 1993 & 1997); Malcolm Smith (Series 6, Episode 6)

LIGHTING GAFFER
Jimmy Wilson (Series 3, Episode 4); Barry Manze (Christmas Special 1997); Peter Robinson (Series 4, Episode 3; Series 6, Episodes 1–3 & 5 and Christmas Special 1993)

PRODUCTION/DESIGN OPERATIVES
Brian Green (Series 3, Episode 4; Series 4, Episode 3; Christmas Specials 1993 and 1997); Max de Nett (Series 3, Episode 4; Series 4, Episode 3 and Christmas Specials 1993 and 1997); Paul Emerson (Christmas Special 1997)

LOCATION MANAGER
Lindsey Chamier (Series 4, Episodes 1–4 & 6); Anthony Garrick (Series 5, Episodes 1, 2, 3 & 6); Gabrielle Lindemann (Series 6, Episodes 1–3 & 5–6); Adam Browne (Christmas Special 1990); Nick Wood (Christmas Special 1993); Jonathan Barden (Christmas Special 1997)

STUNT ARRANGERS
Colin Skeaping (Series 1, Episode 3; Series 4, Episode 3); Steve Whyment (Series 5, Episodes 1, 3 & 6; Series 6, Episodes 1, 5 & 6 and Christmas Specials 1995 & 1996); Gareth Milne (Christmas Special 1993); Mark Anthony Newman (Christmas Special 1993); Bill Weston (Series 2, Episode 5 and Christmas Special 1993); Peter Diamond (Christmas Special 1996); Gabriel Cronnelly (Christmas Special 1997); Tip Tipping (Series 2, Episode 3)

STUNTS

Tip Tipping (Series 2, Episode 3 and Series 4, Episode 3); Wayne Michaels (Series 4, Episode 3); Tracey Eddon (Series 4, Episode 3); Stephen Whyment (Series 4, Episode 3); Lyndon Hellewell (Series 6, Episode 1); Gabriel Cronnelly (Series 6, Episode 5 and Christmas Special 1995); Mark Lisbon (Series 6, Episode 6 and Christmas Special 1996); Tina Maskell (Series 6, Episode 6 and Christmas Special 1996); Seon Rogers (Series 6, Episode 6); Tony Lucken (Series 6, Episode 6); Bill Weston (Series 2, Episode 5 and Series 6, Episode 6); Nick Hobbs (Christmas Special 1995); Roy Alon (Christmas Special 1995); Jeff Hewitt-Davis (Christmas Special 1996); Sarah Franzl (Series 2, Episode 3); Colin Skeaping (Series 4, Episode 3); Stuart Fell (Series 5, Episode 1); Lex Milloy (Series 5, Episode 6)

FIRST ASSISTANT DIRECTOR

Nick Wood (Series 4, Episode 3); Katie Thompstone (Series 6); Angela de Chastelai Smith (Christmas Special 1993); Paul Hastings (Christmas Special 1996); Paul Leather (Christmas Special 1997)

SECOND ASSISTANT DIRECTOR

Simone Dawson (Series 4, Episode 3); Kate Holdsworth (Series 6, Episode 1 & 6); Mark Mylod (Christmas Special 1993); Kristian Dench (Christmas Special 1997)

THIRD ASSISTANT DIRECTOR

Anna Brabbins (Series 6, Episodes 1 & 6)

CONTINUITY

Gail Evans (Series 4, Episode 3); Christine Gernon (Christmas Special 1993)

PROGRAMME BUDGET ASSISTANT/FINANCE ASSISTANT/FINANCE ASSOCIATE

Judith Bantock (Series 4, Episode 3 and Christmas Special 1993); Maggie Kelleher (Christmas Special

1995); Jo Alloway (Series 6 and Christmas Special 1997)

CONSTRUCTION MANAGER

David Channon (Series 4, Episode 3 and Christmas Special 1993); Ron Venables (Christmas Special 1995)

DESIGN ASSISTANT

Linda Conoboy (Series 4, Episode 3); Adrian Uwalaka (Christmas Special 1993)

ELECTRICIANS

Paul Lang (Series 4, Episode 3); Paul Smithers (Series 4, Episode 3); Brian Sullivan (Christmas Special 1993); Rob Brock (Christmas Special 1993)

SOUND RECORDIST

John A. Parry (Series 4, Episode 3 and Christmas Special 1993); Chris Round (Series 6, Episodes 1–3 & 5–6 and Christmas Special 1997)

ASSISTANT CAMERA

John Hembrough (Series 4, Episode 3); Richard Lawson (Christmas Special 1997); Joanna Tam (Christmas Special 1997)

BOOM OPERATOR

Alex Marsden (Series 4, Episode 3); Christian Joyce (Series 6, Episode 6); Chris Round (Christmas Special 1993); Gordon Lester (Christmas Special 1997)

DUBBING EDITOR

Cúan Macconghail (Series 4, Episode 3); Nick Roast (Christmas Special 1993)

DUBBING MIXER

Michael Narduzzo (Series 4, Episode 3); Laurie Taylor (Christmas Special 1993)

MAGIC ADVISER

Brian Miller (Series 4, Episode 3)

ART DIRECTOR
Clara Moreland (Series 6, Episodes 1, 2, 5 & 6); Antony Cartlidge (Series 6, Episodes 3, 4 & 6); Steve Wright (Christmas Special 1995); Sarah Milton (Christmas Special 1997)

CAMERA OPERATOR
Ian Jackson (Series 6, Episodes 1–3 & 5–6)

STAGE MANAGER
Caroline Caley (Series 6)

SCRIPT SUPERVISOR
Caroline Gardener (Series 6); Jane Houston (Christmas Special 1997)

PROP MASTER
Dickon Peschek (Series 6, Episodes 1 & 6); David McCollin (Series 6, Episode 6)

STAND-BY PROPS
Rob Sellers (Series 6, Episode 6); Darren Wisker (Series 6, Episode 6)

FOCUS PULLER
John Fletcher (Series 6, Episodes 1 & 6); John Hembrough (Christmas Special 1993); John Stapleton (Christmas Special 1997)

DRESSERS
Stuart Nuttall (Series 6, Episode 6); Ruth Young (Series 6, Episode 6); Michael Griffey (Christmas Special 1993)

CLAPPER LOADER
Penny Shipton (Series 6, Episode 6)

BEST BOY
Steve Read (Series 6, Episode 6); Paul Lang (Christmas Special 1993)

COLOURIST
Chris Packman (Series 6, Episode 6)

VISION SUPERVISOR
Julia Smith (Series 6, Episode 6)

UNIT MANAGER (PORTUGAL)
Gerardo Fernandes (Christmas Special 1993)

VIDEO EFFECTS
Dave Chapman (Christmas Special 1995)

PAINTBOX ARTIST
Alison Rickman (Christmas Special 1995)

PRODUCTION ASSOCIATE
Jonathan P. Llewellyn (Christmas Special 1995); Lesley Bywater (Christmas Special 1996)

ft 2 TRAINEE
Christopher Stoaling (Christmas Special 1997)

WARDROBE ASSISTANT
Anne Wilson (Christmas Special 1997); George Brent (Christmas Special 1997)

MAKE-UP ASSISTANT
Johanna Bruton (Christmas Special 1997)

PROSTHETICS
Gorton & Painter (Christmas Special 1997)

ACTION VEHICLES
Peter Thompson (Christmas Special 1997)

MERCHANDISE

The following merchandise list details products relating to the series that may interest fans of *One Foot in the Grave*.

BOOKS

Title:	One Foot in the Grave
Author:	David Renwick
ISBN:	0563364289
Format:	Hardback
Publisher:	BBC Books
Publication Date:	1992

NOTES: A novelisation comprising moments from the series, representing a year in the life of Victor Meldrew. A paperback was published in 1993 (ISBN: 0140234985).

Title:	One Foot on the Stage – The Biography of Richard Wilson
Author:	James Roose-Evans
ISBN	0297816624
Format:	Hardback
Publisher:	Orion
Publication Date:	1996

NOTES: Written with Wilson's backing, and including an introduction by the author himself. (ISBN: 0752811150).

AUDIO CASSETTES/CDs

Title:	One Foot in the Grave – Volume 1
Release Date:	1995
Catalogue no:	0563390034

NOTES: Contains four episodes adapted for broadcasting on BBC's Radio 2. Released as an audio CD (no: 0563495049) in 2004.

Title:	One Foot In The Grave – Volume 2
Release Date:	1998
Catalogue no:	056338204X

NOTES: Contains the soundtracks of three televised episodes: 'The Man in the Long Black Coat', 'The Broken Reflection' and 'The Trial'. Released as a CD (no: 0563495057) in 2004.

VIDEOS

Title:	One Foot in the Grave – In Luton Airport No-One Can Hear You Scream
Release Date:	1992
Catalogue no:	BBCV4832

NOTES: The first three episodes from Series Two: 'In Luton, Airport No-One Can Hear You Scream', 'We Have Put Her Living In The Tomb' and 'Dramatic Fever'.

Title:	One Foot in the Grave – Who Will Buy?
Release Date:	1992
Catalogue no:	BBCV4833

NOTES: The final three episodes from Series Two: 'Who Will Buy?', 'Love and Death' and 'Timeless Time'.

Title:	One Foot in the Grave – Alive and Buried
Release Date:	1993
Catalogue no:	B00008T54N

NOTES: The first three episodes from Series One: 'Alive and Buried', 'The Big Sleep' and 'The Valley of Fear'.

Title:	One Foot in the Grave – I'll Retire To Bedlam
Release Date:	1993
Catalogue no:	BBCV5152

NOTES: The last three episodes from Series One: 'I'll Retire To Bedlam', 'The Eternal Quadrangle' and 'The Return of the Speckled Band'.

Title:	One Foot in the Grave – The Beast in the Cage
Release Date:	1993
Catalogue no:	B00008T4UU

NOTES: The last three episodes from Series Three: 'The Beast in the Cage', 'Beware the Trickster on the Roof' and 'The Worst Horror of All'.

Title: One Foot in the Grave – Series 1
Release Date: 1994
Catalogue no: BBCV5387
NOTES: All six episodes from Series One.

Title: One Foot in the Grave –
Warm Champagne
Release Date: 1994
Catalogue no: BBCV5297
NOTES: The last three episodes from Series
Four: 'Warm Champagne', 'The Trial' and 'The Secret
of the Seven Sorcerers'

Title: One Foot in the Grave – Who's
Listening and The Man In The
Long Black Coat
Release Date: 1994
Catalogue no: BBCV5424
NOTES: The Christmas episodes from 1990
and 1991.

Title: One Foot in the Grave –
Re-Arranging the Dust
Release Date: 1995
Catalogue no: BBCV5652
NOTES: Three episodes from Series Five:
'Re-Arranging the Dust', 'Only a Story' and 'The
Exterminating Angel'.

Title: One Foot in the Algarve
Release Date: 1995
Catalogue no: BBCV5183
NOTES: The 1993 Christmas Special.

Title: One Foot in the Grave – Series 4
Release Date: 1995
Catalogue no: BBCV5646
NOTES: All six episodes from Series Four

Title: One Foot in the Grave – Series 3
Release Date: 1996
Catalogue no: BBCV5809
NOTES: All six episodes from Series Three.

Title: One Foot in the Grave –
The Wisdom of the Witch
Release Date: 1996
Catalogue no: BBCV5942
NOTES: The 1995 Christmas Special.

Title: One Foot in the Grave – Starbound
Release Date: 1997
Catalogue no: BBCV6202
NOTES: The 1996 Christmas Special.

Title: One Foot in the Grave –
The Man Who Blew Away
Release Date: 1997
Catalogue no: BBCV6277
NOTES: Three episodes from Series Five:
'The Man Who Blew Away', 'The Affair of the
Hollow Lady' and 'Hole in the Sky'.

Title: One Foot in the Grave –
Monday Morning Will Be Fine
Release Date: 1998
Catalogue no: BBCV4971
NOTES: The first three episodes from Series
Three: 'Monday Morning Will Be Fine', 'Dreamland'
and 'The Broken Reflection'.

Title: One Foot in the Grave – Endgame
Release Date: 1998
Catalogue no: BBCV6593
NOTES: The 1997 Christmas Special.

Title: The Very Best of One Foot
in the Grave
Release Date: 1998
Catalogue no: BBCV6462
NOTES: Contains five classic episodes: 'The
Return of the Speckled Band', 'Dreamland', 'The
Broken Reflection', 'Warm Champagne' and 'The
Trial'.

Title: One Foot in the Grave – Series 6
Release Date: 2001
Catalogue no: BBCV7195
NOTES: All six episodes from Series Six, the final season.

Accompanied by the 45-minute documentary, *One Foot in the Grave – The Story*, which was transmitted on 20th November 2000, prior to the final episode being shown.

DVDs

Title: The Best of One Foot in the Grave
Release Date: 2001
Catalogue no: BBCDVD1062
NOTES: Six episodes from the series: 'The Return of the Speckled Band', 'Dreamland', 'The Broken Reflection', 'Warm Champagne', 'The Trial', 'Things Aren't Simple Anymore' plus the documentary, *I Don't Believe It! – The Story of One Foot in the Grave.*

Title: One Foot in the Grave – Series 1
Release Date: 2004
Catalogue no: BBCDVD1489
NOTES: All six episodes from Series One.

Title: One Foot in the Grave – Series 2
Release Date: 2005
Catalogue no: BBCDVD1657
NOTES: All six episodes from Series Two.

Title: One Foot in the Grave – Series 3
Release Date: 2005
Catalogue no: BBCDVD1727
NOTES: All six episodes from Series Three.

Title: One Foot in the Grave – Series 4
Release Date: April 2006
Catalogue no: BBCDVD1859
NOTES: All six episodes from Series Four plus 'One Foot in the Algarve'.

Title: One Foot in the Grave – Series 5
Release Date: Autumn 2006
Catalogue no: BBCDVD1860
NOTES: All six episodes from Series Five plus 'The Wisdom of the Witch'.

Title: One Foot in the Grave – Series 6
Release Date: 16 October 2006
Catalogue no: BBCDVD2114
NOTES: All six episodes from Series Six plus 'Starbound', 'Endgame' and the documentary *I Don't Believe It – The Story of One Foot in the Grave.*

Title: One Foot in the Grave – The Complete Series
Release Date: 16 October 2006
Catalogue no: BBCDVD2115
NOTES: All six series plus the Specials.

BIBLIOGRAPHY

Donvan, Paul, *The Radio Companion* (London: Grafton, 1992)

Roose-Evans, James, *One Foot on the Stage – The Biography of Richard Wilson* (London: Orion, 1996)

Lewisohn, Mark, *Radio Times Guide to TV Comedy* (London: BBC, 1998)

NOTES

Apart from those listed below, all the quotes used throughout the book were taken from interviews conducted by the author.

INTRODUCTION

i   Interview with *The Look, Daily Mirror*, 6 November 2000.

ii   John Inverdale, the *Daily Telegraph*, 23 November 2006.

iii   Renwick being interviewed for BBC Manchester's documentary, *I Don't Believe It! One Foot in the Grave, The Story*, transmitted 20 November 2000.

CHAPTER 1

i   Recorded in Renwick's journal, 8 August 1991.

ii   Interview with Mary Fletcher, *TV Times*, 14–20 January 1995.

iii   Letter from John Cleese, dated 11 February 1970, to David Renwick.

iv   Letter from Edward Taylor to David Renwick, dated 6 August 1970, re. *Frederick Dunne's Schooldays*.

v   Ibid.

vi   Ibid.

vii   Letter from Edward Taylor to David Renwick, dated 29 December 1970.

viii   Ibid.

ix   Ibid.

x   Ibid.

xi   Ibid.

xii   Ibid.

CHAPTER 2

i   Recorded in Renwick's journal, 23 January 1989.

ii   Recorded in Renwick's journal, 24 February 1989.

iii   Recorded in Renwick's journal, 14 June 1989.

iv   Recorded in Renwick's journal, 12 July 1989.

v   Ibid.

vi   Recorded in Renwick's journal, 1 August 1989.

vii   Recorded in Renwick's journal, 7 August 1989.

viii   Ibid.

ix   Ibid.

x   Ibid.

xi   Recorded in Renwick's journal, 18 August 1989.

xii   Recorded in Renwick's journal, 16 August 1989.

xiii   Recorded in Renwick's journal, 29 August 1989.

xiv   Ibid.

xv   Ibid.

CHAPTER 3

i   Recorded in Renwick's journal, 29 August 1989.

ii   Recorded in Renwick's journal, 16 August 1989.

iii   Recorded in Renwick's journal, 31 August 1989.

iv   Ibid.

v   Recorded in Renwick's journal, 7 September 1989.

vi   Recorded in Renwick's journal, 6 September 1989.

CHAPTER 4

i   Recorded in Renwick's journal, 4 September 1989.

ii   Ibid.

iii   Recorded in Renwick's journal, 21 September 1989.

iv   Ibid.

CHAPTER 5

i   Recorded in Renwick's journal, 18 September 1989.

ii   Recorded in Renwick's journal, 19 September 1989.

iii   Ibid.

iv   Recorded in Renwick's journal, 10 October 1989.

v   Recorded in Renwick's journal, 11 October 1989.

vi   Recorded in Renwick's journal, 31 July 1990.

vii   Recorded in Renwick's journal, 21 September 1989.

viii   Recorded in Renwick's journal, 4 January 1990.

ix   Recorded in Renwick's journal, 4 January 1990.

x   Ibid.

xi   *The Times*, 4 January 1990, p.21.

xii   Ibid.

xiii   Review in the *Daily Mirror* by Hilary Kingsley, 6 January 1990.

xiv   Review in the *Daily Star* by Stafford Hildred, 6 January 1990.

xv   Review in the *Sunday Express* by John Russell, 7 January 1990.

xvi   Ibid.

xvii   Review in the *Evening Standard* by Jaci Stephen, 5 January 1990.

xviii   Ibid.

xix   Ibid.

xx   Review in the *Listener*, by James Saynor, 11 January 1990.

xxi   Ibid.

xxii   Review in the *Guardian*, by Nancy Banks-Smith, 6 January 1990.

xxiii   Review in the *Financial Times*, by Christopher Dunkley, 10 January 1990.

xxiv   Review in the *Daily Mail*, by Elizabeth Cowley, 4 January 1990.

xxv   Recorded in Renwick's journal, 7 January 1990.

xxvi   Recorded in Renwick's journal, 10 January 1990.

CHAPTER 6

i   Article in the *Daily Express*, written by Margaret Forwood, 18 January 1990.

ii   Ibid.

iii   Ibid.

iv   Recorded in Renwick's journal, 24 September 1989.

v   Recorded in Renwick's journal, 25 January 1990.

vi   Article in the *Daily Mirror*, written by Hilary Kingsley, 27 January 1990.

vii   Recorded in Renwick's journal, 4 September 1989.

viii   Recorded in Renwick's journal, 16 October 1989.

ix   Ibid.

x   Recorded in Renwick's journal, 29 August 1991.

xi   Recorded in Renwick's journal, 22 October 1989.

xii   Recorded in Renwick's journal, 4 November 1989.

xiii   Recorded in Renwick's journal, 6 November 1989.

xiv   Recorded in Renwick's journal, 11 November 1989.

xv   Article in *City Limits*, 1 February 1990.

xvi   Article in the *Daily Mirror*, written by Tony Pratt, 18 January 1990.

xvii   Ibid.

xviii   Article in the *Daily Mirror*, written by Tony Pratt, 1 February 1990.

xix   Ibid.

xx   Article in the *Daily Express*, written by Margaret Forwood, 8 February 1990.

xxi   Article in the *Sun*, written by Garry Bushell, 18 January 1990.

xxii   Article in the *Independent*, written by Mark Wareham, 8 February 1990.

xxiii   Article in the *Daily Telegraph*, written by Christopher Tookey, 12 January 1990.

xxiv   Ibid.

xxv   Ibid.

xxvi   Recorded in Renwick's journal, 18 January 1990.

CHAPTER 7

i   Recorded in Renwick's journal, 8 February 1990.

ii   Recorded in Renwick's journal, 9 February 1990.

iii   Ibid.

iv   Ibid.

v   Recorded in Renwick's journal, 6 June 1990.

vi   Recorded in Renwick's journal, 22 May 1990.

vii   Recorded in Renwick's journal, 5 July 1990.

viii   Recorded in Renwick's journal, 3 August 1990.

ix   Memo from Renwick to Welch, titled 'Music Cues', date unknown.

x   Recorded in Renwick's journal, 19 October 1990.

xi   Recorded in Renwick's journal, 1 September 1990.

CHAPTER 8

i   Recorded in Renwick's journal, 26 June 1990.

ii   Recorded in Renwick's journal, 2 July 1990.

xvii   Recorded in Renwick's journal, 25 December 1997.

CHAPTER 15

i   Article in the *Evening Standard* by Patrick Sawer, 13 January 1998.

ii   Recorded in Renwick's journal, 26 February 1999.

iii   Recorded in Renwick's journal, 4 June 1999.

iv   Recorded in Renwick's journal, 6 March 2000.

v   Recorded in Renwick's journal, 14 May 2000.

vi   Extract from a letter written by Renwick to Peter Salmon, 19 May 2000.

vii   Ibid.

viii   Review in the *Daily Telegraph*, 17 October 2000.

ix   Review in the *Guardian* by Nancy Banks-Smith, 17 October 2000.

x   Review in the *Independent on Sunday* by Mark Simpson, 15 October 2000.

xi   Recorded in Renwick's journal, 3 June 1999.

xii   Recorded in Renwick's journal, 28 September 1999.

xiii   Recorded in Renwick's journal, 2 October 2000.

xiv   Ibid.

xv   Recorded in Renwick's journal, 13 July 2000.

xvi   Recorded in Renwick's journal, 16 July 2000.

xvii   Recorded in Renwick's journal, 13 July 2000.

xviii Recorded in Renwick's journal, 17 September 2000.

xix   Recorded in Renwick's journal, 18 September 2000.

xx   Recorded in Renwick's journal, 21 November 2000.

xxi   Recorded in Renwick's journal, 28 July 2000.

xxii   Recorded in Renwick's journal, 11 October 2000.

xxiii Recorded in Renwick's journal, 1 August 2000.

xxiv   Review in the *Independent* by Robert Hanks, 21 November 2000.

xxv   Ibid.

xxvi   Ibid.

xxvii Ibid.

xxviii Review in the *Daily Telegraph* by James Walton, 21 November 2000.

xxix   Review in the *Mail on Sunday* by Jaci Stephen, 26 November 2000.

xxx   Ibid.

xxxi   Review in the *Daily Mirror* by Charlie Catchpole, 21 November 2000.

xxxii Review in the *Sun* by Garry Bushell, 22 November 2000.

xxxiii Recorded in Renwick's journal, 15 November 2000.

PICTURE CREDITS

The author and publisher would like to thank the following for permission
to reproduce their images in this book:

David Renwick: 2, 5, 6, 9, 36, 38, 41, 46, 53, 54, 55, 56, 57, 59, 64, 65, 66, 84, 85, 88, 91, 93, 98, 105, 112, 115, 116, 117, 118, 119, 121, 122, 124, 133, 135, 136, 137, 142, 144, 145, 149, 150, 153, 160, 161, 162, 166, 167, 171, 173, 176, 177, 180, 212, 213, 214, 219, 220, 222, 223; Millennium FX Ltd: 169; Vanessa White: 48, 49, 128, 211, 215; All other photos supplied courtesy of Radio Times/BBC.
Special photography: Andy Eaves; Set designs: John Asbridge.